Syncretism

SUNY series in Korean Studies
Sung Bae Park, Editor

Syncretism

The Religious Context
of Christian Beginnings in Korea

David Chung

Edited by
Kang-nam Oh

STATE UNIVERSITY OF NEW YORK PRESS

Published by
State University of New York Press, Albany

For information, address State University of New York Press,
90 State Street, Suite 700, Albany, NY 12207

Production by Diane Ganeles
Marketing by Patrick Durocher

Library of Congress Cataloging-in-Publication Data

Chung, David, 1917–
    Syncretism : the religious context of Christian beginnings in Korea/
David Chung ; edited by Kang-nam Oh.
        p. cm. — (SUNY series in Korean studies)
    Includes bibliographical references and index.
    ISBN 0-7914-4941-6 (hardcover : alk. paper) — ISBN 0-7914-4942-4
(pbk : alk. paper)
    1. Christianity—Korea—History.   2. Korea—Church history.
I. Oh, Kang-nam.   II. Title.   III. Series.

BR1327.C48 2001
275.19082—dc21   00-041985
                                                                        CIP

10 9 8 7 6 5 4 3 2 1

CONTENTS

Editor's Introduction

When David Chung submitted his Ph.D. dissertation to the Department of Religion, Graduate Studies at Yale University in 1959, his supervisor, Dr. H. Richard Niebuhr, suggested that it be immediately sent to a publisher to be published as a book. Dr. Chung thought that he should have some corrections and modifications made before it could be published. Right after the submission of the dissertation, however, Dr. Chung had to return to Korea to take up a teaching position at the Seoul National University. After a hectic year of settling down in Seoul, he was "snatched" by Konkuk University, a young and vigorously growing university in Seoul, to become its president. During these eight turbulent administrative years, he could not find the time to prepare his dissertation for publication. Thus he lost the chance to have it published as a book.

While I was on sabbatical leave in 1997 in Vancouver, where Dr. Chung lives now, I had the privilege to read his dissertation and was very much impressed by the quality of study and the freshness of its basic presuppositions. It occurred to me that just as his supervisor Richard Niebuhr's work, *Christ and Culture,* even though originally published in 1951, still provides a valuable theoretical framework for students who want to study the relationship between Church and society, Dr. Chung's study could be an excellent frame of reference for anyone who wants to look deeply into the relationship between the religious and cultural elements of Korea and the rapid growth of Korean Christian churches.

There has been a great deal of research on the interesting phenomenon of Korean Christianity. Most of them, however, are studies examining historical, sociological, political, and economical aspects as deemed relevant to the tremendous growth of Christianity in Korea. Dr. Chung's study is unique in that it is mainly a study done from the viewpoint of comparative religions. He investigates deeply into the inner structures of Korean belief systems and tries to find a "religious tapestry," or an internal chemistry, working between the Korean mind and Christian worldviews. For this purpose, he not only analyzes historical and cultural contexts of Christian beginnings in Korea but also contrasts the Christian developments in Korea with those in China and Japan.

It is no accident that Dr. David Chung is the best qualified for this type of research. He was born in Lungjing, Northeast China, in 1917. His father was a Korean Christian minister and one of the well-known Korean independence movement leaders, Chaemyŏn Chung. The young David (his original Korean name is Daewi, which is a modified transliteralization of the biblical name David; "Daewi" literally means "Great Action") attended a Chinese elementary school there in China, during which time he picked up fluent colloquial Chinese at school as well as classical Chinese from his grandfather who was a scholar in Chinese classics. He attended Soongsil Academy in P'ŏngyang, North Korea, and learned English as well as formal Korean languages. He then moved on to Faculty of Theology, Doshisha University in Kyoto, Japan, where he learned not only theology but also languages such as German, French, Latin, Hebrew, Greek, and Sanskrit. While there as a theology student, he even practiced Zen meditation for six months in a Zen monastery in Kyoto. He graduated from the university with a special prize for his distinguished thesis on Karl Barth and his theology.

After serving briefly as a pastor in a small countryside church in Korea, he became a Greek teacher at a theological school in Seoul. Soon after he was asked by the church leaders to go to Canada in order to further his studies at the University of Toronto. Upon finishing his studies in Toronto, he served shortly for a Japanese church in British Columbia. The repeated news about the political and social instability in Korea made him return home in 1949. During the Korean War, which broke eight months after his arrival, he dedicated himself to help his people courageously survive this tragic national ordeal through various capacities. After the war, he became the first Secretary-General of the UNESCO Korean National Commission. While serving in Paris as well as in Korea and associating with the intellectual leaders from many countries, he was able to perfect his French and opened his eyes to new areas of academic pursuit. He became particularly interested in the anthropological approach to the study of religion, and this interest eventually led him to enroll in the graduate program at

Yale University in 1957. By this time, he was fully equipped with all the necessary linguistic tools and methodological articulations.

In this book we witness the fruit of all of the academic preparations that Dr. Chung had accumulated up to that point in his life. He has made extensive use of all the necessary materials drawn from primary sources written in Korean, Chinese, Japanese, French, German, Latin, and others. Some of these sources are highly inaccessible even today. We also see that the kind of comparative method he has employed here is not available for the ordinary scholar with a knowledge of two or three foreign languages.

I believe this study is comparable with similar monumental research done by Dr. L. George Paik, another Yale product, which appeared in a book entitled *The History of Protestant Missions in Korea 1832–1910* (1929). The main difference between the two seems to be that while Dr. Paik's is more descriptive, Dr. Chung's is more theoretical. As the title of the book indicates, Dr. Paik's book is mainly a detailed historical survey of Protestant missions in their early stages in Korea. Dr. Chung's study, on the other hand, is basically an analysis of historical and social contexts of Korean Christianity as an attempt to see the underlying structure of an encounter between different religious traditions.

I am confident that this study of Dr. Chung's is a great contribution for anyone who is interested in Korean Studies, History of Religions, Korean religions, Church history, and Comparative Studies of any kind. This study is not only informative for those in these areas of research but also exemplary in showing how extensively and intensively one's research can be carried out. It seems to me that this book, together with his service of fourteen years as a professor of Religious Studies at Carleton University in Canada (1969–83) and four years as the president of Hanshin University in Korea (1983–87), should be considered as one of his major contributions to the scholarly world of his chosen field.

While editing this book, I have left the main structure intact. I have only updated some information and references. I have also changed all the romanized Korean words following the standard romanization system as found in Peter H. Lee et al., *Sourcebook of Korean Civilization* (2 vols., New York: Columbia University Press, 1993 and 1996). My son Eugene and my former student, Mr. Martin T. Bale, have made many valuable stylistic changes. Dr. Chung has recently translated the frequent French and German quotations found in the dissertation into English. I have left the original quotations in the endnotes, because some of the original sources are not easily accessible to the reader. I also thank Elisabeth Kim and Denise Laville of the University of Regina for their help in verifying the German and French translations of the text, respectively.

I am extremely glad that this significant study is finally available for young scholars, who will now be able to see farther by standing on the shoulders of a "small" giant called David Chung.

Kang-nam Oh
University of Regina,
Regina, Saskatchewan, Canada

Preface

The spontaneous and explosive growth of Christianity in Korea from the time of its first contact with Korean society in the eighteenth century presents a "unique" case in the history of Christian missions. What was the main reason for this "unique" phenomenon? What actually happened in the society when the contact was felt? Is it possible to have a magnified view of the historical and social background of this tremendous event?

This study is an attempt to answer these questions, and for this purpose it endeavours to focus particularly on the question of how Korean society accommodated and assimilated religions of foreign origin, such as Confucianism, Taoism, Buddhism, and Christianity, through crude equation and uncanny or subtle identification of these religions with Korean indigenous beliefs in the stratum of *religio publica*. The study will demonstrate that Korean society, fundamentally shamanistic, received and grafted these religions onto her own and made a remarkable tapestry of beliefs, rites, and values in a comprehensive pattern.

This research is intended to be a historical case study on cultural contacts in the sphere of religion. I believe that an intelligent investigation into the details of the labyrinthine processes involved in these religious contacts in Korea might shed some new light upon the complex semantic problems surrounding this and other similar cases. For practical purposes, I sought a motif that would elucidate the complexity more clearly. The rapidity of growth of Christian churches in the society is chosen, in this manner, as the main theme of the study.

In a brief sketch of the history and the social context of this unique occurrence, I endeavour to illustrate that together with the generally favorable environmental factors, there was another important factor involved, namely, an established habit of *religious syncretism*. The syncretic practice of Koreans in religious matters is reviewed in the context of the "Three Religions Are One" principle, which is dominant in the East Asian societies. Missionary methods which Catholic and Protestant churches employed are examined from the viewpoint of their effectiveness, and their effectiveness is measured by the degree of their intensity and speed in producing Christian impact. It is observed that there was a "danger" of falling into syncretism in each of these effective approaches.

Syncretic phenomena in the East Asian scene are examined with special attention given to the contacts between religions with real or arbitrary "equivalencies." It is pointed out that Christianity, a latecomer to the scene, also produced syncretism, as seen in the T'ai-p'ing Rebellion in China, Hirata Atsutane Shintoism in Japan, and the Ch'ŏndogyo in Korea. Special attention is paid to the fact that these three syncretic movements did not endeavour to establish any official tie with the established Christian churches in the Christian world, whereas Korean Christians, who also had been exposed to the same danger, did their best to abide in the official relationship.

This study, originally entitled *Religious Syncretism in Korean Society*, was a dissertation submitted to the Department of Religion at the Graduate School of Yale University in 1959. Although the harvest of this study gathered here in this volume may be meagre, I would like, once again, to have the privilege of acknowledging my indebtedness to the invaluable instruction received from my professors at Yale, especially from Drs. Norvin Hein and James M. Gustafson, as well as Kenneth S. Latourette and Roland Bainton. In addition, I also acknowledge the honor of working under the supervision of Dr. H. Richard Niebuhr, whose understanding encouragement always sustained me and enabled me to continue my work.

I believed that any research work had a longevity of only thirty years at best. This work was much older than that. It has not even been published formally, except to be included in the series of University Microfilm International, Ann Arbor and London, 1959. It was a forgotten piece. I had hoped to get it published some day as a monograph. Unfortunately, however, I was not able to accomplish it.

Delighted and elated! My younger colleagues in the field of Religious Studies finally discovered my work. They told me that this study still has some value as a reference. They even suggested that it might be worth publishing as a book for easy access.

I am eternally indebted to Professor Kang-nam Oh of University of Regina who saved this dissertation just before it drifted into the ocean of oblivion. He wordprocessed it painstakingly, with the editorial job of standardizing the romanization of the Asian words and updating information and bibliography. He gave this dilapidated work a fresh new look in this way, providing a modern attire. He worked with his computer like a magician, spending his valuable time during his sabbatical year. I also deeply appreciate the efforts of those who rallied around Dr. Oh, especially his son Eugene, to make this publication possible.

David Chung

PART I

THE PROBLEM:
THE UNIQUE EVENT

CHAPTER ONE

Catholicism: *Mirabiliter Ingressi*

In describing the origin of Catholicism in Korea, some Catholic writers do not hesitate to call it a "miracle": Koreans had organized a church in their capital city by the 1770s before any missions had even begun to direct their organized efforts toward this "hermit nation."[1] Adrien Launay, an eminent Catholic historian, records this event with these words: "The Church in Korea has a very peculiar origin, marked by the special character of human wisdom guided by divine wisdom. It was not created by missionary zeal as were the churches in Vietnam, Japan or China."[2] It was a "spontaneous birth, without direct evangelization," like a sprout that came out of the soil in a field where none was expected. The earliest converts were ones who had made themselves Christians. The introduction of Christianity to Korea was accidental. This does not mean, however, that the Christians themselves were scattered individuals. They were united in an organism, a cell—a living cell—that could respond, suffer, and grow. It was this underground cell that met regularly at Kim Pŏmu's Myŏngryedong panggol Street, Seoul in the 1770s. And it was a representative of this group, Yi Sŭnghun, who was sent over the forbidden border to Beijing, China, and was baptized by the bishop who resided there and thereby linked the isolated member to the main body.[3]

In a discourse delivered before the pope on May 9, 1924, on the occasion of the publication of the papal decree that gave official recognition to the martyrs and the causes of the martyrdom of Mgr. Imbert and his company in Korea, 1838–1846, Mgr. De Guebrant gives an account of the origin of the Korean Church.

3

The Church of Korea has perhaps offered a unique example in the annals of modern missions, having originated toward the end of the 18th century in a rather spontaneous manner (that is, not through direct evangelization, but through the sole action of divine grace upon arid souls seeking the religious truth). Just as the Wise Men from the Orient after studying the ancient prophecies followed the star which led them to Bethlehem, so did the doctors of Korea, in the isolation of their solitary domain, study the books in which they hoped to find an explanation of the world. To them as well appeared a mysterious light which shone on the writings that had providentially fallen under their perusal.[4]

The introduction of Christianity to Korea, in this way, was nothing short of a "miracle." Alexandre de Gouvea, the bishop of Beijing at the time, who was chiefly responsible for the cultivation of this newborn church, wrote to Saint-Martin, the bishop of Ssuch'wan on August 15, 1798, a letter which was published later under the title: *De Statu christianismi in Regnum Coreae Mirabiliter Ingressi* (On the Status of Christianity Miraculously Entered into the Kingdom of Korea).[5]

What the author of this letter wanted to do was demonstrate not only the miraculous introduction of Christianity to Korea but also the extraordinary growth of this new Christian community. He repeatedly assured that "within a short period of time, the believers in Christianity had increased. . . . Within five years, the number of Christians had grown to about four thousand."[6]

Threatened by the vitality and potential of the new Christian cell, the would-be self-sufficient society of Korea soon organized a persecution which lasted over a century, leading finally to the last Royal Edict against Christianity published in 1881 and enforced that same year. If a similitude is permissible, "the blood of martyrs had fertilized Korean soil" during this "period of catacombs" before the "rich harvest began."[7] During the Regent Taewŏngun's rule alone, no less than ten thousand Christians paid the supreme price for joy in heaven.[8] Thus Christianity found fertile soil, and a new "Christian nation" was born. The Korean initiative in all this is quite evident.

Of course, it is equally true that "the Jesuits, who have zealously watched over the Imperial Court of China for evangelistic opportunities, have certainly not failed to notice similar occasions

for approaching the representatives of a nation that has not yet
been evangelized."[9]

Korea was one of these "non encore" who sent tributary emis-
saries to China, the Middle Kingdom annually. Matteo Ricci, the
great missionary to the East, himself met with Koreans in 1601 at
the "Castle of Foreigners" in the Imperial city of Beijing.[10]

According to the *Cheng-chiao-feng-pao*,[11] as early as in 1644 a
Jesuit missionary, Johannes Adam Schall von Bell of Germany,
approached for the purpose of evangelism the Korean prince Sohyŏn
who had been detained in China at that time.[12]

> In the first year of Shun-ch'ih, a Korean prince, the son of
> the King Hyojong, was detained in the capital city. He heard
> of T'ang-jo-wang (Johannes Adam Schall von Bell). So the
> prince paid him a visit when possible at the church where
> the priest resided. The prince questioned him about as-
> tronomy and other Western sciences. Jo-wang also came to
> repay the prince his visit on several occasions at the Hall
> of the prince. They had long talks and they understood
> each other deeply. As Jo-wang often explained the truth of
> Catholicism, the prince was glad to hear of it and asked
> detailed questions. When the prince went back home to his
> country (as a free man), Jo-wang gave him many kinds of
> books in translation on astronomy, mathematics and the
> Truth of Catholicism. A globe and a portrait of God (Jesus)
> were included among the gifts. The prince complimented
> him with a letter written by himself.[13]

Unfortunately the prince died soon after his return without achieving anything Jo-wang had hoped for.

Any missionary, given the same opportunity, might have done
the same, and opportunities undoubtedly abounded. Led by their
own curiosity, Korean visitors to the capital city of China were
often drawn to the strange men from the West. They were fasci-
nated not only by the Western scientific instruments found among
the strangers' possessions, but by the personalities of the men
themselves. Ambassador Chŏng Tuwŏn, in 1631, reports of his
meeting with Joannes Rodaniguez: "at the age of ninety-seven he
still seemed to enjoy his clear-mindedness and perfect health. He
was handsome as one of the *shen-hsien* (Taoist immortals)."[14] It is
only natural that the missionaries should have seized every opportunity and used it for their commission. There was, however, no

organized or positive effort on the part of the missionaries to bring forth such explosive results in Korea. When converted, the new Christians had to carry on their work under their own initiative.

The new Christians had no pastor to lead them for ten long years after they were accepted into the world Catholic fellowship. But even before the first decade was over, they had paid heavy prices for their new faith. Thomas Kim Pŏmu (+1785), Paul Yun Chich'ung [Ioun], and his cousin Jacques Kwŏn Sangyŏn (+1791) became Korea's first martyrs for the church.[15]

It is rather remarkable to note that the missionaries to Korea were brought in by the repeated requests of an already established and very active Christian body in the peninsula and through the heroic deeds of the indigenous new converts themselves. They earnestly requested a priest, knowing that more severe persecutions were to follow. Though the presence of a foreigner might aggravate the situation, they felt the need for a priest who could lead them and officiate at the sacraments for them during the period of their tribulation. Their repeated petitions were received by the bishop in Beijing, and in 1790 he promised them to send a priest as soon as possible.[16] A Chinese priest Chou Wen-mo [Jacques Tsiou] was sent and succeeded in entering the forbidden land secretly in 1794, became the first ecclesiastical official in Korea, and was beheaded as a martyr in 1801, after some six years of secret ministry. Chou was sent with the hope that, as a Chinese, he could more easily conceal his identity. After the loss, the new church continued the fight for thirty more years without a pastor.

The resourcefulness of the early Christians of this period is well demonstrated in their devotion and faithful observances of new doctrine in the face of overwhelming adversity.

First of all, it is remarkable indeed to see that these new converts persisted in their struggle to maintain their official relationship with the "Church" through occasional and difficult contact with the Catholic bishop in Beijing. This is in strong contrast to other parallel indigenous "Christian" movements such as the T'aip'ing Rebellion in China and the Hirata Shintoism in Japan, which although awakened under the impact of Christianity, developed independently and created "un-Christian" effects in other societies of the changing Orient.[17]

Maintaining this official relationship through a secret route they established over the border was a vital necessity for this new community; and it is only natural that the energy of the new converts should have been focused around it. The literature of these men during that eventful period is a powerful testimonial to their resourcefulness.

We now have three letters written by the new converts of this period and addressed to church officials in Beijing and Rome. The first one is the "Silk Letter of Hwang Sayŏng" of 1801.[18] The letter, addressed to Alexandre de Gouvea, was written on a length of silk measuring 38 cm × 63 cm with 13,311 Chinese characters arranged in 120 vertical columns. It was written on silk so that it could be rolled neatly into a coat collar of Korean dress and carried secretly over the border by the Christian carriers (Hwang Sim and Ok Ch'ŏnhui). These men had originally planned to join the annual envoy bound for Beijing in the winter of 1801. The writer was Hwang Sayŏng, a noted scholar despite his relative youth. The letter was written under the name of Thomas Hwang Sim, in agreement, because he had already established a personal acquaintance with the bishop during a previous visit with him.

This document, containing valuable firsthand information about the first Korean Christians under the persecution, was given a setting of vivid urgency under the anti-Christian pressure of the age. Hwang recorded it in his village hideout set deep in the mountains, where he had taken refuge from the danger of arrest. Yet the threat of immediate danger was constantly around him as he proceeded to write for forty days in an abandoned pottery kiln on a hillside. Nevertheless, the document contains a balanced view, remarkably free from the usual Oriental exaggerations. It is quite evident that he tried his best to report the situation to the bishop as accurately as possible. This material now provides a reliable source for students of Korean Church history.

Sadly, however, the writer was arrested before he could send the letter away safely, and the letter was seized by the police.[19] Charged with high treason, Hwang was executed with the extreme punishment of Nŭngji ch'ŏch'am[20] before the end of the year. He was twenty-six years old.

The silk letter, soon labeled an "evil letter" (hyungsŏ), astonished the government to an extreme measure. Its capture was immediately reported to the attention of Queen Kim, the great-grandmother and regent of the young King Sunjo. In the government annals we read:

> On the day of Kyŏngsin, October, Sinyu Year, that is, the first year of Sunjo (1800), the police officials Im Yŏl and Sin Ungju came to the palace of the Queen and reported that

they brought with them the "evil letter" written by the pagan prisoner Hwang Sayŏng. She had the letter brought in and saw it. When she gave it back, she commanded them to preserve it in the secret file.

The prisoner Hwang Sayŏng is a noble man who has been unfortunately very much confused and blinded by the evil religion. Knowing that the danger of arrest was drawing nearer he fled to Kŭmo at an early period of police search. He hid himself in a mourner's hemp clothes, used a false name and lived in an earth cave. For more than half a year he was searched for until he was caught at Chech'ŏn.

Police searched through his books and found a document written on a sheet of silk intended to be sent to the Catholic cathedral in Beijing. It is full of evil information such as the event of the executions of Chou Wen-mo [Chinese priest] and others which he intended to report with full details to the Westerners.

There are three points of evil contention: firstly, it [requested the Pope] to move the Imperial Government of China to force us to enter into friendly contact with the Westerners; secondly, it solicited Chinese interference by establishing an office in An-chu [north of P'yŏngyang] to supervise the country [lest it should start more persecutions] and take action immediately [if the prevention does not work]; and thirdly, it asked for an armed intervention of the Christian West by dispatching several hundred warships with fifty or sixty-thousand men in the fighting force and a lot of cannons to threaten us to yield to the freedom of their faith.[21]

The consternation of the government was doubled by the fact that the letter contained a detailed report of the execution of Priest Chou, a Chinese. The killing of a Chinese was certain to stir up a delicate international situation with the sensitive and powerful neighbor. In response, the queen had to send a special emissary to China to explain the government's position in these "religious affairs." The emissary Cho Yundae even carried with him a faked copy of the document.[22]

The copy was an actual extraction of the original text but gave a special emphasis on the points that would help to justify the Korean government's actions. The extraction contains only 923 Chinese characters in 16 columns. But there were no insertions or alterations except the corrections of three Chinese characters.

In the precious original document, which is one of the most valuable sources of information about the infant church and a great literature of martyrdom, one finds how mature and far advanced the Korean Christians were in their devotion and dedication to the supreme cause.

The letter raised three points regarding the maintenance of the secret route between Seoul and Beijing. First, it was recommended that a secret agent be placed at the border to make the contacts safer. Second, financial aid was requested to help with the costly maintenance of the transpeninsular route. Third, the dispatch of ecclesiastical officials was repeatedly urged.

The Vatican was not quite ready to send missionaries to Korea. Yet the Macedonian cry of the Christian community was not a visionary one but an earnest plea and demand in Christian fellowship. The new converts were willing to pay any price to keep their official relations with the main Christian body intact. Hwang wrote:

> . . . . We the sinners are scattered as lost sheep. . . . We dug holes in the ground like the mouse to hide, or slept on the way to escape. We drank our tears, swallowed our lament and went through sufferings in heart and pains in the bones. Our only plea is to partake in the Blessings of Our Omnipotent Lord on High and the immeasurable Grace of Our Great Father [the Bishop]. We earnestly pray for the help of our Lord his Mercy to us to deliver us from this water and fire of the persecution and lead us to the seats of the saints. The Holy Doctrine is proclaimed all over the world and all peoples of the world sing praises for the holy virtues of Catholicism and emulate each other to promote the work of sanctifying the world. As for the miserable beings of this land, there is no doubt that we are also the children of the Lord on High. Only because of the geographical situation of the land in the far corner, unfortunately, we became the latest hearers of the doctrines. Weak in faith we lament that we do not endure the sufferings very well. And yet we spent ten stormy years in suffering. The persecution of this year was beyond our thought in the day and dream in the night. If these extremity persists we are afraid that the blessed name of Jesus may be erased from this eastern land forever. When we think of these we feel that our liver and bowels are broken to pieces. . . . Please hear our plea and extend your help. . . .[23]

Other contemporary pieces of Christian literature bear the same witness to the devotion and resolution of this group. Unlike the ill-fated Hwang Sayŏng's silk letter, two other petitions, written by a François, reached the bishop of Beijing and Pope Pius II. But this occurred during the pope's captivity at Fountainbleau, and he was not able to respond. One of these two earnest pleas for missionaries was quoted by Adrien Launay in its entirety with Launay's own remarks that "This pious and touching supplication cannot be passed over in silence."[24] The letter reads:

Francis and the other Christians in Korea, prostrated on the ground and beating our bosoms, offer this letter to the Head of the Church [Pope], the Father most high and great.

It is with the greatest occasion and the deepest ardor that we implore Your Holiness to have compassion on us, to bestow on us your mercy and to grant us as soon as possible the blessings of the redemption.

We live in a small nation and have had the good fortune of first receiving the holy doctrine through books and, ten years later, through preaching and participation in the seven sacraments.

Seven years later, a persecution has taken place. The missionary Chou who had come to be with us has been put to death along with a large number of other Christians; and all of the others, overwhelmed with fear and sorrow, have dispersed little by little. They have been unable to gather for religious practice, having hidden in fear.

Our only hope lies in the divine mercy and in the great compassion of Your Holiness, which can save us and deliver us from danger. This is the subject of our prayers and longings.

For ten years, we have been subjected to pain and sorrow; many of us have died from old age or other maladies, we do not even know the numbers of us still alive; those who remain do not know when they will be able to receive the holy teachings. They wish to have this grace, as one who is dying of thirst wishes only to satisfy it. They cry out, as in a time of dryness, one calls out for rain. But the heaven is too high, and we cannot attain it; the sea is too vast, and we cannot reach for help on our own.

We, the poor sinners, are unable to express with such sincerity and with such ardor to Your Holiness our desire to receive your immediate assistance. But our nation is so

small, and far away in a far corner of the sea. There is no
vessel or vehicle by means of which we can receive your
instructions or orders. What is the reason for such depriva-
tion if not our lack of devotion or the enormity of our sins?
That is why we now beat our bosom with a profound fear
and anguish. We humbly beseech the Lord who died on the
cross and who has more compassion for sinners than the
just, and Your Holiness who takes the place of God on
earth, and who cares for and truly delivers the sinners of
the world.

We have been redeemed from our sins and have left the
darkness; but the world afflicts our bodies, while sin and
malice assault our souls. Our tears, our sighs, and our
affliction are of little value; but we consider that the Mercy
of Your Holiness is without limits and without measure
and will therefore have compassion on the servants of this
Kingdom who have been robbed of their pastor, and that
you will send missionaries as soon as possible, so that the
blessings and merits of our savior, Jesus Christ, will be
proclaimed, our souls will be saved and delivered, and the
holy names of God will be glorified always and everywhere.[25]

Such petitions were heard at last. And the missionaries began
to arrive after 1831 — only to pay the supreme sacrifice, along with
their flocks, one after another. Bringing the missionaries from their
temporary stations in China safely into the Korean peninsula
through a safer route was the self-imposed duty of a heroic Korean
priest named Kim Taegŏn [Andre Kim], whose stories of adventure
and ultimate martyrdom are well told by Dallet and Launay.[26] He
explored the sea route from the west coast of Korea to Shanghai on
a small fishing boat with a crew of ten who had more faith than
experience in navigation. His initiative powerfully illustrates how
the indigenous Christians played a positive role in maintaining
their official tie with the main body.

The Korean resourcefulness is also well demonstrated in the
activities they organized within their borders. The Hwang Sayŏng
silk letter refers, in several passages, to the "Myŏnghoe Society" of
the catechumen, as well as to the General Conference of the same
body.[27] They kept this organization active even in the face of severe
persecution, in conformity with instructions received in the *Literae
Pastorales* which were sent to them through a secret route, from
Bishop Gouvéa in reply to inquiries from the converts.[28] In this

way, the infant church was administered by an inconvenient remote control, but with extremely satisfactory results.

This underground community even produced Christian literature for the purpose of edification and evangelization. Hwang Sayŏng reported[29] that Augustine Chŏng [Yakchong] had written an *Introduction to Catholic Doctrine* [*Chugyo yoji*] in two volumes in the Korean alphabet, Han'gŭl, so that the uneducated and children might read. It is an excellent work in its own right. The Chinese priest Chou Wen-mo endorsed the book, proclaiming it to be even better than the *Sheng-shih-ch'u-jao* of the Jesuit missionary Fengping-cheng. It was warmly received and well read.

Christian heroism was everywhere evident among the persecuted, who believed martyrdom to be the highest glory for them. Hwang reported the cases of the apostasies also as faithfully as he could. There was a Kim Yŏsam, the Judas-like traitor. But it is of special interest for us to note that, according to Hwang, not only most of those who had broken away were continuously faithful "with resolution of death,"[30] but actually testified their faithfulness at the end of their victorious lives to the greater glory of their triumphant faith.

Among the martyrs there were a number of noted scholars of the day, the most illustrious of whom being Ambrose Kwŏn Ch'ŏlsin, Paul Yun Chich'ung, Augustine Chŏng Yakchong, and Alexander Hwang Sayŏng. There were also faithful women of social distinction like Columban Kang Wansuk. There were believers from the slave class like Peter Cho Taesŏn.[31] There were also martyrs like Martin Yi Chungbae[32] who always attracted a great crowd of people in front of his prison with his medical ability and flair for faithhealing power. There were many, like John Ch'oe Ch'anghyŏn,[33] who made their prison cell a hall of evangelism, and there were those, like Andre Kim, the heroic Korean priest, who made their scaffold their platform to proclaim their faith.

In short, Catholic evangelism was a success from the very beginning. It began "miraculously" and accidentally, and was carried on heroically by the native converts under their own initiative.

CHAPTER TWO

Protestantism: A Success

The same story from Chapter One can be told all over again with Protestantism in Korea. The mystified observers of the explosive growth of the Christian church were the missionaries themselves who, in their reports of success in the brand-new mission field, spoke of such things as "miracles" and "the work of the Holy Spirit."

In 1900, only sixteen years after the opening of missionary work in Korea, the factors of the success were discussed and heatedly debated at the Ecumenical Council, which met in New York that year with representatives of no fewer than forty-eight countries. Some attributed the success to a special method of missionary evangelism adopted in Korea while others objected to this theory.[1]

"Within less than two years after Mr. Underwood's arrival (one of the two first Protestant missionaries who arrived in Korea), he was able to organize in Seoul the 'first Protestant church in Korea.' On October 7, 1887, Mr. Underwood wrote: 'a week ago Tuesday we completed the organization of a Presbyterian church by the election of two elders whom we ordained last Sunday.' "[2] Just like that, the story goes.

However, the statement above about the "first" Protestant church in Korea has to be qualified in order to focus the picture more sharply. The Seoul Saemunan Presbyterian Church is the "first" Protestant church in the sense that it was given an official recognition as such. "There were over a hundred believers in the capital [Seoul]"[3] previous to the date above, gathered around Sŏ

13

Sangyun, an indigenous self-supported evangelist. A strong and effective evangelism was already in progress. The seed had been sown, and the field was "ripe" already, in a sense, and was waiting for the harvest when the first missionaries actually arrived in Korea and started their work.

There were at least two healthy seed-beds in Korea prior to the arrival of the missionaries. One was in Ŭiju, an "entrance" city located on the south side of the Manchurian border; and the other at Sorae, the small village in Hwanghae province and home village of Sŏ Sangyun. Saltau dates the official establishment of the Sorae church in 1888, the date when Underwood paid his first visit there to officiate at a baptism that had been repeatedly requested since 1886 by the delegation from the Christian "group" in this village.[4]

It is evident, however, that this "group" had been a "church" in a broader sense. It had already been functioning as a Christian fellowship in accordance with the teachings in the Bible. It had even extended, on several occasions prior to 1885, invitations to John Ross, a Scottish Presbyterian missionary residing in Manchuria, to come to Korea to officiate at a baptism for them.[5]

The new converts eagerly expected Ross, who had initiated some of the Korean immigrants in Manchuria into Christianity, to come to visit the first Korean church and officially link it to the Christian church. Korea had already opened its doors to the world in 1882. Therefore, they thought the coming of the missionary was not impossible. Unfortunately Ross could not comply with the request, and his visit was delayed until 1887. Instead, Ross asked Underwood to perform this pastoral duty when the latter arrived on the mission field. Underwood wrote of the Sorae converts: "Toward the close of 1886, Mr. Sŏ Sangyun presented himself at my house with a letter of introduction from Mr. Ross and told me that there were a number of people desiring baptism in his village. In the following spring (1887) a delegation of thirteen Christians [of] this village waited upon us [in Seoul], seeking baptism. They were examined before the whole mission and finding they had been believers for some years, and were able to state intelligently the grounds of their faith, the mission unanimously decided that three men should be admitted to the church by baptism."[6]

When Underwood paid his first visit to Ŭiju in 1889, he found a hundred applicants for baptism in the border city.[7] Unorganized, yet unmistakably a "church," this indigenous church was waiting for the work of Sŏ Sangyun. To the Ŭiju seed-bed, Yi Sungha and

Paek Hongjun were the carriers of evangelism. Both these men were converts from the Korean Christian community in Manchuria.

It was John Ross who had been interested in the Koreans whom he met occasionally in Manchuria and began to explore the possibility of evangelizing them. It is reported that he began to preach to the Korean immigrants in 1873. John McIntyre, another Scottish missionary and Ross's brother-in-law, soon came to assist him in his new adventure. A handful of converts were baptized by McIntyre in 1876.

During this period of preparation they undertook a project modest in scope, but explosive in effect. It was the Korean translation of the Gospel of Luke from the Chinese Bible, made by the Korean converts Yi Ŭngch'an and Kim Chingyu. When they printed this in 1882 on a temporary press they had set up in Mukden, Manchuria, they never even dreamed of touching off such a conflagration as that which was soon to follow.

When the Gospel was printed in 1882, Ross sent [a Korean] colporteur to the Koreans scattered in the eastern Manchurian valleys. After six months the colporteur returned with the report that many had become believers, and urged the missionary to go with him to baptize them. Ross did not go; but the colporteur made a second visit of six months and returned with the same encouraging report.

In the winter of 1884, Ross and his colleagues undertook a difficult journey to visit the Korean valleys in northeastern Manchuria. They visited four valleys and baptized seventy-five men, while many were placed on the waiting list for further instruction. These people who received baptism were "all farmers and heads of families." No missionary had ever visited these people; the Gospels and tracts which had been sent to them and the personal witness-bearing of one or two converts in Mukden had alone been instrumental in bringing the great harvest. The result was so gratifying that Ross declared: "It is worthwhile to translate a few books to see such results."

While these missionaries were yet in the fourth valley, they received reports that there were many more believers in other valleys. With much reluctance, they returned to Mukden before the heavy snowfall of the midwinter should check their homeward journey. In the following summer, the missionaries made a second visit and baptized many more.[8]

The most striking feature in all these is that it was the Koreans who took the initiative in their own evangelism. They were more than willing recipients. They were enthusiastic cooperators with the missionary enterprise which was extended to them rather belatedly. It was they who requested Christian fellowship and demanded missionaries to come to them, just as eagerly as the Korean Catholics had done a century before. The mass baptism, comparable to the Charlemagnean experience in early European history, must have been a thrilling, yet heart-warming sight for the Scottish missionaries who had labored for a long time already among the Chinese and never experienced such a tremendous response.

The experience in Manchuria, in fact, was often repeated in "hundreds of villages up and down the peninsula."[9] It was repeated in the towns and cities continuously thereafter throughout the country until Japan, the new master of the peninsula since 1910, began to check the growth for political reasons.[10] Church statistics leaped and jumped during this period of "initial growth" prior to the annexation of Korea by Japan in 1910. Clark's statistics of the Presbyterian Church in Korea,[11] though unfortunately inaccurate for the years prior to 1902, show the magnitude of the growth.

New Catechumen This Year

Year	Number	Year	Number
1884		1902	2,599
—		1903	2,821
—		1904	2,469
1896	2,000	1905	4,755
1897	1,000	1906	8,047
1898	1,000	1907	10,027
1899	1,000	1908	14,008
1900	2,000	1909	17,588
1901	243	1910	14,507

Wasson notes in his interesting study that the growth of membership in the Korean church was arrested immediately after the annexation. He reasons that it was conditioned by environmental factors.[12] But, to be sure, this numerical change reflects but only partially the degree of growth of Christianity. In fact, the numerical increase of church attendants is only one matter, while the expansion of Christian influence upon the minds of the people is another, as Latourette correctly pointed out.[13] For, in some societies, Christian influence is disproportionately large even if the Christian communities are relatively small. In the case of the Korean society, we have every reason to believe that the increase of Christian influence was never seriously checked, even though Shinto Japan tried its best to do so.[14]

On the other hand the Christian Church in Korea saw the serious disadvantage of exposing itself to the danger of too much rapid growth. The churches, therefore, imposed rigid legalistic restrictions upon membership admission to avoid the immaturity of too rapid growth. The leaders felt it necessary to consolidate a church organization fit for a militant and triumphant battle to win the nation. Such extreme, and often excessive, discipline may be considered the main reason for the present size of the Christian population in Korea today.

protect against too fast a growth

By 1912 the infant church had already begun a vigorous evangelism not only in Korea proper but over the border in China. This shows how confidently Christianity took its position in its "newly" adopted land. Rhodes reports:

> The historic meeting of the first General Assembly [Presbyterian] took place in P'yŏngyang on September 1, 1912. . . . The commissioners numbered fifty-two Korean pastors and one hundred and twenty-five elders.
>
> One Sunday during the meeting of the Assembly, one of the Korean members, the Rev. Kim Sukch'ang from Sonch'un preached to an open-air audience of five thousand people.
>
> At this first meeting of the Assembly it was decided to send three Korean pastors with their families to Lai-yang, East Shantung, China, as foreign missionaries to the Chinese.[15]

The Korean church was some twenty-five years old by official count when they passed this resolution at the first General Assembly (consisting of seven Presbyteries). This China mission was maintained until the withdrawal of the last missionary family from the field under the pressure of Communist China in 1957. The church opened a new mission field in Thailand in 1957 and ever since has been expanding the effort among the Thai people.

By 1919 Christianity reached the stage of affecting the ethos of the society in many ways. One can enumerate all the sociocultural changes that took place in this category, because it is Christianity that has played a leading role in this eventful epoch. But we have a more interesting example of the amazing change that took place. As early as 1919, a woman delegate rose to her feet at the "First Korean Congress," a political meeting organized by Korean immigrants in the United States and held in Philadelphia, to move for the adoption of a "message to the people of Japan." The message was prepared by the congress as an echo of the Korean Independence Movement which had grown up among Koreans at home and abroad in response to President Woodrow Wilson's self-determination principle and which had suffered the brutal retaliation of Japanese police. Korea was an occupied country. She said: "Mr. President, on behalf of the ladies here, I wish to make it clear, the way we understand it that we are sending this message out to the Japanese people. It does not mean that we wish to say we are people better than they are, but that we know what humanity is, and that we are not in sympathy with their being barbarous and butchering our innocent people. . . . We want to show them that every Korean will be perfectly willing to act as a Christian toward the Japanese people, whatever they do toward our people."[16]

It came to her so naturally to identify "every Korean" with the nationals, one could not expect to hear such a remark as the Korean woman uttered. In fact, her statement proves to be a fantastic exaggeration when we compare it with the statistics of the date. But the story is not as simple as that. It was taken for granted by that time that a Christian nation was in the making in Korea. Christian leadership in the society was an accepted fact. It was not mere political pretense to draw the sympathy of the Christian West on the Korean side. There was something more to it. It would not be a grave mistake to admit that the Korean public found the meaning of life and a hope, a secular hope, if you like, in Christianity. Even so, it was a religiously oriented hope, as is evidenced in later developments.[17]

Of course, there were great variations and retrogress in this public commitment to Christianity. At one extreme, one finds fanaticism. At the other end, there was something like public recognition or tolerance. Whatever the variations and shades were, it can be safely stated that by that time Christianity occupied a position in the society comparable to that of Buddhism in the Koryŏ dynasty and Confucianism in the Yi dynasty.

A patriotic song of that time, comparable to "La Marseillaise" or the "Star-Spangled Banner," was adopted by the public as the national anthem. It remained in use even after Korea was divided into two, South and North, when Korea was liberated from the Japanese yoke in 1945. All people regardless of their creed or social status were united in the song, the last line of the first verse of which reads: "May *Hanŭnim* protect us. And Hurrah we shout for the Nation."[18] (*Hanŭnim*: Korean term for God.)

The first National Assembly (the House of Representatives) of the liberated Korea opened its first session in 1948 with a Christian prayer. No single voice of objection was heard even though only less than ten percent of the population was Christian. One is perfectly free to say that all this was an innocent imitation of America, with which Korea had entered so close a relationship. But there is something more than that, for she did not "have to" follow the American or any other Western examples. It was the spontaneous and natural thing for the representatives to do on such an occasion. It was taken for granted. This is the "unique event" that took place in Korea.

[margin: imitate West]

There are hosts of witnesses as to how this "unique event" has taken place. Some anticipated a Christian Korea as early as in 1907—only twelve years after the opening of the missionary work in the land. Reporting his visit to Korea in 1907, John R. Mott said: "During my recent tour in the Far East I found the deep conviction that if the present work on the part of the cooperating missions in Korea is adequately sustained and enlarged in the immediate future, Korea will be the first nation in the non-Christian world to become a Christian nation. I know of no mission field where larger or more substantial results have been secured, in proportion to the expenditure, than in Korea."[19]

Next year in 1908, a newspaper correspondent William T. Ellis vented his layman's enthusiasm with these words: "Cannot you say something or do something to make the church in America realize that here in Korea, just now, is the Christian opportunity of centuries? This situation is extraordinary and amazing. The whole country is fruit ripe for the picking . . . If the Christian Church has any conception of strategy and appreciation of an opportunity, and any sense of relative values, she will act at once—not next year, but now."[20]

Another eminent visitor, A. J. Brown, also shared these opinions: "Every year it has seemed that the movement must have reached its climax and that there would certainly be a reaction; but every year has seen the movement broadening and deepening until it now looks as if Korea would be the first of the non-Christian nations to become evangelized."[21]

The happy anticipation of these men has not been proved to be false. In Seoul there were only some thirty churches in the 1930s when the Shintoistic Japanese pressure was acutely felt. This pressure would develop into an organized persecution of a kind seldom seen in modern history. In 1958 there were about three hundred churches within the city limits. One large church had an average of two thousand attendants at every Sunday morning service. An evangelical society built an auditorium in 1957 big enough to accommodate a congregation of five thousand, and it was filled to full capacity whenever revival meetings were held.

In 1997, however, one finds more than thirty thousand churches in Korea including the world's largest churches in Seoul. Korean Catholicism had its one hundred heroes and heroines of faith canonized when Pope John Paul II visited Korea in 1984 to commemorate the two hundredth anniversary of the official foundation of Korean Catholic Church, and this has made Korea the world's fourth largest country in terms of the number of Catholic saints. At the present time, about a quarter of the Korean population are Christians.[22] As James H. Grayson aptly says, "moving into the final decade of the twentieth century, the Christian churches, especially the Protestant churches, are the dominant religious fact of modern Korea."[23]

We will attempt to provide an explanation of this strange phenomenon in terms of religious syncretism.

PART II

CONTEXT:
THE EVENTFUL AGE

CHAPTER THREE

The Historical Stage

In his majestic prologue to the story of the explosive growth of Christianity in the Roman Empire, Rudolf Sohm, the gifted nineteenth-century jurist and historian, used a symbolic expression to outline the historical setting: "die Welt ist leer, weil der Himmel leer geworden ist." (The world is empty, because the heavens have become vacant.)[1] The age, spent in ephemeral glories, lay exhausted on the stage in an intensifying hunger and unfulfilled "*Sehnsucht*" (longing) while the darkness of doubt prevailed on the deserted scene. The heaven was empty, waiting for a dawn.

The Korean world in the sixteenth and seventeenth centuries was empty in the same sense. The Confucian Yi dynasty had gone far in the process of self-idolization after its considerable success in restoring glories comparable to those of the once prosperous Buddhist Silla dynasty. Sadly, however, it also soon took the suicidal course of absolutizing or fossilizing its own systems, ideals, and techniques. This was the age when the impact of Christianity was felt in Korea. A brief account of this process of decline is necessary in order to bring the situation into sharp focus.

For a century or so (1392–1494), the young Chosŏn dynasty seemed to have been destined for prosperity. Succeeding the reform policy of their tragic opponent Chŏng Mongju (who devoted the last ounce of his loyalty to the lost cause of the dying Koryŏ dynasty until he fell under the blow of the founders of the new kingdom, the Yi dynasty), the reformers of the new dynasty revitalized the country. Soon after their seizure of power, they suppressed the monstrous

23

power of Buddhism with strength borrowed from the newly invigorated spirit of neo-Confucianism. Koryŏ Buddhism had fallen into
the ugliest possible form of corruption.

The reform was thoroughgoing. Human rights were greatly
upheld. Land reform was enforced, depriving the nobility of the
privileges of land ownership. It is said that it took several days in
1390 to burn the cadastres to ashes. The feudal system was eliminated, and a strong centralized government emerged. Anticorrup-
tion measures were taken to combat the customs remaining from
the previous dynasty. T'aejong, the third king, hung a bell in 1402
near his palace, so that any one who wanted to appeal directly to
the king when mistreated by officials might ring it to draw the
king's attention. It was called "*sinmungo*," the "bell of petition." A
social welfare office called "*hwalinwŏn*" was instituted in the capital, and services were rendered to the needy all over the country
through "*munminjilkosa*," "social welfare investigators." Agriculture and the silk industry were encouraged through special government agencies. Measurements were standardized. And in 1395 the
collection of the National Code, *Kyŏngguk taejŏn*, was compiled to
maintain the unimpaired prosperity of the new dynasty.[2] Two enlargements of the compilation of the "Code" were added in later
years. Favoritism disappeared from the procedure by which officials
were appointed. Government examination systems were strengthened to select able and conscientious men for the official positions.
The land confiscated from Buddhist temples all over the country
was cultivated to nourish a strong and efficient army.

Scholars, scientists, and artists were encouraged to carry on
their work. Printing by cast copper movable type, invented in the
Koryŏ dynasty two centuries prior to the time of Gutenberg, was
improved greatly during this period.[3] And the printers of this period produced a considerable amount of printed materials.[4] King
Sejong helped the scientists Chang Yŏngsil and Kim Cho to invent
various kinds of ingenious meteorological instruments.[5] Astrono-
mers Yun Saung, Yi Sunji, and Kim Tam improved the lunar calendar. Musicians Pak Yŏn and Nam Kŭp did some rearrangements
of classical music and also renovated some musical instruments.

A medical encyclopedia, *Kogŭm ŭibang yuch'wi*, was compiled
by Kim Sunŭi, Ch'oe Yun, and Kim Yuji. An agricultural directory,
Nongsa chiksŏl, was edited by Chŏng Ch'o and Pyŏn Ch'omun. The
first detailed geography of the country, *P'aldo chiriji*, by Yun Hoe,
Sin Saek, and Maeng Sasŏng, a monumental history of the Koryŏ

dynasty, *Koryŏ sa*, by Kim Chongsŏ and Chŏng Inji were all published in this period.

Sŏ Kŏjŏng's *Tongguk t'onggam*, Chŏng Tojŏn's *Chosŏn kyŏngguk chŏn*, the government editions of *Chip'ŏng yoram*, *Kukcho pogam*, the literary collections of *Tong munsŏn*, historical and geographical surveys of *Tongguk yŏji sŭngnam*, and numerous other literary works are the products of this flourishing period. The most brilliant achievement of all was, of course, the invention of the Korean alphabet which was made possible by scholars such as Sin Sukchu, Chŏng Inji, Sŏng Sammun, and Ch'oe Hang under the supervision and wise counsel of King Sejong. The great scholars such as Kwŏn Kŭn, Kim Chongjik, Cho Kwangjo, Sŏ Kyŏngdŏk, Yi Hwang, and Yi I, who were widely respected even in China and Japan, all accomplished their works in this prosperous age.[6]

The credit for this prosperity goes to Confucianism. To be more specific, neo-Confucianism succeeded the decay of the Buddhist Koryŏ dynasty and became instrumental in bringing the century to its culmination. To undo the fatal entanglement of the society in Buddhist ideologies and institutions, the reformers found handy tools in the neo-Confucian philosophy and system. Neo-Confucianism itself was a "synthesis" of Confucian tradition with Buddhist and Taoist elements.[7] It advocated, however, the combating of Buddhism. In fact, anti-Buddhist fervor was its very impetus. All of the great leaders in the Chinese neo-Confucian school, such as Chang Tsai, Cheng Ming-tao, Cheng I-ch'uan, and Chu Hsi, criticized and denounced Buddhism. The Korean reformers took this advantage to combat Buddhism in their own country, and used the neo-Confucian theories for the purpose.

To be sure, it was the Confucianists of the Koryŏ dynasty such as Yi Saek and Chŏng Mongju who began to propagate neo-Confucianism. Their main purpose, however, was to modernize the nation as a model seen in the Ming dynasty of China and had nothing to do with an attempt at complete elimination of Buddhism as avowedly entertained by their followers in the succeeding dynasty. Though Yi Saek in 1352 and Chŏng Mongju in 1392 advised their kings to restrain themselves from excessive commitment to the cause of Buddhism, they did not—perhaps dared not—renounce Buddhism as such.

It was Chŏng Tojŏn who spoke up clearly and powerfully. He was already an outspoken anti-Buddhist when he was a professor at Koryo's Confucian University Sŏnggyungwan in Kaesŏng, the capital of Buddhist Koryŏ. As one of his students, Pak Ch'o, eulogized, he was "the only one true Confucianist" of the day. When the revolution was achieved with the founding of the new dynasty, he became the first voice "propagating the teaching of K'ung-meng-cheng-chu [Confucius, Mencius, Cheng Brothers, and Chu Hsi), uncovering the madness and poisonous contamination of the long enduring religion of Buddha, breaking the thousand years of foolishness since the days of the Three Kingdoms. He fought ardently against the 'heresies and evil doctrines,' (i.e., Buddhism)."[8] He was not only a clear-minded negative critic on the doctrinal and practical fallacies of Buddhism,[9] but a positive thinker who rendered a great service for the cause of the reform movement by supplying courage as well as theories in law, politics, and economy.[10] Thus the course of history was set for the following five hundred years.

Chŏng Tojŏn as well as other contemporaries of his, however, did not suspect that the philosophy of the indomitable systematic thinker Chu Hsi, comparable to St. Thomas Aquinas in the West on many accounts,[11] would have such extensive fossilizing effects upon the Korean adherents who readily submitted themselves to this ideology. There seems to have been some intrinsically fatal elements in the doctrine itself.

In the first place, this philosophy was an archaism, in spite of the fact that it did attempt some fresh interpretations on traditional text. As an authority on Chinese philosophy relates, it was comparable to the Pharisaism of the first century.[12] With its emphasis on a rigid formalism, patterned on idealized tradition, it pushed back the ideals of society to the dead past. In the long run, it made ultraconservatism the dominant principle in Korean neo-Confucian society.

Secondly, this philosophy was dogmatic in character. The cosmological-ontological doctrines as well as the principles of legalistic ethics were standardized and codified. Authority rather than reason was the criterion of truth. In actual application in Korea, the ultimate authority rested solely upon the "Master's [Chu Hsi's]" interpretations. Every principle was to be derived from Chu Hsi's commentaries and enlargements of the *Shu* and *Ching*, i.e., official Chinese classics.[13]

"*Samun nanjŏk*," meaning "deceiving literati and disturbing rebels," was the quick title given to the daring dissenters or "heretics" of the day. More often, in fact, the title was put into use by accusers to denounce others whom they simply wanted to victimize. The situation was soon aggravated by the fact that powerful political factions made neo-Confucianism the arena in which the struggle for power was fought, from the beginning of the sixteenth century, with swords and shields provided by neo-Confucian doctrines.

Thirdly, the proud man and self-sufficient society were the ideals of the philosophy. And these ideals were the very core of the self-idolization or self-deception of a neo-Confucian society. There was a hierarchy of virtues in this neo-Confucian system. Confucius himself was enthroned as the King of the Literati or *Munsŏnwang* who personified Supreme Virtue. Hierarchical titles were given posthumously to some 130 Chinese and Korean Confucianists according to their virtues and merits in graded levels, the title ranging from Duke to Count. And it was assumed that under this echelon there was *chün-tzu* or *kunja*, a "perfect-man" class to which every decent Confucianist was entitled.

In contrast to the posthumous positions above, this perfect-manship was expected of everyone who proposed to lead a Confucian life. In that sense, it was a kind of standard for aspiration in life, to be attained by the eager pursuance of virtues and the faithful observance of codes of behavior. Pretension, however, was not strictly discouraged. Therefore, everyone had to pretend, at least, to be a *chün-tzu*. Those who were foreign to or excluded from this ideal due to their birth in a lower social class, and those who were unfaithful in achieving this standard were equally despised as *hsiao-jen* or *soin*, "little man." The center of the Confucian arrogance lies here. In an exaggerated view, the *kunjas* were said to be noble animals like giraffes and phoenixes while the *soins* were seen as equals to lambs and dogs.

The original ideal was, of course, to establish a Confucian utopia of "ruling without enforcing law," "spontaneous harmony unsupported with punishment," through edification of all citizens to this standard of perfection. In practice, however, it gave rise to premature pride in individuals as well as to a deceptive sense of self-sufficiency in the community and arrested the normal growth of society.

Under such circumstances, political parties with opposing interests soon found many opportunities to express their hatred for each other in terms of this ideology of perfect-manship. The struggle between the parties took an extreme course, because any one of them could easily claim their possession of "absolute" truth—philosophically defined and religiously sanctioned truth—to add haughtiness to their power. Because of these claims, political fights were fought with atrocities rarely seen except in religious wars. In the name of the truth, excessive measures were taken to punish their opponents. Possibilities of compromise were excluded. No *kunja* was to sit on the same seat with a *soin*.

In the fourth place, the system of seemingly harmonious ethical stages, namely, the "self-family-community-world," had fatal defects within itself. The stages were not presented in a problematic form as an "either/or." Instead, the development of, or comprehensive approach to, all of the four stages was recommended, in spite of the fact that serious conflicts of interests existed between one stage and another. Thoroughgoing self-interest often could not be harmonized with the interests of the family. In practice filial piety and loyalty to the king often conflicted with each other in times of national crisis. The interests of the community and those of the world were always incompatible.

However, offsetting the "harmonious" system, the virtue of filial piety alone was greatly exalted, especially with the publication of the extreme formalism of Chu Hsi's exposition of the "Family Rituals," *Chu-tzu Chia-li*. This oddity perhaps could be attributed to its congeniality to the existing social pattern, an "extended family" type[14] on a grand scale. The Korean society of the sixteenth century is the prime example. It could be said that this Chu Hsian emphasis aggravated the social schism within Korean society by complicating the clanism and parochialism which had existed in the social structure since the early Silla dynasty.[15]

By the sixteenth century, society was completely arrested in growth, poisoned by this ideal of the perfect-man. The veneration of idealized ancestors dried up the stream of progress. Social "mimesis" was to be found only in the dead past as recorded in the "books." Therefore, learning meant nothing more than studying the books, and pursuance of knowledge as such was heresy. Thus the social position of the literati was high at the expense of the suppressed military class as well as of the artisans, industrialists, farmers, and common laborers. As a corollary to this chain reaction, the stratified society suffered greater and greater schism. Thus the society penalized itself.

This was the state of society when Christianity came into contact with it. Korea did not erect a ponderous monument to Victor Immanuel, as Italy did, to mark the death of the creative age of "Dante and Michelangelo."[16] But the numerous stone tablets of the age found all over the country, commemorating usually mendacious "merits" of the members of the dominant party, were heavy

enough to suppress the creative energy of the nation so that no Yi
Hwang or Kim Chŏngjik emerged to produce literature to nourish
the hungry mind of the age. Artistic energy hit its lowest mark.
This tendency encouraged each able individual to direct his aspiration toward achieving the "merits" deserving a new monument, by
following the familiar path of conventionalism. Nowhere was creative effort seen anymore. Only the craving for power was active in
an otherwise static society. The society of the self-sufficient individuals and communities became so rigid under neo-Confucianism
that the creative impulse was stifled.

The signs of death were clearly seen in every quarter of national life. But there was still some flickering of life persisting in
the form of a "*Sehnsucht*." Discontented yet eager-hearted intellectuals of that age were seeking the new light coming from the outside world. They constituted the most sensitive part of the society,
and it was they who responded quietly but surely when the challenge of the West came. Needless to say, these intellectuals were
alarmed by the astonishing achievements of the Western world in
science and technology when they gained some rather scanty information through China. But they seem to have been more alarmed
at this time by their discovery of the utter inadequacies of their
own society. To their utmost dismay they found that the traditional
truth was not "the" truth at all, but an arbitrary enforcement.
Authority hitherto accepted as absolute had been shaken hope-
lessly. Though under the pressures of the age they were powerless
to do anything, they saw their problem clearly.

Scholar Yi Ik,[17] for instance, in his careful observations on the
sciences of the Western world repeatedly wrote remarks like these:
"Their views are absolutely correct"; "Their information is from actual experience, therefore is neither void nor deceiving"; "This theory
is an unchangeable one"; "These are ideas which even the scholars
of China could not dream of." In these words he frankly recognized
not only the superiority of the Western sciences over that of the East
but the fallibility of the "authority" which had been believed to be
unchangeable. In commenting on the accuracy of the solar calendar
Shi-hsien-li of Adam Schall von Bell, the Jesuit missionary to China,
he said: "According to the Han dynasty record *Lu-li-chih*, it was
Hwang-ti who made the calendar; according to the Shih-pen, it was
Yung-ch'eng who made it; and according to Shih-tzu, it was Hsi-ho
who made it. These records are, however, not in conflict with each
other, because Yung-ch'eng was the minister to Hwang-ti and Hsi-
ho to the Emperor Yao." Being attributed to the "Saints," Hwang-ti

and Yao, the calendar was considered something sacred, though its accuracy had to be insured by continuous revisions. "During the period of four hundred years since the beginning of the Han dynasty, five revisions were made on this calendar. From the period of Wei to Sui, thirteen revisions, and from T'ang to Chou there were some sixteen revisions made. During the three hundred years or so in the Sung dynasty thirteen revisions, from Chin Hsi-tsung to Yüan, three more revisions were made. At the beginning of the Ming dynasty Liu-chi advocated a *Ta-t'ung-li* which was known as the publication of the Government but was nothing but the Sou-shi-li calendar of the Yüan scholar K'uo-shou-ching, renamed."[18]

In short, in spite of such an all-out effort for improvement, it only proved that even the knowledge possessed by the saints of the past could not accomplish everything. ". . . The current *Shi-hsien-li* Calendar is the work of a Westerner T'ang-jo-wang [Adam Schall von Bell]. And I believe this to be the final in all calendars, because with this there have been no mistakes in calculating the eclipses. If the ancient saints were to be born again, even they would have to follow this calendar."[19]

No sharp-eyed reader can fail to notice the irony the writer used in this connection. The revolutionary remarks were a shocking statement considering the important role the calendar played in the national and religious life. The shift of the authority to this extent from the Confucian saints to a Western "barbarian" was indeed a matter of tremendous significance.[20] Thus the new ideas caught on among the progressive minority of intellectuals of sixteenth century Korea. But they were too weak to chisel away the solid rocks which surrounded them, to drill a channel through, and bring in the life-giving fresh air from the outside. They firmly believed that a new age was near at hand. But the conservatism was too solid to break through. The power of the dominant neo-Confucians was overwhelming. And it was to take two hundred years more for the dawn to bring the bright sunrise in the self-enslaved "hermit kingdom."

The Chinese writer Hu Shih gives a brilliant account of the successful modernization process of Japan in comparison with the same process in China.[21] The great leaders in the reform and modernization movement in Japan came from the dominant class, the offshoots of the samurai. Since they were from the military class, their interests were naturally directed toward Western firearms and naval vessels and, therefore, to scientific and industrial technologies. In addition to this blessing, the political development

of Japan during the last one thousand years had given her such
stability that she enjoyed complete security while she underwent
the trial period of rapid transformation. The Japanese leaders were
never intoxicated by neo-Confucianism, as the Koreans were, though
that philosophy influenced them deeply enough to enhance their
belief in the "heavenly sonship" of the imperial ruler. In other
words, the self-idolization of the dominant class in Japan had not
yet progressed so far as to harden their reflections and judgments.

In China the story was entirely different. The leaders in this
movement in China, instead of being military or men of the ruling
class, were the literati. Also, they were under the rule of the
Manchus with whom they were reluctant to cooperate. The process
took a rather tardy course there.

Of course, this explanation cannot exhaust the causes of the
different developments in these two countries, and that was not
what Hu Shih intended to do. Nevertheless, it crystallizes for us
the position of Korea at that eventful age. The counterpart of the
Japanese ruling class in the Korean scene was not the men of
military background. They were "scholars," the overenthusiastic
neo-Confucianists. Their only interest was in keeping the precepts
of Confucianism unimpaired and prevalent among themselves. This
concern was well exemplified in the bitter dispute called "Yesong"
carried on between the current two strong factions, Sŏin [Western-
ers Party] and Namin [Southerners Party], over a trivial problem
related to court protocol. It was on the issue of the "period wearing
of mourning clothes" occasioned by the death of King Hyojong.
That infamous and vehement "learned" controversy lasted for thirty-
five years, throughout the reigns of three kings. The issue was how
long the Queen mother Chaui, the step-mother of the late king and
second wife of the late king's father, King Injo, should observe the
mourning period by wearing mourning clothes.

The Sŏins took their stand based on a statement found in the
Wu-li-i, which reads: "The mother shall wear mourning clothes for
her deceased son until his first memorial day," and they insisted
that the queen mother remain in official mourning for one year.
The Sŏin government adopted this instruction. In the said statement, however, there was no elaboration on the kinship term "son."
Nor was the distinction between the first-born son and other sons
made.

To make matter worse, there were conflicting commentaries on
the text in question. Thus commentaries of equal importance were
made by a Cheng Hsüan and a Ku-kung-yen during the Han

dynasty. Furthermore, the commentators had used different copies from the original text which was extant only in the form of fragments by the Han dynasty (*Tai-te-pen, Tai-sheng-pen,* and *Liu-hsiang-pieh-lu-pen*). These three copies themselves were not in agreement, apparently. The corrupted fragmentary documents the Korean Confucianists had at hand were, therefore, conflicting commentaries based on chaotic text, at best. Thus opportunity presented itself for long, bitter, and shameful disputation.

The Namin scholars soon came up with a proposal to amend the decision of the government. They maintained that the queen mother's official mourning should be observed during a full three-year period, for the late king was the "eldest son" to his father though he was born a second son. He was made an "eldest son" when the son of primogeniture, the ill-fated Prince Sohyŏn died.[22]

On the authority of the Ku commentary, they challenged the government's views on the ground that it was a deliberate plan to demote the hereditary position of the late king in the royal family. The said commentary read: "When the eldest son dies and the second son of the lawfully married wife is made the eldest son, the second son then shall be called the eldest son." To this the government spokesman came up with a countercharge on the strength of the *Ta-ming-lu Kuo-chih* and *Sang-li-pei-yao,* the collections of the code and protocol adopted by both the Ming and Korean governments, and declared that the decision was right, after all, because the assertion of the statement which the opposition used did not at all affect the protocol itself. The passage in question says only that when the second son is *made* the eldest, he shall be "called" the eldest. He can only be an "eldest son" *for* the first-born who passed away, but cannot be one in his own right.

Then a complicated controversy followed over the "two natures of the king." As the supreme head of the state he was the ruler of all his subjects, including his parents. But as a son he had to fulfill his filial duty as the supreme Confucian command. The disputants were thereby divided into two opposing parties. A detailed account of this entire disputation is not necessary here.[23] It is sufficient for us to note that the archaic pedantry and conservatism of the leading class had deteriorated to the point where such a controversy was possible. The heaven was empty.

CHAPTER FOUR

Social Environment

The society was changing, slowly yet steadily. Formidable indeed were the walls which the conservatives had built around the nation. But it was evident by the middle of the seventeenth century that the isolation could not last forever. Pressure from without was mounting, and a slow cultural disintegration within was already in process.

If the Japanese westernizing movement had progressed from above downwards,[1] the same movement in Korea took the opposite direction, from lower to higher. And it took the form of fermentation. It started at the lower and inner strata, at first, and developed upward and outward with increasing acceleration in speed and volume.

There are three factors involved in this process: the leaven, the meal, and the climate. Direct impact from the West was relatively slight, perhaps, due to the geographical location of the nation. The Western navigators, in fact, were slow to come to Korean shores. By the time some ill-fated vessels from the Pacific shipwrecked on the shores of the peninsula in the seventeenth and eighteenth centuries, the fermentation had already progressed to a certain extent in the heart of the land, even though it was all quiet on the surface. Rising out of the new ideas that came over the zealously guarded northern border from China, the disintegrating movement had already begun to affect the disinherited intellectuals, the most sensitive class in the society of the day. The affected were only a handful at first, but their influence upon society was deep and profound. Thus a new era began quietly.

It is historically significant for the development of the Korean church that the scientific information from the West, which played the role of the leaven, should have been brought to China and ultimately to Korea by Jesuit missionaries in the sixteenth century. The information which the intellectuals so eagerly sought was presented to the East by the missionaries in the framework of the Catholic *"philosophie chrétienne."*[2] The natural sciences were an integral part of the *"philosophie chrétienne"* of the early Jesuits. Therefore, while aquiring scientific information, the receiving parties were also initiated into some aspects of the Christian doctrines proper, though indirectly.

In this philosophy, "the sincere love of the letters and the knowledge of the Renaissance have been joined with the strict integrity of the doctrine."[3] In fact, it was the spirit of the University of Paris at the time when the institution of learning produced Loyola and Xavier. They are said to have been deeply influenced by the spirit. And it was this "spirit and tactic" that Francis Xavier, the maître és-arts de Paris, brought to the East.

True to this tradition, most of the Jesuit missionaries, especially those who came to China in the sixteenth and seventeenth centuries, carried with them special education in science. Some of them were accomplished scientists of the day. Matteo Ricci of Italy was the most well-known "scientist" in Korea through his first and second revised editions of the World Map with Chinese Nomenclature *K'un-yü Wan-kuo ch'üan-t'u.* His books on astronomy *Li Ma-tou T'ien-wen-shu,* mathematics *Shu-li ching-yün,* and geometry *Hsü-kwang-chi Chi-ho yüan-pen*[4] were warmly received and well studied in Korea.

Next well known was Johannes Adam Schall von Bell of Germany whose calendar *Shi-hsien-li* together with the illustrations on calendar making *Cheng-chieh-t'u* were introduced in 1645. His calendar was adopted in 1653.[5] It was in his *Chu-chi ch'ün-cheng* or "the Creator and His Works" that Koreans found the first concrete information on Western medical science.[6] The *Chu-chih ch'ün-cheng* also provided up-to-date knowledge of Western astronomy in a substantial way.[7]

Sabbathinus de Ursis of Italy is associated with the information on geology. The missionaries whose names were reported among those who directly imparted their scientific knowledge to Koreans were Johannes Adam Schall von Bell, Joseph Suares of Portugal, and Ingatus Kogler of Germany.[8] It was Joannes Rodaniquez of Italy who visited the Korean ambassador Chŏng Tu-wŏn in Peking

in 1631 to give him some instruments including guns, clocks, a
sundial, and a pair of binoculars and scientific books produced in
Chinese. The list and description of these gift items are preserved
in the *Kukcho pogam*.[9]

Thus Koreans were led to Christianity, though indirectly, from
this early date. It is interesting to note that they seem to have been
less impressed by the *"philosophie chrètienne"* than by the men of
science who represented it. I suspect that this may have been true
in China, too. In the preface to his translation of Euclid's Geometry
in collaboration with Ricci, Paul Hsü wrote: "Geometry enables the
students to calm their lusts and purifies their spirits." In other
words, to him natural science had moral quality. Hsü also wrote
about the author Ricci in his own preface to Ricci's famous *Forty-
two Paragraphs*: "I found him by chance in Nanking and after a
short conversation, realized that he was the most learned man in
whole world. . . . In ancient times, the kiosk where the phoenixes
built their nest was considered by the Court a precious object,
ensuring peace and stability in the Empire. Today, we have the
True Man Learned and Great. . . . Is he not a treasure even more
precious?"[10]

In Korea, there were quite a number of writers who referred
in their own writings to Matteo Ricci's influential book *T'ien-chu
shih-i*, the masterpiece of the *"philosophie chrétienne"* in the true
sense. It is evident that this book made a profound impression
upon them. They seem, however, to have been more impressed by
the man, the "True Man Learned and Great," who believed in such
things and whose purpose of visiting the Orient was to deliver the
messages contained in his books.

Ricci's scientific knowledge gave him authority as well as an
opportunity for his evangelism. It is not surprising, therefore, that
those who benefited from his learned teachings in science should
have felt an obligation to listen reverently to the doctrines that the
"wise man" himself brought with him. In fact, this has been a
graceful way of learning in the Orient. In short, the knowledge of
the West which played the role of a leaven in Korean society had
the active Christian element in it.

When the leaven was introduced into society, it was in a form
well adapted to the new environment. It was presented not only in
the literary language of the Korean scholars of the day, but in the
way of expression which perfectly suited their taste. Matteo Ricci,
a man of penetrating insight, employed extensively the "Asiatically
picturesque, poetic form"[11] in his writings, instead of the ice-cold

syllogism of the West. This was the educational method adopted
and used richly by the Jesuits of the day, and it produced rich fruit
in Korea. The leaven was not merely adjustable or acceptable to
the new environment, but also was pregnant with vitality. The
very best knowledge of the West in the post-Renaissance era was
the ingredient. In addition to this, Matteo Ricci and the men like
Adam Schall von Bell were scholars well qualified to present what
they brought with them.

As for the meal, or people, or the matrix for the fermentation,
it was also of good quality. It had racial homogeneity. The predisposition of the people, in general, toward the new ideas seems to
have been, in many respects, healthy and wholesome. Though Korea
is isolated in the far corner of the Eurasian continent, Korea did
have some direct contact with the West beginning in the seventeenth century. And these contacts were carried out in a relaxed
way, contrary to some of the hasty and erroneous views expressed
by writers such as Griffis, *et alli*, as shall be referred to. In fact,
periods of so-called xenophobia are notably lacking in Korean history.

It is true that all but two of the Catholic missionaries from La
Société des Missions Étrangère who entered Korea in later years in
the eighteenth century suffered martyrdom. Yet their deaths were
demanded not because they were foreigners but because they were
antagonistic to the ultraconservative government of Korea. They
paid the supreme sacrifice with more than ten thousand Koreans
in the course of a nationwide persecution. Foreigners were not
unwelcome. Some of them were even forced to stay in the country.
There were occasional armed conflicts with the Westerners.[12] On
closer observation, however, one finds no trace of xenophobia as
such, as we shall see shortly. Despite the fact that the "hermit
nation" zealously guarded her borders against economic and political invasions from the West, she was never unfriendly to peaceful
visitors from abroad.

The general impression of the Koreans by Westerners in that
age seems to have been rather a pleasant one. An eighteenth-
century French observer who met Koreans in China reported: "Koreans are well-built with pleasing physical features and very polite
manners."[13]

There was an unfortunate story, however. A Dutch vessel called
Sparrowhawk was shipwrecked off the coast of Chejudo Island in
1653. And the surviving crew was "detained" in Korea for thirteen
years until they found their way home through Japan. Hendrick
Hammel, the ship's captain, wrote a "Narrative of an Unlucky

Voyage and Shipwreck on the Coast of Korea," the earliest firsthand report on Korea to the West, which was apparently well received by the European readers of the seventeenth and eighteenth centuries.[14] It was an unfortunate story, because the crew had a hard time while they were in Korea—doubly unfortunate, because the narrative tended to give hasty readers a false impression as to the "cruelty" of the host nation. On a careful reading, however, one can find the case to be contrary. Their life was miserable, because the life of the Koreans, especially those in the Chejudo Island where they landed, the most isolated and underdeveloped part of the country, was a hard one. Nevertheless, they were by no means maltreated. The narrator gives interesting accounts of Korean hospitality. He even tells his readers that "he [a Korean] also took such care of our sick that we may affirm we were better treated by that Idolater than we should have been among Christians."[15]

They were discouraged from leaving the country, but they were not prisoners by any means. Their departure was discouraged because the hosts hoped that the guests would make excellent instructors in military training, as Korea at the time was in the process of strengthening her military power. Yi Wan was the commander of the army and had special interest in these visitors. He was given permission by the government to place these men in the military training corps under the supervision of their compatriot John Wettevree of Amsterdam, or Pak Yŏn, a high-ranking military officer of his adopted land since 1627.[16] They could have been treated more courteously if they had accepted the government's offer, rather than attempting single-mindedly to escape.

I feel that Griffis goes too far in describing this incident when he writes: "Like the black potentates of Africa, who like to possess a white man, believing him to be a 'spirit,' or a New Zealand chief, who values the presence of a 'Paheka Maori' [Englishman], Koreans of that day considered their western 'devil' a piece of property worth many tiger skins."[17]

Griffis' literary style is hardly justifiable, because, to the Koreans of the day, the Westerners were neither "spirits" nor "property." They were expected to be military instructors. We find in the Korean government annals the following report:

Kyŏngsin day of August, the year of Kyesa in the Hyojong era [1653]. A report from the Governor of Chejudo Island. A ship was wrecked off the southern coast of this territory. I sent the superintendent of Taejong Prefecture Kwŏn

Kukchong and the police chief No Chŏng with some of their men for an investigation. The investigators, however, failed to find their nationality. It was observed that they lost their ship at sea. They were a crew of thirty-eight survivors. Communication was impossible, because their language and letters were entirely different from ours. The cargo consisted of incense tree 94 bundles, Yong No four drums and fur 27,000 pieces. They had blue eyes, high nose, yellow hair and short whiskers. Some had retained their whiskers only, shaving off mustache. Their clothes were long and tight. There were four pockets on their coat and at the end of each sleeve there was a ribbon attached. Their trousers had folding at the waist like our women's skirts.

One of us who knew Japanese asked them in that language: Are you the Western Christians? They all said Ya, Ya. In gesture language they asked what country this was, pointing to the mainland across the straight. We told them it was the Korean Peninsula. Pointing to the ground where they stood, they asked where they were. We told them it was Chejudo Island. They pointed in the direction of China and asked what country that was. We told them it was the Middle Kingdom, or the Ming. They asked pointing to the northwest. We told them it was the Tartar. They asked pointing to the east. We said that it was Japan or Nagasaki. And we asked them whether they wished to go there or not. They replied yes, ... they wished to go ... there.

In the meantime, the government instruction was to send them up to the capital. We could not do otherwise. Pak Yŏn [Wettevree], the foreigner who arrived in our country earlier and who had been living with us for some time checked them and said they were unmistakably his compatriots.

They were organized into [teams] under Pak Yŏn. Their travel was restricted, for they were skillful in manufacturing fire arms. Some of them could play flute with their nose. And some of them danced weaving their feet.[18]

Such unexpected visitors from over the seas were not infrequent, as the expeditions of the expanding West explored Korean waters more and more frequently. These men met extremely inquisitive, yet not unfriendly hosts on shore in most cases. When they were shipwrecked, they were provided with provisions and sent back home through China. When they were just friendly "visi-

tors," they were entertained accordingly. The country was not
"opened" officially, and, therefore, the visitors were not allowed full
freedom on shore. Nevertheless, the reports from both sides in this
period show no trace of hatred or suspicion.

The story is virtually unchanged for two centuries following the
shipwreck of the Dutch vessel. In his [1816] *Voyage of His Majesty's
Ship Alceste to China, Corea and the Island of Lew Chew*, John
McLeod, the surgeon of the ship, records his interesting observations of the Korean people with a vivid description:

> The next day [we] anchored again among a cluster of is-
> lands, lat. 37° 45' N., long. 124° 40' 30", on the coast of
> Corea. The natives here exhibited by signs and gestures,
> the greatest aversion to the landing of the party from the
> ships, making cutting throat motions by drawing their hands
> across their necks and pushing the boats away from the
> beach; but they offered no serious violence. . . .
>   . . . We anchored [again] . . . in front of a village, a larger
> town being observed at some distance. In the evening, six
> or seven large boats came off Lyra [another vessel on the
> same expedition], being nearest to shore, one of them hav-
> ing on board a chief (most probably of this district) and
> after partaking of some refreshment, proceeded, although
> it was now dark on board the Alceste. He was saluted, on
> leaving the Lyra, with three guns, which was repeated by
> the frigate. As he shoved off from the brig, one of his atten-
> dants, having in some way or other misbehaved, was by his
> order extended on the deck of the boat, and received, in a
> summary way, about a dozen and half blows with a flat
> bamboo over the seat of honour; and, as the culprit squalled,
> a number of his companions standing around him joined in
> the howl, either in derision or to drown his noise. This
> ceremony finished, a flourish of trumpets and other instru-
> ments announced his approach to the frigate. He was a
> man apparently about seventy years of age, of a very ven-
> erable and majestic mien; his hair and beard of a hoary
> whiteness. His dress was a flowing light blue robe with
> loose sleeves, and fastened round his middle by a buff-
> coloured leather girdle. He had on his head an immense
> hat, not less than five or six feet round the brim, made of
> some substance resembling horse-hair varnished over. He
> wore a kind of half-boots, very much peaked and turned up

at the points; and in his hand he held a short black stick, twisted round with a silken cord, which seemed to be the badge of his office. . . .

He was ushered into the cabin, where, in preference to chairs, he sat down upon one of the sofa-cushions placed upon deck. It appearing to be etiquette for the head to be covered, the whole party, consisting of Captains Maxwell, Hall and other officers, conformed to this rule, and squatting on the cabin floor, with gold-laced cocked hats on amid the strange costume of Coreans, looked like a party of masquers.

Much edifying conversation was, no doubt, lost on both sides, but unfortunately not one word was understood; the Chinese interpreter we had on board not being able to write his own language; and some of the Coreans could write, although they could not speak at least that dialect which he comprehended.

Now the old gentleman dictated something which his secretary wrote, and it was put into the hand of Captain Maxwell. The latter, as the shortest mode of communicating that he could not read this, wrote in his turn a line in English, and delivered it to the chief. This had the desired effect, and they seemed astonished to find, that the written characters in use among them were not the only one in the world.

A gentleman of the Alceste having loitered behind his comrades one afternoon on Thistle Island found himself unexpectedly near a number of natives. They seemed to remark the sword he had in his hand, and thinking this a good opportunity to show he had no distrust of them, he threw it on the ground, and spurned it with his foot, as an unnecessary instrument among friends, and advanced to them with open arms. A loud shout of approbation proclaimed that they saw the meaning of this. He now endeavoured himself still more agreeable, by singing a song, and dancing for them. They were not sparing of their applause for his efforts to please; but when he had finished his feats, one of them picked up the sword which he had thrown down and putting it into his hand, tapped him good-humouredly on the shoulder, and pointed to the frigate which anchored not far distant. This sort of conduct we found uniformly wherever we touched.[19]

We find much the same picture of the Koreans in a journal of his voyage recorded by a Protestant missionary who visited the coast and left after a stay of a few weeks in 1832. He was Carl Friedrich Augustus Gutzlaff, the first Protestant missionary to land in Korea.[20] His visit came just during an interval of the Catholic persecution we have mentioned above. He had some information already of this persecution, and that made him the more inquisitive. So upon arrival at the coast he tried to find out what the situation was. It was in vain. He mentions: "According to all accounts which we could collect, there are at present no Europeans at the capital, and Christianity is unknown even by name. We do not know how far we may credit the detailed accounts of persecutions which the Corean Christians endured, and endured with heroic firmness. If so many thousands as is said had been executed on account of their belief, Christianity would live in the recollection of the natives, at least as a proscribed creed; but we could discover no trace of it."[21]

However, the story from a Korean source, as recorded in Dallet's *Histoire*, gives an interesting contrast:

> During the summer of the same year, the British flag was seen off the Korean coastline. A merchant ship, possibly sent by some agents of Bible societies, anchored itself close the Island of Quensan, near the Province of Chungch'ŏng on the West Coast. There was general astonishment, and particularly the Catholic Christians were greatly surprised, for the ship hoisted a banner on which was written in large Chinese characters: *Religion of Jesus Christ.* Some Catholics thinking of meeting their brothers in China hurried aboard the ship without any apparent concern for the disapproval or wrath they might draw from the government. However, they were very surprised to find there a Protestant minister greeting them with the words which were considered sacred among the pagans: "May the Spirit of the Earth bless you!" Upon hearing these words the novices, seeing that they had been deceived and wishing to strictly adhere to their faith, withdrew very quickly without even responding to the greetings and did not appear again.[22]

The picture of the peninsula kingdom and its people which Gutzlaff had in mind previous to his visit was apparently one painted with dark colors by at least two sources, one, the news of the Catholic persecution, the second, Hammel's story. He says: "Their conduct formed a contrast with the behaviour of the Chinese. Had we now left the peninsula, we should have reported to the world, in addition to the accounts of other people in the world, with courage enough to repress every intruder, so that threatening and injury were all which could be obtained there. From our first interview with them, I very much doubted this."[23]

He was glad to find it otherwise. When he left the peninsula, he said: "I should think that a missionary residing here would be less subject to dangers than those in New Zealand, and Greenland. One thing is true, these islands are not inaccessible to Christianity."[24]

Now, we find in Korean documents of the same period the corresponding records to those of the Westerners. A Dutch vessel anchored at Tongnae Port near Pusan in 1797 gave an excellent opportunity for a Korean observer to record the Western physiognomy.

> In Chŏngsa year [1797] of Chŏngjong era, a foreign vessel drifted into the Tongnae harbor. The size of the ship was comparable to ours of capacity of two or three thousand bushels. And there were some fifty men aboard. All of them were very tall, at least a few feet taller than most of us. Their faces looked strange. They had high and stiff noses, the stem of which went right through the forehead. They had no cheekbones. Their cheeks went around from the sides of the nose to their ears without prominent portions as if it were the surface of an apricot seed.
>
> Their clothes consisted of trousers and a coat. But all are so tight that they could barely move their limbs in them. Certainly, they could not bend their knees [because of the tightness] and had to sit on boxes instead of sitting correctly on the floor.
>
> We could not communicate with them through language. We wrote our letters and gave them to them. They did not understand them. They also wrote their letters which looked like a picture of mountains and clouds.[25]

It is apparent that there were some dark-skinned among them. A report from Chejudo Island in the year of Sinyu in Sunjo era [1810] reads:

On the Port of Tangp'o in Taejong Prefecture, Chejudo Island, a big vessel of an unknown nationality sent down five men and immediately sailed away. The appearance of the five were very strange. They wore tight clothes. They had hats made of tropical grass on their heads but no shoes. Their body was black and looked like monkeys. They spoke very quickly with bird's language. There was no way to get any information from them. So we asked them to write something. They wrote with right hand but horizontally from the left. They were neither letters nor drawings, but looked like badly entangled threads.... These men were sent home on land via Peking.[26]

Another record about the same crew: "They had bare feet stuck in mud and little difference from that of animals. There was a hole on their ear lobes. Their hair looked like curly wool. Two of them were pure black like a lacquered box all over the body... The explanation that we could gather [with sign language] was that they were born black ... and did not lacquer themselves. They said a lot of people like them live in their own country."[27]

A report of two British vessels anchored off the West Coast in 1816 relates a glimpse of a Western woman gained by an investigator. "There were also women, at least one. She had a white scarf on her hair and a red skirt on...."[28]

Courtesy was duly shown to such foreigners. Supply of food and water was given when requested. A humorous story is told in the records concerning the shipwreck of a French vessel in the year of Chŏngmi [1847] in Hŏnjong era.

One of the two French vessels was shipwrecked off the coast of Kunsan. But all the crew and cargo were saved. When they left [the port] the French abandoned a few things including two tents, all of which were stored at the warehouse at the harbor. One day a person heard a strange sound, sounds like t'ok t'ak and t'ok t'ak from a box. It continued for seven days. The inhabitants were disturbed by this and thought that the Westerners had left a poisonous devil behind in the box to harm the people. Later they opened the box and found a clock in it. The inhabitants still tell the story with hilarious outburst. They have become a laughing stock since.[29]

Korean hot-headedness is better demonstrated in national cri-ses than in times of peace and leisure. The armed invasions from the West (the French fleet under the command of Admiral Roze in 1866, the American Pacific Fleet under Rear Admiral Rodgers in 1871) were met by Korean armed resistance strong enough to force them to retreat after a fight. Force met force.

The well-publicized tragedy of the American vessel *General Sherman* in 1866[30] is depicted in Korean documents as follows:

Report of Pak Kyusu, the Governor of P'yŏngan Province. I have reported to you through a special horse-express con-cerning the anchoring at Hansajŏng of a foreign ship, which came up the river from the sea. And now I am sending this new report based on the information I received from the Mayor of P'yŏngyang, Sin Taejŏng, dated at 10 p.m., the 19th of this month of July.

Yesterday at about 6 p.m. six foreigners came up to P'yŏngyang on their small blue boat from Hansajŏng, where their ship anchored. Thereupon the police captain Yi Hyŏnik followed them on his own small boat to watch their activi-ties. Suddenly the foreigners approached the police boat and dragged it along to their ship and kidnapped the police officer to their ship. The mayor himself had to go to the ship and demanded his release. The mayor waited for their reply all night long in vain. The next day at about 10 a.m. they took the anchor up and came up the river shooting their cannons and guns noisily until they reached Hwang-kangjŏng where they stopped. Five of them this time came further up near to Madan on the same blue boat for the purpose of measuring the depth of the river. As they came up, a big crowd from the city came to the banks of the river and shouted loudly to demand the release of the police captain. Their only reply was that the crowd would see what happens when the foreigners themselves enter into the city walls.

Unable to restrain their anger the crowd began to throw stones at them. And the soldiers on duty at the city gates also started to fire their guns and shot their bows at the foreigners to warn them away.

The foreigners abandoned their boat and swam to the nearby Yanggakto Island, a little island in the river, and ran down to their ship. The ship went down the river some distance and anchored again at the top of this island. Thereby we took the blue boat and brought it up the river and tied it near by the city gate.

At about 4 p.m. the retired police chief Pak Chungwŏn together with a few police volunteers attacked the ship and succeeded in boarding it from the bow and brought back the police captain alive. When the police chief was in captivity he carelessly dropped his official seal (with which he prints his official title on documents) into the water and lost it. When he was being captured his assistants Yu Sunwŏn and Pak Chiyong who had accompanied him threw themselves into the water from their boat in order to escape. We do not know as yet whether they were drowned or not. They did not come back. . . . I demanded the police captain's resignation not because he had been captured by the foreigners against his will but because he lost his official seal much to our surprise.[31]

Another report of Pak Kyusu reads:

I have received a new report, on the 25th of this month, from the Mayor of P'yŏngyang, Sin Taejong. According to the report, the foreign ship did not show any intention of withdrawing. They robbed food from the Korean boats and shot at the people, killing up to seven and injuring five more. There has been no other vessel so insistent . . .

As they were from a far-away land we expected that they could show us some courtesy and leave in peace. Furthermore, they were well informed of our prohibition of foreigners in the country. . . .

Yet they did not leave; instead, making all sorts of trouble, they even kidnapped our police captain, as is reported in the previous reports. There seems to be no other way now but to destroy them. Therefore, I, your subject, went out to the river and supervised the fight in coordination with the mayor of P'yŏngyang. We attacked them with our canons and we are intending to destroy them by burning their ship. We could not as yet burn her because they ingeniously surrounded their ship with nets to ward off our burning floats. Our gunner Kim Pongjo shot one of them to death. And we fought all the day long. And their ship seems to have grounded as the tide ebbed. So they now can neither

go forward nor withdraw backward. There are only some
twenty of them on board, but everyone has a weapon with
him. Therefore, it seems to be very difficult to capture them
alive. The fury of the military and civilians reached its
peak and morale is high. I will keep reporting . . .[32]

Report on July 27th:

The foreign vessel anchored at P'yŏngyang increased its
madness by gunning and shelling, killing, and injuring our
people. There was no better way to destroy them than with
fire. We sent our fire floats down the river and their ship
at last caught fire. Among them, Ch'oe Nanhŏn and Cho
Nŭngbong leaped out of the ship and came to us to beg for
their lives. We captured them and tied them on the bank.
The angry crowd soon gathered around them and beat them
to death. I believe that all others of the crew were destroyed all together. The trouble is subsided. I would humbly request His Majesty's attention to the fact that the
Commander Pae Nakyŏn and Mayor Sin Taejong directed
well the fighting force under the most difficult military
conditions, thereby, for them military honours are due . . .[33]

Cho Nŭngbong, in this report, was Chinese, but the person by
the name of Ch'oe Nanhŏn was none other than the Rev. Robert
Jermain Thomas, B.A., of New College, Edinburgh, who had set as
his goal to reach the people on this peninsula as the first Protestant missionary.[34] It was, indeed, an extremely unfortunate thing
for him to be on board of this ill-fated vessel. However, it is apparent that he sought every opportunity to come to the people, for
whom he wanted to dedicate his life work, no matter what the price
would be. This was his second visit, some three months after an
unsuccessful attempt to enter the country.
    This tragedy could have been avoided in all probability if there
had been no annoying incident like that of the kidnapping of the
police officer, even if the vessel did force her way too deep into the
interior. We now know that the first contact of the vessel with Koreans, before the fateful incident occurred, was not only cordial but
very happy. She anchored along the west coast of Hwanghae and
P'yŏngan provinces on several occasions on her way to the mouth of
the Taedong River, a week or so before the incident took place.

The officers of the ship made the purpose of their visit to the "Hermit Nation" clear, and it was perfectly understood by Koreans as Korean documents readily show. Meanwhile, Korean officials in the harbors where the ship anchored also succeeded in explaining the policy of the country to the visitors and advised them not to try to open the trade which they desired.

According to the report of the governor of Hwanghae province Pak Sŭnghwi, the ship submitted to the native inspection which was carried out in a friendly atmosphere. Communication with each other through languages and letter was exceptionally satisfactory in this case, because Thomas Ch'oe Nanhŏn "not only spoke Chinese well but understood a few Korean words, too. He understood some vocabulary but failed to comprehend more . . . ."[35]

This report includes the size and construction of the ship, her previous voyages, destination and purpose of the visit, the nationalities of the officers, and descriptions of their individual physical characteristics. It describes Ch'oe Nanhŏn as follows: "Ch'oe Nanhŏn, age thirty-six. Long face, yellow hair, black whiskers and mustache. Gray coat, felt hat, black and tweed trousers, black leather shoes. He had a leather band on his waist, on which he had a pistol on one side and a sword on another. He was a fourth-grade officer."[36]

In another report prepared by Yi Yongsang, military commander in P'yŏngan province, dated on July 18th, 1866, one reads:

Ch'oe Nanhŏn asked what we Koreans do with the white stone pagoda, in the capital city, of which he heard. I answered, I don't know even the date of its construction, but there is really a white tower as he mentioned. And he asked, why should your noble country persecute Catholics? Our holy religion Christianity is in perfect accord with the doctrine of the Heaven and it endeavours to recreate human mind in accordance with the Truthful Way. The reason to do all this is to purify the law and custom of the nations and peoples (in the world). There are doctrines of benevolence, righteousness, faithfulness and filial piety in Christian teachings. This religion encourages all people in the world to follow the Good. And he said that this religion [Protestantism] is different from Catholicism. So, I told him that neither of these are permitted in our country and people do not dare to follow them. . . .[37]

In the above we have endeavored to describe how direct contact of the native Koreans with the approaching Westerners occurred. It was not hostile, except in the few cases of armed conflict. Generally speaking, the initial contacts were made in a friendly way. It is even more important for us to note that these contacts, made from the second half of the eighteenth century, took place while the supposedly anti-Western persecution of the Catholics was being carried on inland.[38]

I believe that the Korean people in that period were, generally speaking, favorably disposed toward new ideas, novel techniques, and the outside world. For not only the intelligentsia concentrated in the capital city, but the less educated local officials in the ports and the general populace along the shores showed an equally intense curiosity toward the West. All were friendly and eager to learn. The dough was in good condition for an effective fermentation; the leaven was present, a favorable climate was required.

So far as the ideological climate is concerned, it was not always favorable. The historico-social environment was extremely severe for the new ideas to grow normally in the sixteenth and seventeenth centuries, as we have already seen. It was an era of fossilization of the old world in Korea, freezing everything to immobility. The modernization movement was, however, not entirely arrested perhaps due to the other two more favorable factors involved, namely, the suitable leaven for the proper meal. These factors may have had something to do with keeping the movement alive during this long winter.

Under such circumstances it took an unreasonably long time for the society to undergo the transition—not throw open her doors to the world until she was compelled to do so, in 1876. Modern Japan, taking geographical advantage, forced Korea to enter into a treaty of friendship with her in 1876 and made her open the doors to the world in 1882. Thus, the hermitage came to an end. Korea made treaties with the Western countries after 1882 and came out of the hermitage rather in an awkward way.[39]

Once the doors were pushed open, the cultural climate within, too, changed abruptly. It was suddenly summer, though it was soon proved to be only an "Indian summer." Belatedly, the government realized the necessity of modernization and in 1881 sent a team of observers calling themselves "Traveling Gentlemen" to Japan to inspect the effective modern system that its ingenious neighbors had adopted. Some sixty-nine students were sent out to T'ien-jin, China, that year at the government's expense to study

Western sciences. It was certainly a great stride taken by official action. It was, however, almost nothing in scope and lasting significance when one compares it with the immensity of the popular response at this opening for a new epoch.

It was the time for progressive ideas of every shade to sprout through the cracks of the long barren ground of conservatism to turn it into a weedy grassland almost over night. It was weedy because all kinds of good or bad ideas and institutions suddenly and spontaneously sprang from the ground, for the long winter was dead. The age embraced the warmth and moisture of life. Bustling activities filled the peninsula with cries and echoes of life and joy.

Literature was quick to change its ideology as well as its form from that of the Chinese classics to the colloquialism and naturalism of the modern style. The first Korean weekly paper published its first issue in 1883. New schools of the "new learning" mushroomed everywhere and quickly became the centers of the modernization movement in all Korean communities. The greater number of such mushroomed schools, of course, were painfully inadequate. They were poor in facilities but not in spirit.

As for Christianity, this was the era when the first Protestant missionaries arrived and started their rewarding work among the enthusiastic population. Gale, a Canadian missionary writer, has a very interesting story to tell us about the explosive growth of the Korean church in this period.

> ... Still there are other 'theological schools' that have played a great and important part in the work of missions, and one of the best of all was the old *Kamok*, or Criminal Prison. Filthy, cold, infected by all the germs that flourish in the East, crawling with vermin, associated with crime, torture, and horrible death, and yet a *pok-dang* or house of blessing, it has become. The old emperor in his days of absolute power locked in this pest house Lee Seung-man [Syngman Rhee], Yu Song-jin, Kim In, Lee Sang-jai, Lee Won-gung, Kim Chung-sik. He thought that these men meant reform along Western lines, and they did.
>
> Without trial by judge or jury, they were shut behind the bars; some of them wore the cangue collar and worked in the chain-gang. Here they suffered from cold, from ill treatment, from the constant fear of execution, although in their veins, there was a deadly desire for revenge in the heart. They hoped for escape, for the opportune moment,

the keen knife, for accounts squared for time and eternity, when all unexpectedly, there came into their company the New Testament, Bunyan's *Pilgrim's Progress*, and some of Moody's tracts in Chinese. Their prison, visited regularly by the Rev. and Mrs. A. D. Bunker, became first an inquiry room, then a house of prayer, then a chapel for religious exercises, then a theological hall, and when the course was completed, God let them all out of prison and set them to work. With their high social standing, with their political influence, with their superior training in Chinese, these men have become the first Christian leaders of the capital.

The year 1909 found Lee Seung-man [Syngman Rhee] in America, taking a postgraduate course at Harvard; Yu Song-jin is a consistent Christian in the service of the government; Lee Sang-jai, formerly Secretary of the Cabinet, and once Secretary of Legation in Washington, District of Columbia, is Director of Religious Work in the Seoul YMCA, and Kim In is General Secretary of the native branch of that organization while Lee Won-gung, one of the most noted Confucian scholars living, is an elder in the Seoul Presbyterian church; and Kim Chung-sik, once chief of police of Seoul, is now in charge of Religious Work among Korean students in Tokyo.

Not established under either Methodist or Presbyterian auspices, this old unwashed *Kamok* prison has been one of our best helps. When such a means as this can be used for God's glory, it teaches one to go slowly and prayerfully and wait to see what he will do. . . .

Sadly, however, this thriving summer did not last long. When Japan finally realized her cherished ambition from the eighteenth century onward by "annexing" Korea in 1910, she was a ruthless conqueror. The Indian summer was over, and the winter chill returned at once.

It is true that Japan "modernized" Korea considerably during her thirty-six-year occupation which ended in 1945. But, in truth, she abruptly arrested the normal growth of the indigenous modernization movement already in progress. She did it deliberately by cutting off all the possibilities of positive action on the part of the natives toward that end. In fear of revolt, she took drastic measures to block the growth of the people. Her blow was powerful enough to paralyze Korea's efforts, forcing progressive ideas to retreat into another hibernation.

Instead, Japan demanded her version of modernization as a part of her assimilation policy. That version was not only repulsive to Korean nationalism, but failed to meet the public demand or the aspiration of the younger generation of that age. Fundamentally speaking, the Korean and Japanese approaches were entirely different in character. As has been briefly surveyed, the process of modernization in Korea was initiated, though indirectly, by the Jesuits in China within the context of their "*philosophie chrétienne.*" Therefore, it definitely had a Christian component from the very beginning. Furthermore, Christianity as a religion had special appeal to Koreans, as shall be explained below.

But the story of the same process in Japan was entirely different. It was comparatively free from Christian influence. In the process of adjustment, only the technical side of the Western civilization was successfully adopted and utilized in Japan, while the religious side was very much suppressed for the sake of her own fundamentally Shinto nationalism. By providing its theology, Christianity had rather assisted Shintoism in shaking off its long-standing syncretic partner, Buddhism, to enthrone itself in the newly invigorated Japanese nationalism.[40]

When Japan compelled Korea to accept the new version of modernization so that the newly annexed territory could be quickly and efficiently exploited for the prosperity of the "Empire of the Rising Sun," she also forced Korea to accept her Shinto ideology, oddly enough, as an integral part of the entire modernization-assimilation program. Japan placed Shintoism in the place which Christianity had previously occupied in the Korean version of modernization. She tried to teach Western techniques to Korea within the Shinto framework, but found it did not work. In doing so, she also started to check the dangerously growing Christian influence among Koreans. In this way Japanese colonialism very quickly found her bitter enemy to be the rapidly growing Christian church in Korea. To put it bluntly, could one expect a Korean student to be willing to learn English with the peculiar Japanese accent under a Japanese instructor when he could learn it from the missionaries directly? This was roughly the situation at that time.

In reaction to this Japanese demand, Koreans seemed to have been inclined more to Christianity and regarded the church of the missionaries as the authentic channel through which they could get more of what they desperately needed. Needless to say, the injured Korean national pride also played an important role in strengthening the position of Christianity among Koreans. This is the background of the well-told story of Paik in his excellent dissertation. According to him, "In spite of these handicaps [imposed by the Japanese government], the Christian schools were popular and those who did not go to school flocked to the Christian institutions. This turning of the Korean youth to Christian institutions at once commanded the attention of the Japanese. They built fine-looking schoolhouses with public funds and provided Japanese teachers, but very few went to their schools."[41]

Unfortunately, however, the popularity and prestige of these private institutions did not last long, because the government's "supervision" policy over the private institutions was strengthened greatly to check this undesirable current. By the 1930s, this institutional prestige was almost completely transferred to the government schools, as the assimilation policy was greatly stepped up, and the private and Christian institutions suffered the more under the enlarged pressure. That was the pre-Pearl Harbor era. In this way Korea's acculturation proceeded not on a self-determined and therefore natural course. It took rather a politically determined artificial and purposely ineffective, tardy course.

Nevertheless, it is interesting to note that in spite of the deliberate effort on the part of the Japanese westernizers, the Korean public seems to have never ceased to identify the Western civilization with Christianity. In fact, the church-centered modernization movement has never been seriously curtailed, although it was suppressed severely by the harsh political climate.

It is necessary for us, now, to turn to the economic factors involved in this environment. Korea has long been a stratified society. At the time when the waves of the expanding West struck upon her shores, Korea was a society having a four-class structure: nobility, *yangban* (literati and high-ranking military men's class), commoners, and outcasts.

Each class, in turn, was differentiated into several subclasses by the vicissitudes of history. And it was the disinherited portion of the *yangban* class, victims of the political struggle, that was hit first by the new ideas from the West in the seventeenth and eighteenth centuries. They were the members of the minority group, the disinherited Namins (the Southerners). We have every reason to believe that the politically disinherited Namins were also the economically deprived, as has been exemplified in a typical Namin Christian Chŏng Yagyong's life.[42]

This pattern is repeated once again when the new ideas from the West began to flourish in the later part of nineteenth century Korea.

It was also this stratum, *i.e.*, the disinherited intellectual class, that supplied the human resources and energy for the modernization movement. Perhaps this was due to the fact that only the intellectuals of this class were the ones who were capable of responding effectively to such religious-intellectual challenges from abroad. The fermentation started here and grew wider and stronger. The social classes that quickly responded to Catholic and Protestant evangelism in the seventeenth and nineteenth century were the same.

History witnessed the mass conversion of the people during the twenty-five years from 1886 to 1910. In the process of this quarter of a century it became apparent that the most progressive provinces of P'yŏngan and Hwanghae coincided with the most strongly Christianized areas in the peninsula. It was also true that with the most strongly Christianized provinces coincided the most deprived areas of the country. P'yŏngan and Hwanghae provinces were the most discriminated against and deprived provinces during the rule of the Chosŏn dynasty. The people of those areas were alienated from the dominant parties in Seoul for the very reason of their strong parochial tendencies, which, in turn, were made worse by the discriminating action of the government toward them. This made them revolutionaries in many ways. Once ignited, they went far in burning their hitherto suppressed energy in white heat, as in the cases of the Myoch'ŏng and Hong Kyŏngnae revolts.[43]

It proved to be the same when they embraced Christian zeal. The Protestant church, especially Presbyterianism, grew so rapidly and strongly that a prominent visitor[44] to the provincial capital, P'yŏngyang, is said to have named it a "Jerusalem." The socioeconomic disinheritedness apparently assisted in the evangelism of Catholics and Protestants in Korea.

On this ground, I disagree with Wasson, who makes an interesting observation on the growth of the Southern Methodist Church in Korea from 1896 to 1930.[45] He observes that there have been, statistically speaking, clearly visible periodic growths and arrests during that period. But it is misleading to attribute the arrest of growth to the economic predicament of the people in those particular periods in generalized terms. On the contrary, it could speed growth. The "sect-type" character[46] of the Korean church, born in the context of this economic disinheritedness, met the need of the society superbly, providing plenty of opportunities for satisfactory compensations for the discontented people and society. And this, I think, greatly aided, rather than harmed, the growth of the church throughout its history.

Within a decade or so after the "annexation," the class structure
of the Korean society went through a period of radical disintegration, not caused by the normal Industrial Revolution, but by the
Japanese colonial economic policy. The indigenous industry of the
ex-hermit nation was in the initial stage when she was occupied.
Korea soon became a victim of a ruthless economic exploitation.

Korea then began to change her outward look. The building of
communication systems was greatly stepped up. The Japanese built
a railway system and operated it efficiently. Highways were built,
harbors were improved, the postal system and telecommunications
were greatly developed. The rivers were harnessed to provide water for the new irrigation system. Dams were built to supply elec-
tricity for the rapidly growing industries. The banking system was
greatly improved; weights and measures were standardized.

The improvement was so impressive that a secretary of Foreign
Missions of the Presbyterian Church U.S.A. reported on his third
visit to Korea in 1926 with these words: "There can be no doubt
that Japan has sought and is seeking the economic well-being of
the country. It is her interest to do this and it is her duty. And no
one can read the Reports on Reform and Progress issued annually
by the Governor General or see with one's eyes the changes which
have taken place and not realize that Japan is eagerly seeking the
prosperity and happiness of Chosen [Korea] for the sake both of the
Koreans themselves and of the Empire as a whole."[47]

But the inside story of the seemingly prosperous colonial Korea
was, unfortunately, very different. McCune aptly summarizes the
situation as follows:

In terms of the percentage of the aggregate gross value of production represented by mining and industry as shown in the following table, Korea appeared to have made great strides toward
industrialization.

Table I
Distribution of Aggregate Gross Value of Production
by Economic Activity, 1938

	Percentage
Agriculture	46.4
Forestry	5.5
Fishing	4.8
Mining	5.5
Industry	37.8
	100.0

But the distribution of the population occupationally reveals a quite different picture:

Table II
Distribution of the Population of Korea
by Occupation, 1938

	Percentage
Agriculture	73.6
Fisheries	1.5
Industry	3.1
Mining	1.2
Commerce	7.0
Transportation	1.0
Public Service and	
Professions	3.9
Others	8.9
	100.0

This discrepancy between the percentage of the aggregate gross value of production attributable to agriculture and the percentage of the population engaged in agriculture indicates that a disproportionately small share of the national product was being received by those engaged in agriculture. Agricultural prices were depressed vis-à-vis those in other sectors of the economy and the great mass of the Korean people were engaged in agriculture. The further breakdown of the above figure of 73.6 per cent of the total population engaged in agriculture shows how decidedly this was the case: 75.6 per cent of the Korean population were occupied in agriculture in 1938, while only 5.4 per cent of the Japanese had usurped the farm land that would yield the greatest return for themselves; a very large share of them were landlords or held the more lucrative managerial positions, as in the Oriental Developmental Company.[48]

In the process of this ruthless exploitation, the great majority of people became desperately poor. The ex-hermit nation emerged in the modern world finding herself painfully in bankruptcy, politically as well as economically. Deprived of a "fair" chance for adjustment in this way, the society inevitably became a disinherited one, in the literary sense, from the very initial stage.

The characteristics of the Korean church, especially that of Protestantism, could have been that of "middle class" Christianity, if the sociological terminology designed for the American society could be applied tentatively here, because the greater majority of the members came from the educated and comparatively well-settled class of people. They could be classified in groups of upper middle, middle middle, and lower middle class, so far as their relative economic and social statuses within the deprived society were concerned. But the economic margin between the classes was actually very small, indeed, because they all shared the predicament of the entire society.

Under such circumstances the Korean Christians seem to have sought compensation in their new spiritual community life. In a Troeltsch-Niebuhrian sense the Korean churches as a whole, regardless of their affiliation to the various missionary organizations from various social backgrounds, universally demonstrated the "sect-pattern" outlook. With its emphasis on otherworldliness and legalistic doctrines, discipline under the ideals of the mystico-ascetical pattern of Christian life, and administration of the spiritualized hierarchical organization, the Korean church amply fulfilled its expected function as a religion in the deprived society while it grew steadily and powerfully by means of its own merits.

The liberation from the Japanese colonial yoke in 1945 marked the watershed. Korea entered a new era. Dwarfed by the constantly threatened destruction from the North and under the heavy load of the immense task of building a new nation, the new Korea more often staggered than strode on the road to her promised prosperity. Nevertheless, the society began to function normally, healing the wounds inflicted during her enslavement.

As the war debris was gradually cleared away, the social structure emerged with a definitely capitalistic outlook. Some groups of Christians began to show their inclination towards middle-class values, shifting from their former sect-type of Christian life. At present, some of the urban churches are discernibly in transition from the sect-type to the church or denomination-type, from the disinherited to the privileged, the process of which in an American scene is so masterfully analyzed by Liston Pope.[49]

The rapid growth of the churches in Korea took place within this context of a changing society.

CHAPTER FIVE

Method Employed

In exploring an explanation of the explosive growth of Christianity in Korea we have tried, in the previous chapters, to survey the historical and sociocultural environment in which the event took place. We came to a tentative conclusion that the pre-Christian scene in seventeenth century Korea was set quite properly as if it were a stage during an intermission, just before the curtain of the next act is raised. We also noticed that the material preparation for the fermentation was satisfactory. The climate was not always favorable, but the severity was enough to stimulate the society to respond.[1] A Christianity-centered type of acculturation took place in the society as its response. We also mentioned that the growth of Christianity kept pace with the progress of modernization in society.

Now our attention is turned to the specific points worthy of consideration in delineating the picture in more detail. Some writers have held that the main cause of the "unique" development of the Church was the effective methods the missionaries employed. This brings us to view the event at closer range.

Our first topic is the "method of accommodation"[2] which the Jesuit missionaries to China, notably Matteo Ricci and his colleagues, had adopted. Although Korea was never a parish of the Jesuit order, and was occupied in later years by the *Société des Missions Étrangères* of Paris and Dominicans who actually opposed the Riccian approach as mission policy, it was the Jesuit work in China that became the leaven to bring the cultural and religious revolution to Korea.

"Accommodation," as a missionary approach, can be defined with the cautiously chosen words of the Catholic historian Josef Schmidlin. According to him, it is the method of a missionary who must "fight and eliminate all those elements in the concepts and customs of the people which originate from the paganism proper and are in direct opposition to Christianity, but with as much moderation and wise timing as possible under the consideration of the permissible usage of the people in the greatest extent."[3] This was the method adopted by Matteo Ricci, the grand developer of this missionary tactic in the East.

And this method was, according to Huonder, in good accord with the spirit of Ignatius Loyola, the organizer of the Jesuits:

> It is abundantly clear that the so-called Jesuit Accommoda-
> tion Method does indeed go back to Ignatius Loyola him-
> self. He is a convinced believer in the method, although in
> his own particular way. For him, it is a logical consequence
> of the great basic thought to which he gives a place of
> priority in his spiritual exercises. According to this thought
> there is but one absolute value: the greater glory of God.
> Everything else, whatever it may be, is of merely relative
> value. It is good if it serves the greater glory of God, and
> the more it does so, the better it is. The principle of *tantum
> quantum* applies to all that has been created such as tools,
> means and ways. They are to be used if and insofar as they
> serve the purpose, i.e. the glorification of God and the sal-
> vation of souls.[4]

Of course, in Loyola there was no clear "theological distinction" between the essence and the additives of Christianity. This was destined to become a bitter issue thereafter among his followers. Nevertheless, though vague in theological terms, a militant missionary spirit was well displayed by him in his conviction as to what should be the central point and what should be the peripheral and, therefore, compromisable elements for the church to grow on a new soil.

Though the spirit of a "positive missionary approach" had found a powerful expression in Loyola, he was not the author. Schmidlin elaborates the point very convincingly with rich examples from the missionary-minded leaders in the Middle Ages as well as in early Christianity. Schmidlin maintains that Paul himself employed this method basically. It was evident that the framework he used for his messages was a flexible one so that it would accommodate the historical or cultural situation when and where he preached to the Jews. He preached, however, to the Gentiles within the context of natural revelation and the philosophy of the non-Christian world.[5] According to Schmidlin, the accommodation method was older than Paul. Even the exclusive Palestinian Pharisaism before Paul had used the method for Jewish proselytism.[6] In fact, not only in the Judeo-Christian missionary enterprises but in the historical phase of the expansion of the other religions as well, whose influence overflowed their respective cultural boundaries, accommodation has been an inevitable and necessary procedure.[7]

As a "method," however, the problem of accommodation has always been a touchy and difficult subject to solve. The issue involved is not only the question of to what extent and degrees of accommodation should be granted to the unavoidable alien elements which came in through the contact, but it also involved the question of maintaining the purity of the enterprising missionary religion itself. To be sure, Ricci did not provide any answers to this question. We could say that he rather brought up the issue anew with an important example, an issue which eventually gave rise to a painful and long-lasting controversy known as the Controversy of Rites.[8]

When Ricci arrived in the Middle Kingdom in 1582, he was a resolute missionary "equipped with" the "Akkommodationsmethode" with which he was destined to shake the foundation of the East. On the pattern of the Pauline dictum ("I have become everything to everybody, so as by all means to save some of them. And I do it all for the sake of the good news, so that I may share in its blessings along with the rest.");[9] and in accordance with the rules in the canonical law concerning the clerical clothes;[10] and encouraged by his understanding superior Alessandro Valignani, Ricci changed his soutanes into the cloak of the Buddhist bonze and shaved off his hair and beard to identify himself as a "cleric" in the Chinese sense. In this way, he became a Chinese "man of religion." His companion Michele Ruggieri wrote to his friend on February 7, 1583, saying "so, before long, we became Chinese to win China for Christ."[11] Thus, the first step toward "attire accommodation" ("*die äussere Akkommodation*") took place dramatically.

However, the bonze's cloak was a mistake. Ricci and Ruggieri soon found out that the social situation of the Buddhist bonzes in China was very low in contrast to the situation in Japan. Based on the experience of the Jesuit missionaries in Japan, they had hoped to be accepted in China with the due social respect as bonze-like "religioso." Valignani advised him to occupy, as soon as possible, a social status equal to that of the ruling class, so that he could have access to the important few in the society to win the nation for Christianity. Now, however, he realized that it was impossible so long as he remained a Western "bonze." Therefore, "he let his hair grow and put on the costume of the Literatus to gracefully comply with the civilization where he came to live."[12]

He became a Li Ma-tou, adopting a compromised form of trans-literation and a pure Chinese three-syllable name. He did this kind of modified transliteration in both directions. It is he who translit-erated the name of Confucius from K'ung-fu-tzu into Latin form as it is spelled in Western countries now. In addition to his attire and name, he also adopted the Chinese type of courtesy.[13] He mastered, of course, the complicated art of using the honorific titles correctly when addressing mandarins. He learned the table manners. He also adopted the graceful way of giving and receiving presents and exchanging visits on proper occasions.[14]

He "accommodated" Chinese language and literature success-fully into his Catholic sermons. He was a gifted linguist,[15] though in later years he confessed that he had almost forgotten his mother tongue. It is extremely interesting to note that in Ruggieri's *"catechismo ossia Ttienciu Sce Lu (T'ien-chu-shih-lu)"* (1584) Bud-dhist terms are extensively used. The Jesuit writer may have thought that his literary style should match his monk's cloak. Ruggieri called himself a "bonze" and even he signed his preface as a bonze from "India," India being the representative of the Western countries in the contemporary Chinese literature.[16] But this was soon corrected by Ricci. Ricci replaced Buddhist terminology with that of Confucianism when he changed his appearance from bonze to literatus.

It is not surprising to see that Ricci put emphasis on "aesthetic accommodation," for art is the "means of expressing ethical-religious and national ideals" (*Ausdrucksmittel sittlich religöser und nationaler Ideale*).[17] Chinese architecture and fine arts were skill-fully accommodated to blend a splendid new species in Christian art. In the phase of *"sozialrechtliche Akkommodation"*[18] Ricci faith-fully followed the strategy adopted by the Jesuit mission in general and persisted in his effort to win men of the ruling class (*das Streben nach der Gewinnung der Vornehmen*) in the society. He was willing to compromise with the "civil ceremonies" of the Con-fucian ancestral worship, if the ruling class could be won through concession. The number of converts was of no concern to him. He devoted a disproportionate amount of energy and time to the single purpose of winning the best few, the court, and King Wang Li himself, if possible. Under such circumstances the social structure of the society was also accepted to the greatest possible extent as it was. The system of Chinese social values also found its secure place in Ricci's Chinese Christianity. Only when a concrete problem such as polygamy or slavery actually became obstacles was he willing to come to deal with them, but mainly in accordance with the idealized version of Confucianism. In fact, "idealized Confucianism" to him was no other than Orientalized Christianity.[19]

In this way, Ricci became Chinese purposely. But we do find in him genuine respect and affection for the great civilization in addition to his purposive method. He admired the intellectual achievements of the people whom he was more than willing to accommodate. In Ricci's literary works one finds not only proof of his mastery of the Chinese cultural heritage but his love and devotion toward it. He has given an important place to Chinese intellectual achievement in his Christian message which he prepared for Chinese readers.

He preferred the literary style of dialogue so widely used in Chinese literature. His *T'ien-chu shih-i*, mistakenly called a Catechism, consists of a soul-searching conversation between a Confucian scholar and a Jesuit missionary. And the dialogue is presented in such a way as to show their deep mutual understanding and respect. His *Chi-jen shih-pien*, which consists of his ten conversations with the "important few" on various occasions, also clearly demonstrates the author's profound admiration for the traditional oriental literary style, to which he actually has given much refinement with a touch of the Western wisdom.

With regard to the religion of China, Ricci was accommodating toward Confucianism, but rejected Buddhism and Taoism, because he perceived in the latter two religious enemies of his evangelism. For Ricci Buddhism was the "sect of gods," the most heathen of all religions in China.[20] He employed very often, with contempt, the words *"Idoli"* and *"Pagode"* to designate the Mahayana pantheon at the head of which was the Buddha, or the "Highest Master" of the "sect." To the male gods he appropriated the masculine form *"Pagode"* and to the female deities *"Pagod."* To this "sect" he took up direct opposition, contrary to his earlier borrowing of the bonze's cloak and identification as the *"religioso dell' India."* When challenged by the leading Buddhists of the day, he encountered them in a most uncompromising manner.

The occasion presented itself when the Buddhists found in Ricci's Christianity a powerful rival. The famous Catholic-Buddhist disputation took place in 1599.[21] The influence of Buddhism in China had diminished considerably as the permeation of neo-Confucianism (which Ricci repudiated as "recent materialists")[22] progressed. But by no means had it lost out completely. Buddhism played, therefore, the self-confident host in this disputation.[23] The issue at stake was mainly the question of "the Lord of Heaven" (*Signor del cielo*).[24]

Ricci could not tolerate either the godlessness of the learned Buddhists on the one hand and the "superstitious" aspect of popular Buddhism on the other hand. He wrote to a bonze by the name of Yü Te-yüan: "Buddha placed himself in opposition to the Lord of Heaven, *T'ien-chu*, and denied Him, intending to place himself upon the throne. This is why I reject Buddha."[25] Buddha was a man, "not more than an ant," to Ricci. To this strong assertion a countercharge came from the Buddhist camp with the same harsh tones. Bonze Shen came up with an argument based on an etymological consideration regarding Ricci's accommodated term *T'ien-chu* or *Signor del cielo*. He said the Christian word was derived from the *T'ien-chu* of Buddhism. And this *T'ien-chu* was no other deity than the Trayastrimsas, the Lord of the Thirty-three Heavens in the four continents of the world. Ricci confessed that he had not read Buddhist books and, therefore, was ignorant.[26] But in spite of the accidental coincidence, he maintained that the Christian *T'ien-chu* was the creator of the heaven and earth, the Supreme Lord over all things therein. He fought Buddhism on the ground of the doctrine of a personal God and His oneness.

And it is extremely interesting to note that when he attacked the doctrines of Buddhism he was a sharp science-minded rationalist *par excellence*. His favorite topic seemed to have been the Buddhist transmigration theory, against which he devoted a large portion of his *T'ien-chu shih-i* (Chapter V).

One thing is very clear in all this blow and counterblow. To Ricci Buddhism was not a religion of Chinese origin.[27] Therefore, there was no need for him to accommodate the apparently alien elements of that religion to Christianity.

With Taoism the story could have been entirely different, because it was an indigenous Chinese religion. Consequently, the accommodation could have been more generously extended. But Ricci chose to do otherwise. He opposed it no less vehemently than he did Buddhism. This was the case mainly because his attachment to Confucianism was so strong that perhaps he had to choose to reject this "superstition." The so-called religious Taoism (*tao-chiao*) in particular was "superstition" to the leading Confucianists of the day, in addition to his own observation on the practices. King Shen-t'ung, the contemporary of Ricci who declared in his decree on May 18, 1602, that Buddhism as well as Taoism were paganism in China, was an exponent of this scholarly tendency of Confucianism of that age.

It could be speculated that Ricci's attitude toward Taoism might have been less rigid if he had perceived its possible historical relationship with Nestorianism or other Syriac types of Christianity. In fact, Ricci may have been aware of its doctrinal morphological analogy to Christianity, because in actuality, perhaps driven by necessity, he had accommodated from Taoism some useful terms for his evangelism, while bitterly repudiating the concepts attached to them. He adopted the most important terms for him, *Shang-ti*, or Emperor on High, and *T'ien-ti*, or the Emperor of Heaven, from the Taoist-Confucian stock, to denote the Christian God in Chinese, there being no more suitable word in Chinese. He rejected, however, the concept of Taoism originally implied in these words. He wrote: "The vocabulary Lord of Heaven *T'ien-chu* of our country is correspondent with the 'Supreme Ruler' *T'ai-shang* in Chinese [Taoist] language. But, the Christian concept is entirely different from that of the gods that the Taoist fabricated with names such as 'the Secretful One' or the 'Purely Elevated One' *T'ai-ch'ing*. The deity called by these names cannot be other than a being like a man who had some merits and lived on the Wu-Tang-Mountain. He belongs entirely to the human species if there was such a being. (Taoistic assertion is absurd.) How can a man make himself the 'Purely-Elevated-Heaven-Ruler'?"[28]

T'ien-t'ang, or Paradise, and *ti-yü*, or Hell, were terms Ricci borrowed from the Taoist-Buddhist stock.[29] *Hsien*, the spiritual being, another widely used Taoist vocabulary, was adopted by Ricci to signify the "holy man" in the Christian sense during the period from 1582 to 1602.[30] He later substituted for it the Confucian "*sheng*," or "holy," in his writings including the *T'ien-chu shih-i*.[31]

His repudiation of Taoism was based, however, on solid doctrinal ground. In his dialogue *T'ien-chu shih-i*, Ricci had the Chinese literatus, the visitor, bring out a topic concerning Taoism for discussion with the host, the Western literatus. "The Taoists say that all things are originated from nothingness and the consummation of all things is found in this nothingness" (then he goes on to further referring to the doctrine of void in Buddhism and the *t'ai-chih*, or

Sumum Extremum, in Confucianism.) To this the Western literatus, Ricci himself, replies bluntly: "Both of these schools which preach nothingness or void are absolutely in opposition to the true doctrine of God. It is clear that one cannot follow their doctrines."[32] That was Ricci's final word for these two religions.

With Confucianism Ricci's attitude was diametrically different from his attitude toward the two above-mentioned religions. One finds the zenith of Ricci's *Akkommodationsmethode* in his treatment of Confucian ideology and practices.

This attitude of Ricci's could be interpreted from both ends of a continuum. At the extreme practical end there is Ricci's missionary tactic. He perceived that the surest and, therefore, best way to win China for Catholicism was to win Confucianism, the most deep-rooted and prevalent religion in China to his side. Although the neo-Confucianism of the Sung period, which Ricci interpreted to be a materialistic deviation from orthodox Confucianism,[33] had introduced some unwholesome elements into the original and therefore, pure Confucianism, he strongly believed that this poisonous philosophy of the *"quelques lettres de ce temps"*[34] would be eliminated ultimately, to reveal the great wisdom which was discovered by the "saints" of ancient China. Therefore, he endeavored to enter into an alliance with this powerful religion to use its influence in establishing a strong foundation for Catholicism in the Middle Kingdom. He thought it was possible, because he found a strong analogy between the two religions. He saw the possibility of making this analogy a useful tool, not only for combating Buddhism and Taoism but also for winning Confucian society itself as a whole. In his apologetic writings, therefore, his knowledge of the literature of Confucianism was extensively utilized. It was used as an offensive and at the same time as a defensive weapon. In his instruction in Christian doctrines, the tool was put into use so convincingly that his influence reached far beyond the boundaries of China proper and produced strange effects beyond his expectation, notably in Korea and Japan.

His collections of maxims from Christian sources in his books, "The Treatise on Friendship," or *Chiao-yu-lun*, "Ten Discourses of a Stranger, " or *Chi-jen shih-pien*, "The Twenty-five Sentences," or *Erh-shih-wu chang-chü*, and so on, were intended to bring out this analogy. It was so intended not only because he knew that it was the best way to introduce Christianity to Chinese people but also because he himself strongly believed that these maxims actually "accommodated the genius of China so that he could remember our philosophies, our saints and our other ancient and modern thinkers."[35] At the same time, it was reported that he was encouraged by Valignani, his superior at the time, to write a book to replace Ruggieri's "Catechism," *T'ien-chu shih-lu*, which was heavily dotted with Buddhist vocabulary, for the reason that there was a need for "a writing in which the natural order was emphasized by means of the arguments drawn from Chinese literature."[36] This book was the *T'ien-chu shih-i*. In the process of preparing this book, he testified that "I have noticed many passages which are in favor of our faith, such as the the unity of God, the immortality of soul, the glory of honor, etc."[37]

At the other end of the continuum mentioned above, one finds the "philosopher" Ricci. Trained under the Thomistic synthesis of Jesuitism,[38] he was quick to find in Confucianism an *"Ursprunglich Reinheit der Naturreligion"* (original purity of nature religion) in the most perfect form known to him. To him this "pure natural religion" seemed to be based on the "voice of Reason," and, therefore, in an ideal harmony with the religion of Revelation in the Thomistic hierarchical relationship. Therefore, he treated Confucianism as an important preparatory beginning toward the true religion, and Christianity as the fulfillment of the ideals of Confucianism.[39]

To be sure, Ricci's Confucianism was not what he encountered around him. He disagreed with his contemporary Chu-hsian neo-Confucianists, because of their materialism. That was to him a degeneration from the traditional pure belief. He was in sympathy more with the personalism of the Wang Yang-ming school. Nevertheless, Ricci's Confucianism was something else. Detaching himself from the degenerate Confucian commentators of the Sung dynasty onward, Ricci preferred to go back to Confucius himself whenever possible. But Confucius was no more than an organizer and compiler of the already existing beliefs of his day. So, Ricci went further back to the idealized *"Ursprung"* in the *"Urzeit."* Ricci's idealized pure Confucianism with Christianity-like ideology was postulated in that mythological *"Urzeit."*

He was so detached from the living Confucianism of the day that Longobardo, his immediate successor as the superior of the Jesuit China mission after his death, rebelled against the Riccian version, arguing that Ricci had disregarded completely, erroneously, the traditional orthodox Confucianism. By evading Confucian commentaries on traditional Confucian texts, Ricci rather read into the ancient ambiguous vocabulary of the texts something very new. He "took up the text which is more favourable and in conformity to our doctrine and rejected the commentaries entirely."[40] Longobardo declared: "For me, with the permission of the good father [Ricci] and those of our fathers who follow him, I feel differently, and I believe that ancient Chinese were atheists."[41]

Whichever the case was, we find it strange that the leading Confucianists of the day were more than willing to argue or agree with Ricci on the ground of the Riccian understanding of Confucianism as provided by Ricci. Hsu Kwang-chi (Siucoamchi) and Li Chih-tsao (Licezao) were the best known and most influential persons among them.

As was mentioned above, Ricci was willing to compromise the peripheral matters of Christianity if he could thereby win the heart of the great nation for the Church. Therefore, he boldly accepted not only the names for God in the (Taoist-Confucian) usage: *T'ien, Shang-ti,* or *T'ien-chu,* but also the Confucian concepts and notions attached to the vocabularies.

The "civil rites," or the cults of ancestors and of Confucius, were also accommodated on the interpretation that they only signify personal veneration and filial piety in a conventionalized form. According to Huonder,[42] Ricci demanded of his Chinese Catholics that no prayers be offered to Confucius. But limited participation of Christians in the ceremony was thought to be justified. Riccian Christians, therefore, were allowed to make prostration to the ancestral tablets and to the image of Confucius. And it went further; incense was burned and sacrifices were offered. These gave rise to bitter controversy among the Catholic missionaries in China as well as to the Vatican theologians at home.

Nevertheless, it would be a grave mistake to assume Ricci's original intention was to identify Christianity with Confucianism. He did not neglect to indicate Confucius's *"silence sur les choses de l'autre vie"* (silence on matters of the other life). Bernard-Maître said: "It was therefore necessary to a certain extent to overlook Confucianism."[43] I agree with that statement.

All in all, insofar as the "Accommodation Method" remains a "method," method is method. "Worauf schliesslich doch alles ankommt, ist nicht das System, sondern der Erfolg."[44] The results speak of the value of the method. What counts most, in this context, is the result.

From the standpoint of the result, the Riccian Accommodation Method was effective and powerful, dangerously powerful. It could nourish a strong resisting power in the new converts and help them withstand the pressure of the age. This was well demonstrated in China proper.

The influence of the neo-Confucianism of the Sung (Chu Hsi school) and Ming (Wang Yang-ming school) dynasties was too harsh a climate for the infant Christianity to grow normally among the literati, to whom all the Riccian effort was directed. Riccianism, however, did not perish. It lived on. It produced Ku T'ing-lin (1612–1681) and his successors Yen Jo-chü (1636—1740), Hui Shih-chi (1709–1741), and others who were the rebel spirits against the tyrannical Chu-hsian commentators and their orthodox rationalism. They were the creators of the "Fourth Renaissance"[45] in China, which brought back the scholarship of the seventeenth century directly to the classical Confucian documents and not through the labyrinthine commentaries of latter day Confucianism.

This school of neo-Han, or Han-hsüeh, the leading spirit of the Fourth Renaissance, not only successfully survived Chu Hsiism but became eventually the destroyer of the tyranny of orthodoxy in the later development of history.

Ricci's method proved to be very effective in breaking new ground. It is splendidly demonstrated in Korea. It wrought a "miracle."[46] We see that the Riccian documents, notably Ricci's *T'ien-chu shih-i* and Pantoja's *Ch'i-ko-ch'i-shu,* stirred up heated responses among the intellectuals of the day immediately after they were introduced. That was a sign of their effectiveness. They were disturbing, because the literature explained a "new" belief in a surprisingly familiar framework and in a precise language never known before. Behind the facts which the literature describes, there was a surprisingly compact system of thought or "philosophie chrétienne," supported by rational as well as scientific speculations. This added great strength to the impact.

The newness and the familiarity of the literature seem to have caused all the excitement. In commenting upon the *T'ien-chu shih-i,* Yi Ik, the Korean Confucian scholar says: "In their doctrine, the *T'ien-chu,* Lord of Heaven is their supreme deity. The Lord of Heaven 'is' no other than the *shang-ti* of Confucianism though the way of reverence and worship is rather similar to that of the religion of Shyaka [Buddha]. They use our familiar concepts of the Paradise and Hell for the purpose of exhortation and premonition. The universal master and savior is Jesus. Jesus is the Western name for the Saviour of the World."[47]

In commenting on *Ch'i-ko-ch'i-shu* Yi Ik says also: "The *Ch'i-ko* is the book written by an author called Pantoja from the West. The contents of the book 'are' the teachings of our Confucian wisemen on Self-denial. In short, the book is a Confucian one."[48]

In contrast to these statements of the progressive Yi Ik, who repeatedly expressed his favorable opinions on Christianity, extremely hostile opinions were also expressed by influential scholars of the other camp. The representatives of the latter group are Pak Chiwŏn, the author of *Yŏrha ilgi* and Hong Yangho whose literary works were collected in *Igye chip*. "As for the doctrine of worshipping Heaven, it is not surprising, because they have modeled their belief and vocabularies on our ancient Confucian Shang-ti. But it is too much for us to take when they say that the Creator created the world through Jesus. There can be no more excessive arrogance and pomposity as this."[49]

Pak Chiwŏn says: ". . . thereafter, Matteo Ricci seduced China [into utter confusion] with the help of his doctrine of the heavenly deity. [Christians] believe the spiritual existence and destiny of man as the Buddhists do in their own belief in transmigration. It is the theory of Paradise and Hell. Yet, they reject Buddhist doctrines and attack them as if they were the enemy. But why? Buddhism is . . . absurd itself, because it contradicts the teaching of *Shih-ching* in their negation of reality as existence. Christianity is absurd also, because, according to the *Shih-ching*, the Supreme Being in Heaven has no voice nor smell. Christianity fabricates the voice and smell for the same."[50]

It is extremely interesting for us to note that both advocates and critics of the receiving parties reacted equally to the Christian challenge in a very similar pattern. They both readily "identified" Ricci's God with the concept of a deity they already possessed. They only differed in their decision by either accepting the "new" Christian elements as the fulfillment to the old beliefs, or refusing the same as a contradictory assertion to the traditional ways.

The spontaneous growth of Protestantism that came later is partly attributable to Ricci's method, too, because the Protestant literature when first spread among the people took the same route already opened by the Riccian "*Bahnbrecher*." To a large extent, Koreans had grown familiar with the Christian concepts and doctrines already, on the merits of the Riccian approach, by the time Protestantism was introduced.

The penetrating effect of Ricci's method was clearly demonstrated in Japan. Jesuitism had been well established in Japan even before Ricci reached his field of life work in Japan. But, curiously, the Riccian literature exerted influence upon the zealous neo-Shintoists, namely Hirata Atzutane (1776–1843) and Ohtano

Nishiki (1764–1824), and helped them to systematize their Shinto theology on the Christian model.

The fundamental tenet of the Motoori Noringa's powerful neo-Shintoism was to make Shintoism purely Japanese by eliminating the long-lasting influences upon it from Buddhism and Confucianism.

Hirata, who succeeded Motoori after his death, was the developer and systematizer of this Shinto theology which exerted its decisive influence upon the entire national life thereafter. It was destined to become the guiding spirit of modern Japan.

Hirata's theological contributions[51] can be summarized in two points. Firstly, he elevated the Three Creator Deities in the Shinto mythology (Master-of-the-August-Centre-of-Heaven Deity *Amenominakanushi*; High-August-Producing-Wondrous Deity *Takamimusubi*; Divine-Producing-Wondrous Deity *Kamimimusubi*) and made them transcendental deities of the Judeo-Christian type. He elaborated the first sentence of the *Kojiki*: "The names of the deities that became in the Plain of High Heaven when the Heaven and Earth began" with a new Book-of-Genesis-like concept and changed it into a new sentence which reads: "At first before the Heaven and the Earth were born there were the deities in the plain of High Heaven, whose names were. . . ."[52]

He also changed the spirit-producing deities *Izanagi*, or Male-Who-Invites Deity, and *Izanami*, or Female-Who-Invites Deity into the mankind-producing deities A-Da-Mu [Adam] and En-Ba [Eve] respectively.[53]

Secondly, Hirata enlarged considerably the domain of the "Master-of-the-Great-Land *Ohkuninushinokami*," the deity of the Land of Dead, into a comprehensive spiritual world including heaven and hell, so that a separate accommodation could be provided for the departed according to their deeds on earth.

It is apparent that he was an ingenious thinker who could adapt a framework so foreign for the use of the Japanese mythology which was very much different from the one for which the framework was originally designed.

He went further. He wrote a book of two volumes when he was thirty-one years of age, entitled *Hon-kyo kai-hen*, which may be rendered in a free translation: *Significant Doctrines Originated Outside of Shinto*. This book was kept from the public until it was published in the second volume of his complete works in 1911.[54] This remarkable book opens with the two hymns[55] quoted without acknowledgment from the eight "hymns with musical accompaniment" by Ricci, published in his *Chi-jen chih-pien*. In fact, there was no harm done if it was used for the purpose of exalting Shintoism, because there was no direct mention of Christian terminology in them. The religious terms used in the hymns were by no means monopolized by Christianity. Christianity was the borrower, in the first place, of these religio-poetic terms from Oriental literary expression.

He devoted a good portion (pp. 5–18) of his first volume to a Shinto adaptation of Ricci's *T'ien-chu shih-i*. The original dialogue between the Chinese and Western literati became a dialogue between a Confucianist and Hirata himself. Hirata put himself into the position originally taken by the Jesuit Ricci. It is a remarkable feat—with only a slight alteration Ricci's words are placed in a Shinto theologian's mouth with no scruple or hesitation. Among the alterations there is a passage that reads: "Blessed are those who have endured persecution for their uprightness, for the Kingdom of Heaven is already theirs and they will never die. For this is the mystery of Shinto which is beyond man's wisdom."[56]

The next largest section of the book (pp. 18–47) is devoted to the literary adaptation of Matteo Ricci's *Chi-jen shih-pien*. Ricci's ten conversations with ten Chinese literati are made into a long conversation between Hirata himself and a Confucianist.

The entire second volume (pp. 47–83) is a somewhat abridged copy of Pantoja's *Ch'i-ko* seven volumes. In contrast to the first volume, in which Ricci's words are translated into Japanese, the abridgment in this second volume is made entirely in straight Chinese. Hirata may have thought that there was virtually no need to alter the ethico-religious life, which the Christian writer delineated in order to transplant it in the new Shinto soil.

The above facts seem to indicate how powerful—dangerously powerful—the effect of Ricci's accommodation was. Along this line, Longobardo, Ricci's successor and opponent, certainly had some good reasons to object to Ricci's approach. It had the danger of engendering syncretism!

As a missionary method employed by the Protestant side, the well publicized "Nevius Method"[57] is worth mentioning. It is worthwhile not because it has been a persistent method of an important mission in Korea, but rather because it had a powerful effect in molding peculiar characteristics of Korean Protestant churches as a whole.

This method was developed by a not-very-successful[58] missionary to Shantung, China, by the name of John L. Nevius, who published in 1885 in the *Chinese Recorder* a series of articles entitled: "Planting and Development of Missionary Churches."[59] The articles caught the attention of newly arrived missionaries in the Korean peninsula in 1884. They invited Nevius to come to Korea to initiate them into this method, and that was realized in 1890. He stayed in Seoul for two weeks, and his method was adopted by the Korea Mission of the Presbyterian Church, USA in that year. H. G. Underwood, one of the first missionaries, recalls the occasion and mentions: "after careful and prayerful consideration, we were led, in the main, to adopt these [methods]."[60]

Though the method is linked to the name of Nevius, the high points of it are by no means his invention. It was a notable new trend in the missionary movement of the day. The days of making "known the glorious gospel for perishing men" were over.[61] The already grown-up native churches in the various successful mission fields demanded a "new" method, a wiser method, to deal with them.

There were two distinctive phases involved in the situation. One was a theological evaluation of the native Christians and their churches. The other was a practical evaluation of the native resources in view of the fact that there were limitations on the part of the supplying missions to meet the need, while the growing native churches seemed to present a limitless demand. On the meeting point of these evaluations a principle of "a self-supporting native church with assistance from foreign missions" was born.

The first keen-sighted advocate of this method is said to be Henry Venn (1790–1873),[62] the secretary of the Church Missionary Society of Britain, who began to express his views on the matter with his first memorandum of 1851, prepared with special attention given to the situation in South India. But his views took decisive form as a missionary program in his second memorandum of 1861 entitled, "Minutes on the Organization of the Native Churches in Missions," that was to influence the missionary work in Korea deeply. It was in this document that the elementary principles of self-support, self-government, and self-expansion were fully formulated.

This idea was given more refined presentation by his American contemporary and friend Rufus Anderson (1796–1880)[63] who, echoing Venn's memorandum, delineated this method in 1856 as follows: "If we resolve the end of missions into its simplest elements, we shall find that it embraces (1) the conversion of lost men, (2) organizing them into churches, (3) conducting them to the stage of independence and (in most cases) of self-propagation. Occasionally the labors of a missionary society will terminate when its churches shall have become self-subsistent; but generally it must carry its work to the point of reliable self-development . . ."[64]

They reasoned that it would benefit both the old and the young churches, because it would lessen the burdens of the mission considerably while utilizing the resources of the new churches and giving them opportunities of full participation in progress. Venn had said: "It may be said to have been only lately discovered in the science of missions, that when the missionary is of another superior race than his converts he must not attempt to be their pastor; for they will be bound to him, yet if he continues to act as their pastor they will not form a vigorous native church. But as a general rule they will remain in a dependent condition and make but little progress in spiritual attainments."[65]

The real contribution of the "prophet" Nevius[66] is found in his vigorous programming and application of this method to the Korean scene with the help of the young American Missionary statesmen.[67]

It is very interesting to note that the "formulation" of this method prepared by Nevius with compact yet detailed directions for missionaries was remembered differently by his notable followers, Underwood and Moffat, who heard him directly. They "summarized" the method in their own distinctive ways.

Underwood seems to have understood it as a missionary approach with special emphasis on the necessity of native participation. He summarizes it in the following four points:

1. Let each man abide in the calling wherein he was found, teaching that each was to be an individual worker for Christ, and to live Christ in his own neighborhood, supporting himself by his trade.

2. To develop church methods and machinery only so far as the native church was able to take care of and manage the same.

3. As far as the church itself was able to provide the men and the means, to set aside those who seemed the better qualified, to do evangelistic work among their neighbours.

4. To let the natives provide their own church buildings, which were to be native in architecture, and of such style as the local church could afford to put up.[68]

On the other hand, "the more important missionary statesman" of the day, S. A. Moffat, gives a one-sentence summary which includes only two clear-cut points: "from him [Nevius] came the seed thought of the two great principles of our work: the Bible training class system and self-support."[69] To Moffat the "Bible training class system," an effective tool to implement his approach was the more important feature, as shall be explained below.

These two missionaries took somewhat different courses in their work. Moffat took his station at P'yŏngyang and made it a stronghold of Presbyterianism within twenty-five years' time. He had brought with him from America an ultraconservative type of Christianity, derived from the old Convenanters of Scotland, with which he blended the Nevius method to produce a type of vigorous legalistic Christianity that is peculiar in modern Church history.

Meanwhile, Underwood, who was stationed in Seoul, took up a modified form of the Nevius method free from Moffat's orthodoxy. The disagreement between the two was brought to light dramatically in the "college question," a bitter dispute that lasted for more than ten years from 1909 onward.

The Board of Foreign Missions of the Presbyterian Church USA was also deeply involved in the dispute throughout the period, only to find that the Convenanter missionaries' decisions were too strong to alter. The Moffat-centered Korean mission repeatedly refused to comply with the recommendation of the Board or of the special commission incorporated by the General Assembly to solve the question. The fervent missionary group advocated that "the object of the mission is to develop a self-propagating, self-governing church which shall complete the work of evangelism,"[70] in conformity with the Nevius method as far as possible. In order to carry out this purpose they declared that it was necessary to prevent Underwood and his friends from establishing a college in Seoul with a liberal approach to Christianity, so that the "college" already in operation in P'yŏngyang under their supervision would be the only Christian institute of higher learning in the land. It is not difficult to imagine what the curricula of this "college" were, in view of their education policy. In accordance with the method in general, they deliberately discouraged positive effort in education, as we shall see.

The unsatisfactory solution to this problem gave an upper hand to the prefundamentalistic Convenanters, enabling them to dominate Presbyterianism in Korea and use the Nevius method as if it were a weapon specially designed for them. In a doctoral dissertation a missionary of the Moffat school gives a faithful description of the actual description of this method in Korea.[71] With him we can make a journey to see with clarity how the method was put into use by these men. The following are excerpts from the missionary program:

—How Should New Converts Be Dealt With?[72]

Each individual Christian should be led to work for his neighbors and friends, without pay, remaining in the vocation wherein he was called.

Utilize and capitalize on the new enthusiasm of the young Christians to the limit, even though it involves making more demands upon them than the blase Christians in America ordinarily give to work.

Do not coddle the Christians too much financially. Hardship, and even bitter persecution, will put iron in their blood.

—How Shall the Christian Groups Be Managed?[73]

Expect every man, woman and child in the congregation to be at the same time a learner from some one better informed . . . with whom they come in contact.

From among the ordinary laymen believers of the groups, select one or more "Leaders" who shall voluntarily conduct services on Sundays and attend to the spiritual interests of the little company of the believers, working under the superintendence of the missionary in charge.

—What Shall Be Done about Self-Support?[74]

As a matter of course, expect the Christians to provide their own chapels. These chapels are usually simply dwellings at first . . . Later, there may be buildings especially erected for worship, but, even then, they should be similar to the dwellings as long as possible . . . Keeping the church thus inconspicuous has disarmed village hostility.

No paid pastors are to be installed in local single congregations. The unpaid "Leaders" are to do the work until the people are able and willing to pay their pastors. The local churches should also begin at once to pay towards the salary of the "Helper" of the circuit.

—Standards?[75]

The Bible is made the basis of all the work, and the aim is to fill the minds of the people with it so that it will control conduct. The Bible is the only authoritative guide to answer questions. If the teachings of the Bible are unreliable and inconclusive, the authority of scripture is shaken at its foundations.

—Schools?[76]

The great mission of the Christian church is not to teach mechanics and civil engineering or foreign languages or science, not to Christianize heathen nations by civilizing them.

—Medical Work?[77]

. . . of the greatest importance.

—The Missionary's Work?[78]

His business is to plant independent, self-supporting Christian institutions and to raise up a native ministry.

These are the germs of the method by which the North Presbyterian Mission USA has persisted so faithfully and pugnaciously (in the face of many objections and criticisms from the "liberal missionaries"[79] as well as thoughtful Koreans[80]). The mission even passed a rule that every new missionary, upon arrival, "should be handed a copy of the Nevius book, and be required at the end of his first year, along with his examination in the language, to show that he also had come to understand the principles."[81] It is a tradition of the mission that still has force.

A *coup d'oeil* of the whole scheme soon revealed to us that the real aim of this method, as it was applied in practice, was to formulate an effective program designed rather for the "self-discipline" of the native Christians than anything else. The natives were trained intensively, under the principle of self-support, not to be independent from, but to be more "docile" toward the missionaries and their method.

It is evident that this method technically separated the missionaries from the natives on a hierarchical scale. It led the native

into the self-supporting and self-binding activities on their own
initiatives within the preplanned limits set by the missionaries.
Under the conditions set forth by this ingenious method, group
psychology gripped the Christian communities so that the members drove themselves even into excess.

Morning prayers at 5 a.m. every day were urged upon every
decent Christian. There were usually four meetings on a Sunday:
the 5 a.m. prayer, 11 a.m. adult Sunday school, 2 p.m. main service
and 6 p.m. evening worship. All members were expected to be
present at all of these meetings. There was a Wednesday evening
prayer meeting and the Friday evening "section meeting" which
was held separately in a home in each section in the community.
In addition to these, family worship including the hymn-singing,
which made Korea famous,[82] was encouraged. Tithe was the standard scale of offerings. Supervision of the elders over the discipline
of the congregation was something comparable to that of the
consistory of Calvin's Geneva.

In order to give the natives full freedom, the missionaries usually did not participate in these activities. Instead, they kept calm
and observant eyes on the natives. They were to command the
marching militia, instead of mixing themselves among the hard-
working rank and file.

What did their deliberate negligence in education and leadership training mean? They represented the precontroversy Funda-
mentalism of America and succeeded in transplanting the attitude
toward higher education in their mission field manifested by ultraconservative Presbyterians in the United States. The timing of their
arrival in Korea was perfect for launching an ambitious program in
education. The stage was perfectly set. It was to be some twenty-
five years before Korea was to lose her freedom to Japan. Therefore, they were perfectly free if they wished to launch an ambitious
program. The age demanded it. But they calmly turned it down
because they believed it would be rather harmful, as was indicated
in the method. They believed that if the intellectual stature of a
native leader should stand out above the rest of the group from
which he came, it would make the leader detached from his fellow
men. They feared that, as the result of education, a schism would
follow due to a possible aloofness on the part of the educated and
popular jealousy on the part of the uneducated. They were cautious
about letting this happen. The original "mission school" was not a
"school," but an "orphanage" or "Jesus' doctrine school."[83] These
schools refused to teach English,[84] being reluctant to give the fruit

of knowledge to the Korean Adams and Eves lest they should fall. What they actually aimed at was a conditioned growth of the entire Christian community, so that there would be no serious intellectual division among the educated from the entire group. And the fruit reaped was "contempt for learning" as a Korean writer put it, in 1917:[85]

> ... another bad fruit is the contempt for learning. To say that the Church, which founds schools, despises learning sounds like a contradiction; but a real Christian, so-called, treats learning with the greatest contempt, calling it 'worldly knowledge.' Arguing that 'worldly knowledge' weakens faith, he regards learning as a temptation of the devil and an enemy of the soul.
>
> Those who desire to acquire an education higher than that of a special school or to go abroad for study, are considered to have already stepped inside the gates of hell. 'Faith is all important. To learn ever so much—what is the use of it?' is the instruction ...
>
> In Church schools no attention is paid to natural science, geography or history—the essential subjects in a modern curriculum. Remember that Koreans of today must seek learning as the thirsty seek water ...
>
> Be the cause what it may, to despise knowledge is the sure road to destruction. It is indeed a regrettable attitude.

To be sure, the leaders' training program was by no means lacking in this method. But the aim was something very different from the "conventional" method. Clark argues: "Dr. Mateer (a contemporary missionary to China with Nevius and his bitter critic) quotes approvingly some remarks made by Dr. Fitch (another influential missionary to China who also was critical) in the 1898 Conference (at the meeting the "experiment" of the Nevius method in China was discussed), 'the Nevius plan is opposed to building chapels and hiring preachers, but it does not provide for the training of Christians.' That is one of the strangest statements in all of his (Mateer's) book. Certainly the Bible Class System invented by Dr. Nevius and carried over into Korea could not be accused of being lacking in that one line."[86]

Under such circumstances no one will be surprised to find that theological education was nothing but an extension of this Bible Class System. "Coming to the seminary, as in the case of the Bible classes, every man paid all of his own expenses...The seminary, for the first ten years or so, was deliberately planned to run but three and one-half months per year, in order that the men might serve the other months in the circuits...The first students were not men of modern education, but it did not matter much."[87]

It is rather remarkable to see that this method based on a "self-supporting principle" did not even include any consideration of "devolution."[88] The formulator of this extraordinary method may have assumed that the control of leadership by the missionaries in the beginning may have remained to be so in practice for an indefinite length of time if not permanently.

It seems that the Vennian ideals of "euthanasia" of the missions actually had no place at all in this "method." It is true that some progress has been made, however, along this line of "devolution" since the nation's independence in 1945. Nevertheless, the hierarchical structure between the natives and the missionaries was still powerful. And so far as there remains this conditioning factor which hinders its full growth to maturity, the Korean Presbyterian Church will never be able to stand on its own feet.

Thus, the Nevius method, which has been unduly glorified by some missionaries, betrayed itself in its own ingenious way during the early crucial years of history. The Korean Presbyterian Church today looks like an infantile giant under the mission's too careful protection and overly one-sided diet. The self-assertion of the Moffatian missionaries was once again heard loudly in recent years when they came out to "protect" the church from the danger of "liberalism" or "Barthianism" or "neoorthodoxisms" brought in by the "returnees"[89] from abroad.

Regardless of these demerits, the Moffatian impact on the Korean church history is significant in some ways. Firstly, it created an active and functional church in Korea. With its powerful, direct, and simple approach it created an active church with all its members striving to do their share in the "big business" of Christianizing their communities. It gave humble folk free opportunity to express themselves in Christianity. Thus they found an open channel of catharsis in a religiously oriented way. They found the meaning of life in the Bible, spiritual delight in prayers. In short the "folksy" approach met the need of the common people well. Sermons were delivered not by learned preachers in theological language, but by "leaders" as humble as the members of the congregation themselves. It was not an absolute necessity for them to build or purchase an expensive building for a church, because using common dwellings for the purpose was encouraged. Other churches organized by other missions soon began to copy this approach, because they perceived its effectiveness and ease. In this way the Moffatian type of church became the model of all Protestant churches in Korea.

Secondly, its Biblicism and legalistic discipline had a special social appeal. This approach easily attracted the attention of the people because they had undergone the necessary training already during the preceding centuries under Confucianism. The strict interpretation of the Bible as the Law simplified the message. It would have taken a much longer period of time to establish a church if the missionaries had tried to explain the paradox of the Gospel and Law in theological terms. The Moffatians took the shortest route. The Moffatians themselves were fundamentally Calvinistic legalists. Therefore, the shortcut was a natural course for them to take.

Thirdly, the Moffatians approach provided ample opportunities for the native asceticism to find a proper place in their devotional life. The missionaries had to allow the Koreans to grow in this direction because they realized that in their emphasis on Biblicism they actually led the young Christians very close to the Biblical Primitive Church in which mystical asceticism was certainly an integral part of the Christian life. Fasting, praying through the night, vision, prophesying, faith healing— all had their proper places there. These practices all had their counterparts in the indigenous religious life of the Koreans. To the Korean Christians of those early days, St. Paul or St. Peter or Abraham were more contemporary to them spiritually than the missionaries themselves who actually lived among them. Weak in theology but emphatically strong in Biblicism, legalism, and ascetic mysticism, the Nevius-Moffatian type of Christianity grew quickly in Korean soil. And other churches gradually followed this model also.

To sum up, it seems that these two effective methods, which the Jesuits and the Northern Presbyterians employed, produced noteworthy results in two successive periods of Korean history. They share some common features, regardless of their different origins and different approaches. In the first place, both methods ignited strong responses. Ricci's method touched off the spark with its pinpoint impact on the ignition point of native religious ideas, which the society had developed and accumulated through the vicissitudes of her long and painful history. The newness, maturity, and the get-to-the-point approach of the Jesuit enterprise made the Korean ignition decisive.

Arriving at the scene a century later, the Nevius method made the flame jump anew and spread wide with a new and greater velocity by breaking the windows of the stagnant room for the purpose of ventilation, and by adding a tankful of oxygen—American enthusiasm. It achieved its great results thus by providing the necessary conditions.

Secondly, these two methods equally well accommodated and nourished native elements. With Ricci's way the native theology found its place in an inclusive superior system and framework. With sophistication in the later years, a gradual transformation of the native elements into the "authentic" Christianity was achieved. That was the success of Catholicism.

With the Nevius method, the native energy and the indigenous pattern of devotional life were given an opportunity to come into full bloom in Christianity. The American optimism those missionaries brought with them also worked wonders. Just a few drops of this life-giving spirit could change the whole depressed community into a hallelujah-singing congregation. In this way, the Christianization of Korea became a "success," though there is a long way to go yet to attain the aim.

In surveying the entire context of the growth of the Korean church we find that our problem is as complex as the entire labyrinthine syncretic process that took place between the two worlds which came into contact. Korean society became soaked with Christian influences through numerous labyrinthine channels during a most eventful period of Korean history, acting, but also being acted upon; influencing but also being counterflowed, throughout the process.

A possibility, however, presents itself to us at this juncture of another effective approach to our problem of why this "miraculous" expansion of Christianity occurred. The response of the people to the Christian challenges was extraordinarily explosive. Their spontaneity, initiative, resourcefulness, and energetic contributions to the cause demand our special attention. We sense here a strong possibility of religious syncretism. Certainly, syncretism is a "danger,"[90] a grave danger involved in the missionary enterprise. And yet, nonetheless, it is an indication that alien ideas were being absorbed and appropriated; and indeed an exceptionally active syncretism may indicate that something in the cultural climate of the receiving country was especially receptive and congenial toward the incoming concepts.

PART III

SYNCRETISM:
TAPESTRY IN THE EASTERN SCENE

CHAPTER SIX

Concept and Meaning

In this chapter we will endeavor to lay out a certain analysis regarding the universal nature of syncretism in the expectation of using it in the understanding of interreligious relations in Korea.

James Moffat, in his excellent article in the Hasting's *Encyclopedia of Religion and Ethics*, traces the word "syncretism" back to its usage among the Cretans, as Plutarch records in his essay *De Fraterno Amore*: "For, although the Cretans were frequently at faction and feud with one another, they became reconciled and united whenever a foreign foe attacked them. This they called 'syncretism συνκρητισμος'." However, it is said that it was the great Erasmus of Rotterdam who salvaged the antiquated word and put it into practical use. He urged Melanchton in a letter to come into a *"syncretizein"* (common) defence against their opponents regardless of the minor differences between themselves, emphasizing their points of consensus instead. This ironic usage of the term was soon adopted by Zwingli and other Protestants who lived in the aftermath of the Reformation era.[1]

According to Paul Tschackert,[2] the term "syncretism" is also "misused," wrenched from its original usage and forcibly applied to denote a confused mixing of religions. He traced back etymologically this misused form to *"synkerannumi"* (to mix up). In any case, the widely used German synonym *"Religionsmischung"* may be regarded as responsible for making the "misused" form decisive in the modern uses in the sciences of religion.

In a comprehensive way Pinard de la Boullaye presented a *"sens divers"* of the term "syncretisme" as follows:[3]

Sens a) : *Indifferentisme plus ou moins absolue*
Tolerance and blending between cults which contain
more or less equivalent elements.

Sens b) : *Indifferentisme relatif*
Consensus of all Christians, for example, on the essential
issues regardless of their disagreement on other matters.

Sens c) : *Melange philologique et historique*
Accidental (historical and philological) combination of
the borrowed elements which more or less reflect different
origins in different cults.

Further elaboration of each of these three meanings of syncretism is required. We notice that one factor that stands out in the
sens a) is "equivalence." In order to create syncretic phenomena,
"equivalence" must be present when two or more religions come
into contact. What is "equivalence"? It has several meanings:

i) It means the antecedent analogy between some particular
elements on each side. Convergence is usually the case. Sometimes
diffusion from a common stock in the forgotten past can also be the
case.

Both types of syncretism occur generally in the "time of troubles,"
when "the parochial gods who came to be identified with one another in a disintegrating society, as a consequence and an acknowledgment of the unification of the parochial states."[4] Under such
circumstances the ancestral gods of different sections usually become "equivalent."

ii) It could also mean a purely arbitrary "equation" which is
brought into being by the political or cultural environment. Of this
type we have plenty of historical examples which, in more precise
language, are "no genuine religious phenomena, but merely politics
under a religious mask." It also includes the cases of metamorphosis of deities within the historico-environmental context. Perhaps,
the "fortune" of the formerly obscure local god Amon of Thebes
which came to be identified with the high god of the Egyptian
Pantheon[5] is a suitable example. "But, for this immense aggran-
dizement, Amon had to pay the price of ceasing to be himself."[6]

Such glorification and ultimate metamorphosis of a deity occur,
as a rule, in the course of "time of troubles." In exceptional cases,
however, such arbitrariness can also be manifested in peaceful times,
too, in a genuine cultural contact. This can be seen in the
identification of the Latin *numina* with the Olympian divinities.

iii) Thirdly, "equivalence" could also denote a "contextual equivalence" which disregards any particular items of belief on each side of the religions in contact, but emphasizes the similarities in the contexts of those corresponding beliefs. One finds good examples of this in the early Christian missionary enterprise, as it has been majestically arranged and interpreted by Harnack.[7]

Christianity has shown its capacity for altering its missionary approach according to the predisposition of the receiving parties, since the first centuries onward. It sought the contextual equivalents in the particular pagan societies in order to establish points of contact. As a matter of fact, this Christian capacity "was the secret of its fascination and a vital condition of its success" in evangelism.[8] For example, in preaching the "Gospel of the Saviour and of Salvation"[9] to the Hellenistic world, Christianity emphasized purity, consolation, expiation, and healing of the savior. It changed its "original temper,"[10] in light of the demands of the particular pagan world in which the gospel was proclaimed, to suit the world seen in the writings of the Seneca, Epictetus, and many others. Its endeavor to fulfill the need of the society, the witness-bearing Christianity produced an unexpected result on both sides. Christianity deliberately and consciously assumed the form of a "religion of salvation or healing"[11] in this case. The soul of man is moribund from his birth; but now the remedy is available. Baptism, "a bath for restoring the soul's health," Eucharist, "the potion of immortality," and penitence, *vera de satisfactione medicina*" were provided by Christianity. Also on the pagan side a profound change took place. Jesus was identified with the spiritualized physician Aesculapius.[12] Thus, metamorphosis was achieved and a special type of Christianity was born in Hellenistic society.

iv) In the broadest sense, "equivalence" could also imply the Javanese dictum: "all religions are one."[13]

This is a telescopic view of the religion of a weather-beaten sage. It implies tolerance, of which Toynbee writes:

[T]he right motive for toleration is an intuition that all religions are alike, from the highest to the lowest, are quests in search of a single common spiritual goal, so that they do not differ in their aim but merely in the extent of the progress which they are able respectively to make with the aid of their varying lights. This intuition makes it apparent that the propagation of one religion at the expense of other religions through the employment of methods of barbarianism,

on the ground that the religion in whose name the persecution is carried on is a religion of a higher order, is a moral
contradiction in terms, since oppression and injustice and cruelty are negations of the very essence of spiritual sublimity.[14]

This monistic intuition could be attained in many ways. First,
spiritual sublimity, in Toynbee's words, is a way. We have a good
example in the ideas of Sebastian Frank of sixteenth century Germany.

He was fond of talking of the non-partisan God who does
not and cannot allow himself to be comprised within the
categories of man because his being is so vast and so in-
comprehensible that it can be described only in terms of
antinomies. Whatever is said of God, the opposite will also
be true. This God makes himself known in partial measure
to all men and not exclusively to a chosen few . . . "Wherefore
by heart is alien to none. I have my brothers among the
Turks, Papist secretaries, or will remain so; in the evening
they will be called into a vineyard and given the same wage
as we. From the east and from the west children of Abraham
will be raised up out of the stones and will sit down with
God at his table."[15]

Secondly, rational deism also could lead the way. The Latitud-
inarianism or the Religion of the Universe approach of Kang-hi and
Leibniz[16] are good examples.

In contrast to the deductive approach of mysticism, the rational approach finds its starting point in inductive methods, because
they are deemed to be the best way to discard the stumbling block
of boastful dogmatism. Troeltsch, in his famous lectures delivered
almost a century ago (in 1901), yet still edifying, frankly told his
audience: "The construction of Christianity as the absolute religion
is impossible from the historical way of thinking and historical
means" (*die Konstruktion des Christentums als der absoluten Religion ist von historischer Denkweise aus und mit historischen Mitteln
unmöglich*).[17]

To "solve" the problem, he suggested that Christianity is the
"Hohepunkt" or the culmination of all religious experiences. It is
extremely interesting for a student of religion to see that his view
has found a new modern exponent on a grand scale in Toynbee.[18]

Thirdly, the "intuition" could be attained through disturbing
experiences on the part of the religious people who live in a world

that spreads its horizons to all directions with a speed the parochial absolutists could not cope with. In this way the sense of human solidarity makes previous claims appear to be only relative ones in a larger and expanded context.

Fourthly, sometimes the particular situation is molded externally. The situation can be created either artificially or naturally. The territories governed under the constitutional religious liberty, generally speaking, are the former case, while Radhakrishnan's Hindu tolerance represents the latter case. It has been proudly maintained that Hinduism is the most tolerant of all religions. But fundamentally and practically, the Hindu tolerance is corollary to the social structure of the particular society, India. The caste-ridden society believes in the birthrights of individuals. And those who were born in the "twice-born" status were excluded from the direct possibilities of achieving *moksa*, at least until the next round of transmigration. In that sense, there can be no direct proselytism in Hinduism, though it tries to inculcate Hindu ideals for the benefit of the society as a whole. Therefore, in Hindu tolerance there certainly is the social basis besides the much advocated doctrinal grounds. It has to be tolerant to other religions for its own survival in the world community.

What are the motivations of "blending"? It can be motivated by political, economic, or cultural conditions. Yet, under each condition above, the psychological factor stands out. Attraction to foreign elements and yearning for excitement in exotic cults plays an important role. This psychology is what Toynbee called "sense of Promiscuity,"[19] a product of the interactions between the sociohistorical environments and human nature.

The fundamental character of Pinard de la Boullaye's Sens b) is "Consensus," a consensus among the religions in alliance in one way or another regardless of their varieties. This he called *"indifferentisme relatif."*

What does "consensus" mean in this regard? In a societal situation, it is the "framework" of the so-called popular belief. In simpler and smaller primitive societies, "consensus" is easily crystallized and institutionalized. But in the larger and more complex societies the "consensus" often assumes more flexible and therefore hard-to-define forms. Though flexible, the "popular belief" is a reality in every society. It is the *"religio publica."*[20]

i) In the Plutarchian sense, the "consensus" among the religious bodies may arise from a retrospective view on their fraternity, or their real or fictitious kinship bifurcation in history. It remains a sad story that a united front between the heterogeneous Protestant groups, Lutherans and Zwinglians, which was to be organized at the Marburg Colloquy in 1529, proved to be a failure.

Yet, consciousness of togetherness among the Protestants themselves did not falter. The hostility between the various orders in the Catholic Church has been demonstrated time and again, but they maintain an efficient unity under their Supreme Pontiff. The thorny words, uttered some time ago by an Eastern Buddhist in front of an imaginary Christian audience composed of those who ridicule the two great divisions of Buddhism, can still be heard with dull sharpness. He charges: "Taking all in all these contradictions do not prevent them, Protestant as well as Catholics, from calling themselves Christians and even good, pious devoted Christians ... The same mode of reasoning holds good in the case of Mahayanism, and it would be absurd to insist on the genuineness of Hinayanism at the expense of the former. Take for granted that the Mahayana school of Buddhism contains some elements absorbed from (alien sources); but what about it? ..."[21]

In Islam the principle of unity is already set in the alleged words of Muhammad: "Difference of opinion in my community is a (manifestation of divine) mercy." (*Ikhtilafu ummati rahmatu(un)* ...) Accordingly the four *madhab* (*Hanafi, maliki, Shafii and Hanbali*) can exist side by side. Islam also recognizes Judaism and Christianity on the basis of their common belief in special revelation.

ii) Secondly, the "consensus" may be formed in the public mind by a blurred composite picture consisting of the various creeds actually existing in the society.[22] Despite the fact that a great number of different shades of opinion, according to the individual inclinations of the members of a society, could be harbored in it, the "consensus" becomes a reality if enough time is given for the public familiarity to those diverse religious systems to grow.

The pre-Christian popular belief of the Greeks is an example. Not only was a pantheon incorporated in due time, but the various religious beliefs could also form an alliance to resist a new faith when the latter appeared on the horizon with strong enough power to attract their attention. There seem to be two elements involved in this situation. One is the time element,[23] and the other is the ideological affinity: relativism *inter se*, absolutism *inter se*.[24]

The fundamental character of the Sens c) group is the "accidental combination of the un-equivalent portions of the 'equivalent' elements involved in the syncretic phenomenon." This situation arises with the contact and merging of two societies with different cultural configurations. The difficulty they encounter at the outset is the problem of communication. This brings us to the problem of the "semantic features" of the respective communicants.

i) First, communication is carried through the channel of language. "How are they to believe him if they have never heard him?"[25] Paul said. But language is a symbolic system in a given culture; each vocabulary in a given language has its own culturally determined and socially accepted semantic feature which cannot be detached from its innate cultural setting or transplanted into another language in another setting. Therefore, what has been achieved at the end of the conversation is more often not identical with the original feature which the speaker tried to convey to the other from a different cultural background, due to the linguistic limitations.[26] "Each language draws a magic circle round the people to which it belongs, a circle from which there is no escape save by stepping out of it all together into another."[27] This is the difficulty and frustrating experience that those translating religious literature from one language to another have to face.

In spite of these obstacles communication occurred again and again as an "adventure," inevitably creating "open chances" for syncretism. In the worldwide missionary enterprise of Christianity, the problem has been raised anew by the immensity of its scope, never before known in history. As a dogmatic religion with a claim of *Absolutheit*, Christianity must make itself universal in diffusion; and at the same time, it must preserve its creed in a vigorous exactitude. Therefore, the missionaries are entrusted with a task that includes the fundamentally impossible task: communication in exactitude. In that regard, missionary effort is intrinsically an "adventure."

In order to work efficiently some of the Christian missionaries must exhaust their ingenuity to "Christianize the native languages" (*Sprachverchristlichung*), by means of a "change and enrichment of the language" (*Wandlung und Bereicherung der Sprache*) for the purpose of evangelism.[28] They have to create new vocabularies "if expressions for higher concepts are lacking" (*wenn es an Ausdrücken für höhere Begriffe fehlt*).[29] They have to adopt or accommodate the native vocabularies "if expressions for higher concepts are available (*wenn Ausdrücke für höhere Befriffe vorhanden sind*).[30] In either case, the missionaries should try their best to give Christian meaning to these created or accommodated words. And they are advised to be very cautious. It is pointed out: "He who knows from experience how vital a part religion plays in the lives of these archaic peoples, but who also knows how vague and nebulous the concepts are on which their religion is based, will know that Christianity, in order to be a triumphant counterforce, must include that which can be immediately experienced as well as a clear and sharply defined knowledge. Only in this manner can the missionary be spared the disappointment of concocting the crassest pagan-christian syncretism which will cause whole groups to fall victim to the preacher of a Christian heresy."[31] When there is danger, there is always the possibility of falling into it.

ii) Secondly, communication is also carried through artistic expressions. Artistic expressions in aesthetic symbols consist primarily of the highly conventionalized forms of an individual culture. We know that so-called primitive art has as long a history as the art of civilized societies, and its styles and forms are the conventions and symbols accepted by the particular society. Therefore, if a transcendental aesthetic value should be given artistic expression in a society of all, it has to be expressed in the conventionalized artistic form of the particular society. Otherwise the product cannot satisfactorily communicate the idea to the cultural group. This is how native cultural elements are interwoven into the tapestry of all transcultural religions. Furthermore, we are not surprised to find in a work of creative art the objectivity or historicity of the subject evaporated to crystallize on the canvas the inner reality or the sublimated subjectivity of the artist himself or herself. The objectivity or historicity of the "subject" itself has little value. Therefore, any version of tapestry has its own independent value insofar as it remains a product of sincerity on the part of the artist whose subjective reality could not be expressed otherwise than through the conventionalized forms and symbols of the society in which he or she lives and creates.

iii) Third, in the processes of symbolic communication there always are ample opportunities for the native religious concepts from the background of the native myth, *Weltanschauung*, philosophy, custom, and social structure to come to play an auxiliary part.[32] Like a powerful testimony to human solidarity such tapestries colorfully adorned the stages of religious history. We witness today that Christian tapestries are still in the making on the worldwide scale especially with the multicolored threads provided by the younger churches.

CHAPTER SEVEN

The Eastern Tapestry:
The "Three Religions Are One"
Principle

The "national religion" of Korea puzzled the early Western visitors who tried to find some counterpart of the organized Western religions in that peninsula. Opinions differed:

> ... from those who think that Koreans have no religion, to those who would say ... that they are very religious. If you were to ask the average non-Christian Korean about his religion, he would say "no religion."[1]
>
> He [a Korean] personally takes his own education from Confucius; he sends his wife to Buddha to pray for an offspring; and in the ills of life he willingly pays toll to Shamanist "Mootang" [sorceress].[2]
>
> As a general thing, we may say that the all-round Korean will be a Confucianist when in society, a Buddhist when he philosophises, and a spirit worshipper when he is in trouble.[3]
>
> Korea's is a strange religion, a mixing of ancestor worship with Buddhism, Taoism, spirit cults, divination, magic, geomancy, astrology, and fetishism. Dragons play a part, devils of natural gods are abundant; "tokgabi" (elves, imps, goblins) are legion.[4]

A missionary even tried to give this "religion" a name: "Shin-gyo," or Teaching of the Gods.[5]

Such syncretic phenomena seem to have left strong impressions on the visitors who observed the "religion without a name" in action, as is evidenced in the quantity of literature they produced.[6] To single out a typical case among the host of bizarre practices, in Korean funerals,[7] for instance, it is Confucianism that dresses the mourners in sackcloth, while the Buddhist bonzes chant their sutras for the departed to the Western Paradise, a Buddhist heavenly kingdom. It is a shaman who exorcizes the evil spirits that may annoy or harm the departed on his or her journey, while Taoist geomancers engage themselves in supervising the digging of the grave on the site that they believe to be the most "profitable" location.

Each religion plays a different note here, but in a strange harmony. Confucianism provides the religious etiquette; Mahayana Buddhism the ritual and the vision of future life. Taoism ensures the safe journey of the deceased to the spiritual world, while keeping an eye on the expected prosperity of the bereaved conformists to the rites. A shaman is needed to deal with the several souls of the dead directly.

It is no wonder, therefore, that Western observers should be confused when confronted with such a tapestry with extremely complicated designs and colors. They did not know what to make of it. To be sure, there were "independent" Confucian, Buddhist, and Taoist religious organizations functioning separately in the society. Shamanists did not incorporate themselves into any type of organization, but nonetheless it was a religious institution.[8]

Furthermore, it would be entirely erroneous to suppose that the attitude of one religion to another was basically indifferent. Especially since Confucianism ascended to a position of a state religion in the early years of the Chosŏn dynasty, it never hesitated to persecute other faiths as "superstitions," "abominable deeds to embroil heretic sacrifices," or "evil-causing heresies." This Confucian persecution was checked by the fact that Confucianism itself was the exclusive religion of the *yangban* class. Women as well as the commoners were excluded from the rituals. On the other hand the suppressed religions were not entirely silent in their protest. It is not surprising to find that the revolts of Hong Kyŏngnae (1811), the Paekkŏndang of Chinju (1863), and the Tonghak (1894) were all colored with Taoist and Buddhist beliefs though basically they were the movements of the oppressed people against the ruling class.

Hong Kyŏngnae, the leader of the revolt that was named after him, assumed the role of the Taoist mystical general who was believed to have possessed supernatural powers. Some five years after his death in the abortive rebellion, some of his followers in the southern provinces still believed he was alive and organized another series of unsuccessful revolts on the strength of this belief. The Tonghak revolt in later years definitely took the course of a religious war against the ruling class.[9] Ch'ŏndogyo and the host of the similar "indigenous" religious sects in this group are the off-shoots of this rebellion.

Regardless of all this, the most outstanding feature in the complexity is that an "ideal type" of (in the Weberian sense)[10] Korean could always give his or her allegiance to all of these religions at the same time. This situation led a student in Uppsala to exclaim: *"Die Religion Koreas ist synkretistisch."*[11]

It is syncretic; but in what sense? What is the structure of this version of syncretism? Looking at its history, this syncretic attitude of the people had a long standing. Ch'oe Ch'iwŏn, the great scholar of the ninth century Silla dynasty wrote of the "national religion" of his age, which "embraces the three religions of Confucianism, Buddhism and Taoism, grafting them to its own body and nourishing the divergent understandings therefrom in harmony. . . ."[12] This clearly shows that already in his century the seemingly *"indifferentisme plus ou moins absolue"* of the "Three Religions Are One" principle of Chinese origin was rooted deeply in the Korean soil.

The Tangun legend itself has a strong syncretic setting. This foundation myth tells that the nation was founded by Tangun, the descendant of the heavenly deity Hanŭnim or Hwanin.[13] The Koryŏ dynasty's thirteenth century versions of the legend recorded in *Samguk yusa* and *Chewang ungi* are thickly colored with Taoist and Buddhist mythologies and terminology.

If one were inclined to accept the hypothesis of Kim Chewŏn[14] in the face of the much disputed problems of the origin of the Tangun legend,[15] one would find that the Tangun mythology was set already in the syncretic framework, with strong Taoist influences, when it was recorded on the stone slabs of Wu Liang Tzu of the Chinese Han dynasty.[16] If Kim is right, the Han dynasty stone-slab version could be dated safely around the second century C.E. The northern part of the peninsula was under the occupation of Han previous to that date.

If one were inclined to apply the time-depth measurement of the *Kulturekreise-methode*[17] prepared by Wilhelm Schmidt, the

Austrian anthropologist, on this Korean legend, one would find
that the origin of the syncretic attitude in the story could be pushed
further back. The legend depicts the marriage between Hwanung,
the son of the primitive monotheistic deity Hwanin or Hanŭnim,
and the bear-woman Kom,[18] a deity widely worshipped by the North
Asiatic tribes in Manchuria and Siberia.[19] If the marriage meant
the hybridization of two societies with different cultural and religious backgrounds (one, a patriarchal and nomadic with a monotheistic male deity, the other, matriarchal and agricultural with a
totemic female deity), we may be able to trace the lost memories of
the people into the realm of prehistory via the legend. Even in that
stage, which was free from Taoist and Buddhist influences, it is not
difficult for us to infer that the legend was also in a syncretic form:
the marriage of the two deities.

Despite the fact that these ideas, individually, are but hypoth-
eses, one thing is clear. The religious attitude of the people has
been syncretic for a long long time. In what sense, in what character and structure? Kraemer introduces the "Three Religions Are
One" principle, the pre-Christian Eastern syncretism, as a fitting
example of his own thesis. He supposes that it was the relativism
of the Eastern religions based upon the "inherent natural monism"[20]
that gave rise to such a strange phenomenon. He observes: "The
religious allegiance of the average (Chinese) is not related to one
of the three religions. He does not belong to a confession or a creed.
He participates, unconcerned as to any apparent lack of consis-
tency, alternately in Buddhist, Taoist or Confucian rites. He is by
nature a religious pragmatist. Religiously speaking we find him
"prenent son bien où il le trouve." . . . We are repeatedly told, especially of the Chinese and Japanese, that they have a deep-rooted
indifference towards dogma and doctrinal differences."[21]

On closer view, however, Kraemer's interpretation is misleading on several accounts. Firstly, the "average" Far Easterners,
including the Koreans, are not "relativists." They do not philoso-
phize in terms of the *"Absolutheit,"* of course, but they know the
absolute norm with which they must conform. They have indeed
elevated the norms to the absolute height attributing them to the
will of the Heavenly Being. It was the voice of Heaven that spoke
to them through the wise men whom they canonized as their saints.
They are by no means progress-minded relativists. On the contrary, they are conservative absolutists oriented in archaism.

Secondly, they are not pragmatists, religiously speaking. Their
devotion and piety does not allow impartiality in their religious

duties. The *"Prenent son bien où il le trouve"* attitude is psychologi-
cally contradictory even to the sincere "idolators." If they were
pragmatists, why was Christianity, for instance, not accepted in
those countries without undergoing the tragic persecutions? It was
not xenophobia alone that caused the persecutions. They were most
of all religious persecutions.

De Groot provides us with more acceptable explanations on the
matter. According to him: "The three religions are actually branches
of a common trunk which has existed since ancient times; this
trunk is the religion of universism ... Universism, as I will call it
from now on, is one single religion of China; the three religions are
simply its integrating components. This is the reason why the
Chinese feels equally at home in all three of them without being
burdened by conflicting and incompatible dogmas."[22]

In short, the "Three Religions Are One" principle is a coherent
system although it looks on superficial observation like a chaotic
conglomeration of heterogeneous and bizarre elements. In this sense,
of the fraternity of the three and more religions in the East Asian
societies of Animistic character, including Korean shamanism,
Japanese Shintoism seems more likely to be the one that belongs
to the Sens b) group syncretism; *Indifférentisme relatif.*

Regardless of their very much exaggerated doctrinal differences,
Confucianism and Taoism maintained a propinquity throughout
Chinese history. In spite of their antithetical philosophies as to the
ontological theories of the universe and ethical attitude and in
spite of their roots in different social strata, they were inseparably
united by the fact that they shared the same animistic ideologies
as well as identical religious vocabularies. It is very interesting to
note that the *Chung-yung*, a classic hitherto believed to be one of
the most important literatures in Confucianism, has been thoroughly analyzed recently by competent scholars and attributed to
be rather a book of Taoist origin.[23]

Of course, Buddhism is a religion of foreign origin, but it was
accepted into the society having been acculturated successfully
through various stages of syncretism. Today the term "Chinese
Buddhism" is a denotative name for a branch of Buddhism that is
peculiarly Chinese. To be more specific, Mahayana Buddhism in
China came to occupy an integral part of the religious life of the
people through the syncretic processes for which we have appropriated our Sens a) and Sens c) groups. Happily, the conditions of the
Sens b) group (spatial proximity and enough time) were added
later on to make Mahayana Buddhism a truly Chinese religion.

A study of the processes of this integration will bring us one step further into the hidden structure of the Principle. When Buddhism was introduced into China, it was accepted on the merits of its "equivalence" to Taoism. This Chinese version of Buddhism, as was accepted in the later Han dynasty, was a religion of Taoist *Shen-hsien Fang-shu* (Occultism and Magic).

There are a lot of opinions expressed as to the earliest date of the introduction of Buddhism to China. Some even maintain that Confucius himself knew of Buddha.[24] Early accounts of the "mysterious" introduction are bewildering.[25] The related documents could be graded according to the degrees of their exaggerations.[26] But they all seem to agree that Buddha revealed himself (c. 63 C.E.) to Emperor Ming of the Han dynasty in a dream—for three years (*Fa-pen-nei-ch'uan*), ten years (*Kuang-hung-ming-chi*), seven years (*San-pao-chi*), or eleven years (*Ti-wang-nien-p'u*) as a luminous golden deity who could fly over the emperor's court freely as if he had embodied in himself all the magical power the Taoists of that age were hankering after.

Of course, the documentary evidence shows that most of these accounts were the latter day additions of overzealous Buddhists.[27] But that is the very point we are interested in. Buddha was deliberately made to be a Taoist "deity." It is not surprising at all, under such circumstances, that the myth of Lao-tzu's visit to India, namely, *hua-hu-shuo*, should appear and make a strong appeal to the age.

By 166 C.E. Hsiang-chieh reported to Emperor Huan that: "Some people say that Lao-tzu went to the barbarian country and became Buddha. In *T'ai-p'ing-ching*[28] it was only mentioned that Lao-tzu went to the West and stayed for eighty years and lived through the Yin and Chu Dynasties. But another Taoist-Buddhist document *Hua-hu-ching* amplified it and mentioned: 'Lao-tzu . . . was made an official to the Government during the reign of Yü-wang. But again with Yin-hsi he went to the Western country and became Buddha. He gave the King of the barbarian country *Hua-hu-ching*, consisting of 640,000 words. After he came back to China, he wrote the *T'ai-p'ing-ching*."[29]

The first royal convert to Buddhism was Prince Ying of Ch'u, who was definitely a syncretist. Emperor Ming himself testified that "Prince Ch'u believes in the mysteries of the Emperor Hwang-ti and Lao-tzu and worships Buddha and goes into mystical union with gods."[30] Lao-tzu and Buddha may have even shared an altar together in the reign of Emperor Huan. According to one record,[31] Emperor Huan worshipped Lao-tzu at a *chia-lan* (apparently a

Buddhist temple, as the name signifies) called Yo-lung-ko in 166 C.E. The Leaping Dragon Hall, Yo-lung-ko, a name definitely Taoist, was reported to have been renamed previous to the emperor's worship with a Taoist-Buddhist name: Ch'ung-hsü-ssu or "Temple of Admiration for Nothingness."[32]

Such Taoist-Buddhist syncretism seems to have been approved not only by the prince and the emperor, but also by the average general attitude of the devout Buddhists of that early age. The *"Biographies of the Eminent Monks"* of Hui-chiao of the Liang dynasty makes An-shih-kao (Lokottamer), the missionary from Parthia who translated the Buddhist texts, a highly competent Taoist occultist. The famous monks of the Wu dynasty, K'ang-seng-hui and Wei Chih-nan, and the Wei dynasty's T'an-k'o-chio-lo were among those who were depicted to be accomplished Taoist magicians. The composite picture of Buddha himself during the Han and the Three Kingdoms period found in the biographical literatures of that period is definitely a Ta-hsien, or the "Great (Taoist) Immortal" from India. This is how "equivalence" has taken its place in the syncretic phenomenon in the Chinese scene.

In the process of translating Buddhist literature into Chinese, we find the Sens c) group phenomenon gradually emerging on the scene. Anyone who is familiar with the Taoist literature and the Chinese Buddhist texts of the early period will be able to indicate without serious difficulty how many identical words are used on both sides with different meanings. A careful comparative study on this extremely interesting problem is beyond the scope of the present thesis. Nevertheless, we are able to pick a few fundamental common words that had distinctly different semantic features from the view of the respective religions. One is *Tao*. The second is *wu*.

"*Tao*" in the early Buddhist texts was the translation of *bodhi*. A keen observer will immediately see the fundamental disagreement between the two terms which were parsimoniously joined. Taoist *Tao* is the principle of inaction or *wu-wei*, naturalness, or *tzu-jan*, while *bodhi* is an inspiration and goal of aspiration. One may "return" to Tao while he has to "strive forward" to *bodhi*. It is Hsüan-tsang who gave new translations. *Marga* was translated into *Tao*, and *bodhi* was translated into *chieh* by him. *Wu* in the early Buddhist texts is the translation of *nirvana*. The latter is an absolute negation while the former is the principle of *Ursein*.

At any rate, under such linguistic limitations and the ambiguity involved in symbolic communications, Taoism and Buddhism have been proximated in the early contact and were made to be religions of the same principle. A syncretic writer even writes: "The *Tao* of *yin* and *yang* created with their harmony everything in the world. Tao [Lao-tzu], being born in the East, became a tree (Lao-tzu's family name is Li, an apricot tree) of *yang*. Fu [Buddha], being born in the West, became Golden *yin*. Tao is the father; Fu is the mother. Tao is the heaven; Fu is the earth. Tao leads one to live peacefully; Fu leads one to die peacefully. Tao's causality and Fu's corollary are like the *yin* and *yang* and could not be, therefore, separated."[33]

The benefits of this syncretism went in both directions. Buddhism found a secure place in the arrogant society through this process, while Taoism equipped itself with the newly introduced doctrinal, ritual, and institutional refinement from the "West." As its position in the society became more and more secure, Buddhism expanded itself into a whole gamut of Buddhism, eliminating as far as possible its previously assumed roles as the conciliatory partner in the syncretism. But the effort of purifying Buddhism from the syncretic state was the business of the experts or specialists[34] whose works affected only their faithful followers. The *"religio publica"*[35] of China remained virtually unchanged regardless of the unceasing efforts of the leaders from both camps, who tried to clarify their respective positions.

We can repeat the same story with the syncretism between Confucianism and Buddhism. However, in this case the mutual influence between them following the initial translation period is more interesting. It also started with an "equivalence" and ended with a "consensus."

It is only natural that from the Buddhist camp the spirit of fraternity should have appeared. Its early representative is Sun Ch'o, who identified the Buddhist seven *Tao-jen* with the Confucian Seven Worthies in the Bamboo Forest in his conciliatory *Tao-hsien-lun*. In his other thesis *Yü-hsien-lun*, he solemnizes the unity of the two religions, saying: "Confucius of Chou is Buddha. And Buddha himself is Confucius of Chou. For these two names are nothing but the foreign and native names of one and the same person. Confucius saves [humanity] from the ultimate calamities while Buddha enlightens and teaches the ultimate causes. They are the beginning and the end. Their fundamental truth is not inconsistent . . . Therefore, a radical inquirer may find them to be two, but a man of comprehensive understanding finds them not to be two."[36] This is the case of the "contextual equivalence" in our Sens a) group above.

On the other hand, there were not a few in the Confucian camp proper who were ready to embrace the conciliatory spirit, though they did not bother to mention explicitly their indebtedness to the "alien" doctrines. What they tried to do was show the Confucian contextual equivalence with Buddhism. In the model of the Buddhist dogma on emotions and desire as defilement (a strong contradiction to traditional Confucianism), Li Ao, for instance, maintains that the "essence of human nature is tranquillity"[37] and evil comes from the disturbance of emotions. Of course, Li Ao's terminology as well as concept has its origin in the traditional Confucian texts. But the more important thing to note is that such expressions and ideas were newly taken out from the hitherto neglected contexts and revived in meaning under the new stimulus of Buddhism. This kind of contextual equation became clearer with the Sung dynasty neo-Confucians. They were supposedly anti-Buddhist. But it is not too much of an exaggeration to say that "if there were no Buddhism, there would be no Sung Learning [neo-Confucianism]."[38]

The founders of the neo-Confucianism that was destined to rule the minds of the intellectuals during the following six centuries until the end of the Ch'ing dynasty established a school mainly with their counterproposals to Buddhism. They did so abiding in the mute presumption that there is a contextual equivalence between Confucianism and Buddhism. In other words, it was Buddhism that provided neo-Confucianism with the doctrinal framework which the Sung philosophers tried to fill with the material drawn from ancient sources and some fresh interpretations of their own. Their interpretations are what Matteo Ricci and Leibniz were against, because they believed it to be a serious materialistic deviation from the "pure" Confucianism under the influence of Buddhism.[39]

In spite of their anti-Buddhist attitude, Chou Tun-i, the founder of the Southern Branch of the school, and Chang Tsai, the founder of the Northern Branch of the school, developed their teachings of *T'ai-chi* (Supreme Ultimate) and *T'ai-ho* (the Great Harmony), respectively, only by positing Confucian equivalences to the idea of emptiness (*sunyata*) found in Buddhism. Chou Tun-i's *T'ung-shu* especially reflects clearly the traces of the influence from Ch'an Buddhism in its ideas as well as vocabulary. Though Chang T'sai's *Chen-meng* contains radical criticisms of Buddhism, it is also full of counterproposals to the Buddhist doctrines that make the book's real contents a Confucian reflection on Buddhist teachings. His *T'ai-ho*, which nourishes the principles of action and inaction as well as their reciprocal harmony, seems to have been given the equivalence to the Buddhist One Mind. This includes two aspects, *sui-yüan* (result from conditioning causes) and *pu-mieh* (*anirodha*). His "Great Void" and "Temperamental Energy" seem to reflect equally the relationship of the *chen-ju* (*bhutatathata*) and *alaya-vijñana* of Buddhism.

It is rather amusing to see that the vehement critic of Buddhism, Chu Hsi, attacked Buddhism for several reasons, but especially for Buddhism's resemblance to Confucianism and Taoism in its doctrines. He enumerated the resemblance and insisted that they were due to borrowing and "stealing" of Buddhism from wisdom of Chinese origin.[40] Of course, through effort Chu Hsi and his followers could bring out to some extent several distinctive features of Confucianism in contrast to the "contextual equivalences" or counterparts in Buddhism. But what they actually accomplished in the public mind was not the idea of Confucianism as absolute religion, but rather the relative validation of Buddhism in light of the traditional truth in China. The "consensus," namely, the "Three Religions Are One" principle, gradually crystallized itself and took its permanent place in the religious life of the people.

To sum up, what strongly impresses me in the whole complicated process that took place in the "capillary system" of the society are:

On the part of the giver:

1. The effective challenge suitable to stimulate an eager native response (precondition) and

2. The ability of voluntary or involuntary compromise to the environment to produce the effectiveness of the challenge (selectivity in action).

On the part of the receiver:

1. The keen receptivity to the particular challenge and

2. The ability of active participation with its own resources to exploit the maximum benefit from the alien stimulus by acclimatizing or acculturating it (selectivity in action).

The whole thing looks as if it were a partial absorption or assimilation of the encountered religions with the price of metamorphosis paid to some extent by both sides. With a price, Buddhism was accepted by the Chinese public to be an "*intergrieerenden*

Bestandteile" of their "natural religion." This is the general picture of the Eastern tapestry: the "Three Religions Are One" Principle.

This same process can be well illustrated again with the coming of Christianity, a religion of absolute truth-claim with well-systematized doctrines and militant organization, to the Eastern scene. Christianity easily became involved in syncretism in the East Asian societies. We have three examples, one in each of three countries: China, Japan, and Korea.

On the grand scale, we have an important example in the T'ai-p'ing Rebellion (1851–1864) of China.[41] In this shocking incident there were many aspects involved: political, economic, and religious. It was the Han people's movement in revolt against the ruling Manchus, first of all. Recent Communist press reports from Beijing portray the movement with some justification as the first "organized movement of the Chinese proletariat" against the ruling class.[42] But the battle was fought in the name of "Christianity" as "a bizarre syncretism of misunderstood Christianity and native beliefs" or "a strange compound of Christianity and Chinese beliefs and practices."[43]

The victorious army was led to occupy Nanjing under Christian banners. Hung Hsiu-chüan, the leader who fanatically believed himself to be the brother of Jesus, ruled his "Heavenly Kingdom of Great Peace," *T'ai-p'ing t'ien-kuo*, as the Heavenly King *T'ien-wang* with strongly legalistic administration based on the Holy Bible, *Shen-t'ien-sheng-shu*.

The special feature that attracts us in this movement is the understanding of Christianity by the rebels. The T'ai-p'ings "declared that their doctrine was not new but that the ancient classics had taught it in part and later generations had departed from it."[44] This claim, we find, is in perfect coincidence with what the Riccian Jesuit missionaries had tried to announce in seventeenth century China.

However, "the T'ai-p'ing religion still was not Christianity" in all accounts.[45] But we have strong reason to infer (with Latourette) that: "[H]ad it had the immediate contact through missionaries with Christian communities in other lands, it is possible that in time, it might have developed into a movement which, while preserving many peculiarly Chinese features, would have caught the meaning of Jesus and have become a church which would have deserved both the adjectives Chinese and Christian. As it was, it was quite clear that even the leaders had never really understood the Christian message."[46]

Let us turn to Japan. As Buddhism was once the stimulus in China that made Taoism and Confucianism leap into their own organized systematic actions, Jesuitism was the stimulus in Japan that awakened Shintoism to leap into proclaiming its own independence against its long-time partner in *Ryobu* Shinto-Buddhism.[47] As has been observed above,[48] the ingenuity of the neo-Shinto theologians successfully accommodated the Riccian Christianity into its own doctrinal system.

Had the mission method been effective enough it would have not been impossible for Christianity to occupy a stronger foothold in Japan. It would have been more effective if the Jesuits (the Longobardian) were a little bit more willing to accommodate these kinds of native responses within the Christian fold at that historical juncture.

A disastrous thing happened to Francis Xavier, the father of the Jesuit Oriental mission, who preached the *"Dainichi"* upon his arrival on the Japanese Islands, misunderstanding it to be an appropriate Japanese term equivalent to God in a Christian sense. He had been misinformed by a Yajiro, or Nanjiro, a Japanese of little education and an escapee to India. "He believed that the term Dainichi could designate the Deity in the Japanese language. This term was completely displaced since, among other meanings, it signifies the 'primal substance,' or the Great Sun or its dininity . . . Even the human sexual organs! As soon as the scandalized people informed him of it, he returned to the various places where he had preached before, shouting, 'Do not pray to Dainichi!' "[49]

Alarmed and dismayed, the Jesuits in Japan too hastily initiated the work of the transliteration from the Portuguese terms directly to produce the bizarre series of the remarkable Kirishitan terminology. The entire terminology was purposely ineffective to convey Christian ideas to the natives.[50] It must have been a painstaking experience on the part of the missionaries who were forced to teach this entirely new vocabulary to the Japanese in order to convert them. Nevertheless, the syncretic native elements soon crept in just the same from the moment when the influence of the missionaries began to ebb under the persecution, permitting the tropical jungle to reclaim the abandoned city. The jungle-like results are still seen among the "Kirishitan Remnants" who have totally alienated themselves from the Catholic Church.[51]

Longobardo's opposition to the Riccian approach was actually influenced by this hasty policy of the Jesuits in Japan and created the long-lasting futile "controversy over the rites."[52] And it was Yi

Kyugyŏng who introduced Longobardo's transliteration of Christian terms into Korea.[53] According to it, Ricci's *Shang-ti* was substituted with *Tou-ssu* (Deus) and the *T'ai-ch'in* with *Ju-te-ya* (Judea), etc. However, the introduction fortunately came after Riccian Christianity had already set roots in the soil, and it had no negative effect on the development of Catholicism in Korea.

We still have a third example to review. In Korean society, Christianity gave a subsidiary impetus to a syncretic religion of Ch'ŏndogyo, the religion of the "Heavenly Ways," which placed itself in an artificial opposition to Christianity. But, as will be observed,[54] Ch'ŏndogyo not only acquired its theological framework from Christianity but its institutional aspect as well. There are no statistics available, but it is not erroneous to state that not a small number of the Korean Christian converts came from this syncretic stock, as Augustine came from Manichaeanism.

PART IV

THE CLUE:
DIFFUSION AND CONVERGENCE

CHAPTER EIGHT

Confucianism and Christianity: Morphological Analogy

In the following chapters we will attempt to look into the pre-Christian religious heritage of Korean society. We have a double purpose in mind. First, in doing so we would like to find some clues which, we hope, would lead us into the heart of the religious understanding as to why the people of Korea showed keen receptivity to Christianity to such an extraordinary degree when the evangelism from the West reached its shores. We believe that this receptivity is in its greater part due to the fact that the already established belief of the people, prior to the arrival of Christianity, had elements congenial to Christian doctrines. And we believe that the congenial elements were the fuse which, when ignited, touched off the explosive growth of the Christian churches in the land.

Second, we will attempt to bring out the alleged congenial elements only, disregarding others (in a somewhat exaggerated way) in order to rigorously focus our attention on them with the aid of magnified views. We disregard the other elements, because we believe that a highly selective process took place in the minds especially of those who were inclined to accept Christianity when they were exposed to the Christian challenges. We also believe that the crystallized picture through this selective process was composed mainly of congenial elements.

We will start to investigate these congenial elements in a chronologically reversed fashion. Confucianism should come first, because Korea's first contact with Christianity was made in the seventeenth century when Confucianism was the state religion.

107

And those who actually responded quickly to Christianity were the avowed Confucians.

However, this Confucian society in Korea was not entirely Confucian. Buddhism, though oppressed, exerted its influence continuously upon the people even after Buddhists were ostracized by the Confucian society. Buddhism in Korea had a thousand years of history when Confucianism came to power. So Buddhism comes to our consideration following the discussion of Confucianism.

The Confucian society was not entirely free from Taoist influences, either. Taoism was introduced into the land even before Buddhism was. Taoism, however, has never been a dominant religion in Korea, although it has persistently exerted its influence upon the society as a philosophical system (*tao-chia*) as well as religious practices (*tao-chiao*). Although the Confucians were monopolizing the position of a state religion at the time when the Christian impact was felt in Korea, the spirit of the "Three Religions Are One" principle of East Asia was the religious tenor of the society. In these syncretic phenomena Taoism played an important role as the catalyst.

Behind all these imported religions there existed a pre-Confucian, pre-Buddhist and pre-Taoist religion, an indigenous belief. It is true that this belief has been dissolved into the imported religious systems and did not maintain its own independence after the introductions of those religions. But, to our own interpretation, it is this indigenous belief that gave the Korean character to each of those imported religions. We have reasons to suspect that the Korean type of "Eastern Tapestry" was woven, in fact, in a basically monotheistic pattern, which is the fundamental character of this indigenous belief.

Thus, as shall be seen, Confucianism, Buddhism, as well as Taoism assumed in Korea the more distinctive theistic-monotheistic characters. We feel, therefore, that we are compelled to look into the multiple religious heritages of the society in order to find out our anticipated congenial elements to Christian faith which, we think, made it possible for the "unique" event to take place. Our task is complex, but it will be rewarding. We will begin with Confucianism.

Morphological analogies exist between Confucianism and Christianity. It was "sensed" early by Ricci and brought to the attention of the world by his colleagues in the bitter Controversy of Rites which ensued after his death. In an excessive form the Riccian understanding of Confucianism found an expression in Le Comte, himself a Jesuit missionary to China, who was by the Longobardians "accused of having preached indifference in religion, driven by illusion of a church in China before Jesus Christ, and of having substituted the Chinese people as the chosen nation in place of Israel. And so forth."[1]

To Ricci, Confucianism which preserved the original purity of nature religion (*Reinheit der Naturreligion*)[2] was a postulate, an *a priori*, a basis and cornerstone for future Catholic evangelism in China. But to Le Comte the story was a different one.

Le Comte believed that the Chinese once had been in possession of "the original truths revealed by God to the first human beings." (*les première vérités révélées par Dieu aux premier hommes.*) These are what Le Comte interpreted to be the same undeniable "vestiges" of "primitive piety" (*la piété primitive*) which the Israelites possessed. He saw a rather deep-rooted fundamental agreement in the doctrinal analogy of Christianity to Confucianism that he interpreted to be derived from the same sources in the *Urerfahren* which mankind had from the beginning. This presumably existed before degeneration and defilement set in, especially from the "superstitious" religions, such as Buddhism of the East Asian scene. According to him:

> The Chinese religion seems to have kept intact and pure throughout the ages when the original truths revealed by God to the first human beings. "China, more blessed in its beginnings than any other people of the world, has drawn almost from the beginning on the saints and the original truths of her ancient religion." The ancient first Emperors built temples to God, and "it is not a small glory of China to have sacrificed to the Creator in the oldest temple of the Universe." This primitive piety is conserved among the people due to the Emperors who were careful to maintain it so well that idolatry did not gain a foothold in China. "Before the arrival of the superstition such as impiety toward Buddhist god infested China, there was no idol or statue among the people . . . so that people have conserved for almost two thousand years the knowledge of true God and have honored Him in a manner that could serve as an example and instruction to Christians."
>
> The Chinese religion has the unique privilege of showing us what human life could be in this fortunate age when peace, good faith, and justice reigned in China and, at the

same time, it explains to us the facility that the Jesuits had in gaining converts in China. In summary, Chinese only rediscovered in Christianity, but with greater clarity and evidence, this primitive religion, of which the memory has not been entirely vanished, despite the progressive changes that have taken place with idolatry and atheism.[3]

Le Comte did not stand alone in such a magnified and exaggerated Riccian view. His views were supported by many of his colleagues, such as Bouvet (Pe-Tsing-Ming) (1656–1730),[4] Foucquet (Fou-Fang-Tsi) (b. 1663),[5] Noel (Wei-Fang-Tsi) (b. 1651),[6] Alexis de Gollet,[7] and most of all Joseph-Henri (ou Marie) de Prémare. Bouvet, for example, high-spiritedly stated in his letter of November 8, 1700, to the Protestant philosopher Leibniz as follows:

> Having continued this year to apply myself to the study of the ancient books of China, I have had the good fortune of making some new discoveries . . . practically the entire system of true religion is contained in it . . . the principal mysteries of the incarnation of the Word, of the life and of the death of the Savior, and the principal function of His holy ministry are contained as if in a prophetic manner in these precious monuments of Chinese antiquity. You will be surprised as much as I have been to see that it is like an extended thread of shadows, figures and prophecies of the truth of the New Law (Christianity) . . . Let me add that I believe one thing is certain . . . that the Chinese classic books and the Chinese written characters are much older than the Chinese themselves, and that these are faithful monuments to the most ancient tradition which the fathers of all nations have left to their descendants and which the Chinese have conserved more carefully than others.[8]

Despite the vehement opposition of the Longobardians, as exemplified in the accusations of Maigrot (1693) in which the views above were presented as "being false, alarming and scandalous,"[9] this school of thought was far from being checked. It seems rather that the criticism poked the fire to leap up anew.

We have evidence of this on a grand scale in de Prémare's work entitled: *Selecta quaedam Vestigia praecipuorum Christiane religionis dogmatum ex antiquis Sinarum libris erute.* This work was preserved in the form of a manuscript in the library[10] when it was discovered in 1837 by A. Bonnetty and Paul Perny, who translated it into French and published it in 1878 under the title: *Vestiges de Principaux Dogmes Chrétiens Tirés des Anciens Libres Chinois* (Vestiges of Principal Christian Dogmas Pulled from Ancient Chinese Books).[11]

According to Prémare himself this remarkable book was written under the general plan as follows: "This will be the plans of this work— I. Firstly I will explain various points of which the knowledge is necessary for an adequate understanding of the book. II. I will talk about God as the one *and* the Trinity. III. I will deal with the question of the state of nature in its integrity and innocence. IV. Then of the state of corrupted nature, and separately, of the rebellion of angels and the fall of Adam. V. Of the state of nature restored by Jesus Christ. This point, God willing, will deal with the importance of the subject as much as with the abundance of the material."[12]

With this plan in mind de Prémare divided his book into four divisions or topics he called "articles." The first division is more than a general introduction to the pertinent Chinese literature. It is a restatement, with skillfully extracted excerpts from the Chinese documents, concerning his favorite theme which he had previously expressed in more concise language. The previous statement, made in regard to his other work *Notitia linguae sinicae* (auctore p. Prémare, in 4e, Malaca 1831), reads: "The final and ultimate purpose that I pursue in this study is that the whole world shall know that the Christian religion is as old as the world and that the God-man relationship has certainly been known by those who invented the Chinese hieroglyphs and composed the Chinese Canons."[13]

This general theme is more powerfully presented in the present work in which the Riccian motives, i.e., 1. The pure Confucian tradition of the Doctrine is lost, but not without leaving some traces *(la tradition de leur doctrine de la Confucianisme pure s'est perdue)*; 2. The Books of Canon has been corrupted by the interpreters, but can be restored somewhat by correct reinterpretations *(Les livres Kings ont été corrompus par leur interpretes)* are restated. However, he believed that this attitude was not peculiarly Riccian or an invention of this school of thought. De Prémare was convinced that the Riccians, including himself, were standing in an authentic tradition in Catholicism.[14]

The second division consists of the "traces of the Christian doctrines on One and Triune God" which he "rediscovered in the ancient Chinese books." To be sure, de Prémare was too cautious to let his "traces" imply that some of the Chinese indigenous religious notions were identical to the corresponding Christian doctrines. He says:

> I should once more inform the reader that I do not claim that *T'ien* or *Shang-ti* is the true God that we Christians worship. This is why I will always translate the term *T'ien* as "Heaven" and *Shang-ti* as the "Supreme Lord." As for the Chinese understanding of *T'ien* and *Shang-ti*, I leave that to the judgment of experts and especially to that of the Sacred Congregation of Propaganda [of the Vatican]. And in the same manner, as my private judgment, if I should even dare to express it on this matter, I am prepared to renounce it without hesitation and with all sincerity if I am concerned that it is even slightly disagreeable to the Holy Church, outside of which there is no salvation.[15]

What he really means here is that the historical facts could be established through comparative studies in the religious-historical literature on both sides. He repeatedly assures that "These traditions were confused in later works and were poorly amalgamated as often as not, but still offered some recognizable articles of belief."[16] If these "recognizable articles" could be purified and supplemented, de Prémare believed, they could be put into good use for effective evangelism in the Middle Kingdom.

Along this line of thinking, de Prémare tries to show the affinity between the Chinese notion of the Supreme Deity to that of Christianity with extensive extractions from the important texts including *Shu-ching*, *Shih-ching*, the main writings of Confucius, Mencius and other writers, as well as the popular proverbs. He also tries to show by quoting from the pertinent texts that the attributes of *t'ien* or *shang-ti*, or *t'ai-i*, or *t'ai-chi*, or *Tao* were expressed actually in terms of "One and Three" in a theological framework which resembled that of the Christian church to a remarkable degree.

He devotes only a small space to his third division. But he further demonstrates his basic contention by pointing to the memories and glimpses of the paradises lost and regained (in anticipation) in heaven, Pu-chou, and on earth, the Koullun Mountains as recorded in the ancient Chinese literature.

The fourth division is devoted to the purpose of identifying Christian-like accounts of the fall of the angels and humankind and the origin of sin and death in Chinese mythology. Chinese mythologies are full of mystical animals, and de Prémare took pains to identify them with their respective spiritual beings in Christian mythology. Kung-kung, who had "the face of a man, the body of a serpent,"[17]is ingeniously identified with Lucifer. The Christian understanding of the predicament of fallen humanity is well depicted with the mosaic of quoted words from Chinese sources.

The most remarkable feat is found in his fifth division in which he tries to extract from the texts the Messianic hope of the ancient Chinese. According to him, the "divine man" (*l'Homme divin, shen-jen*), "holy man" (*l'Homme-saint, sheng-jen*), "great man" (*l'Homme grand, ta-jen*), "good man" (*l'Homme-bon, shan-jen*), "beautiful man" (*l'Homme-beau, mei-jen*), "faithful man" (*l'Homme fidele, hsin-jen*), "heavenly man" (*Ciel-Homme, t'ien-jen*), "One man" (*Un-Homme, i-jen*), "separate man" (*l'Homme-séparé, chi-jen*), "perfect man" (*l'Homme très parfait, chih-jen*) are no other than the terms that the ancient Chinese have used to designate their Messiah.

De Prémare goes further and decides that they also knew that their Messiahs were to be born of virgins, because "in ancient times the Divine and Holy ones were born of mothers who conceived them under the influence of Heaven. Therefore, they were called the Sons of Heaven."[18] "The ancient Holy men were all born without their fathers. They were conceived by Heaven."[19] Furthermore, the Messiah will sacrifice himself for the salvation of the world. "An evil man will die to amass a fortune. The philosopher will die to acquire fame. The nobility will die to keep their position. The saint will die to save the universe."[20] The death of the Messiah on the cross is anticipated and prophesied.[21] The sacrifice in the form of the "meal" (*repas*) in a similitude to Christian practices is the core of Chinese ritualism.[22] The Lamb is the sacrificial animal. "The lamb loves society, but it flees the rebellious crowd. When it is seized, it does not resist; when it is killed, it does not cry out; during its life, it does not fail in its duty; by its death, it fulfills all justice."[23] Therefore, the Chinese character for lamb, *yang*, is always hierographically associated with other Chinese characters for beauty (*mei*), good (*shan*), happiness (*hsiang*), justice (*i*), sacrifice (*hsi*), and so on.[24] In short, "sacrificial lamb" (*l'agneau immolé*) is the symbol of the Saint who is the Saviour of the World.

How could it be possible that "Christian traces" of such an extent were found in Chinese literature? It was understood on the basis of natural theology. But it is extremely interesting for us to notice that de Prémare also tried to provide a diffusionistic explanation for this by identifying Ch'in with Syria.[25]

With these bases "established" he could now proceed to point out the "identity of the first ten generations of Chinese with the ten biblical generations before the flood."[26] Thus Huang-ti is identified with Adam, and Lui-tsu with Eve.[27] In the same way Seth is identified with Shen-nung or Ch'ang-i, Abel with T'ai-hao or Fu-hsi, Cain with Shao-hao, or Hsüan-hsiao, or Ch'iung-sang. The entire Biblical genealogy down to Noah is given in such a manner: a biblical family tree with Chinese mythological personalities. The flood which the *Shu-ching* dated to the time of the Emperor Wu is identified with that of Noah.

We cannot give any serious consideration to these prescientific "discoveries" provided to us by de Prémare and his school, though we cannot restrain ourselves from admiring the ingenuity and energy of the missionary scholars.[28] In our opinion, what they have imposed upon themselves was an impossible task from the very beginning. In the first place, contrary to what they assumed, there is no unilinear religious thought in China. The texts de Prémare often used do not agree among themselves, and thus are not of any real value for this purpose. No conclusive facts can be derived from such imaginary "*souvenirs.*" Nevertheless, despite these fatal defects, their work makes one thing very clear. They are successful in pointing out for us that, if not "vestiges," some analogous points did exist actually and coincidentally between Confucianism and Christianity.

It is true that from Matteo Ricci's *T'ien-chu shih-i* onward these missionary writers depicted the ideal type of Confucianism under the Christian "bias" with thickly Christianized pictures. But it is equally true that those Chinese readers, especially of Ricci's work "have never accused him of being mistaken or of having misunderstood the ancient books; on the contrary, they have for the most part granted him the highest praise."[29] They were willing to accept the analogical accounts as were provided by the missionaries. This is a noteworthy feat indeed.

It is apparent that the Emperor K'ang-hsi himself, who was hailed by the Riccian missionaries as "*un ideal de monarque éclairé*" (an ideal of enlightened monarchy) comparable to the "*Roi-Soleil de la France*" (Sun King of France) Louis XIV,[30] had been won for the time being by the Ricci-Prémare camp when the imperial declaration of November 30, 1700, was decreed.[31] Furthermore, as has been observed,[32] the very impetus of the *Han-hsüeh*, or the "Fourth Renaissance," was nourished among the Chinese scholars by those who were friends of the Riccian missionaries. They were the ones who willingly consented to the Riccian interpretations of the Chinese texts.

On the other hand, the analogies between Confucianism and Christianity are limited on "certain points," as is evidenced in the thorough comparison carried out by de Prémare. The lack of eschatology or the *"silence sur les choses de l'autre vie"* (silence on the matter of the other life)[33] is especially noteworthy. Nevertheless, the existing analogies, which roughly cover the areas of theology proper, soteriology, and anthropology in terms of Christian theology, provided enough of a matrix out of which the Riccian missionaries intended to set Christian zeal aflame. The evaluations of this matrix from the Christian viewpoint could be various, of course. But we suspect that the more imaginative evaluations such as those expressed by Pascal and Leibniz are closer to the truth in this case, because we believe that it was those who accepted the imaginative Riccian interpretation who were the more imaginative Chinese.

Pascal mentioned the problem of *"la révélation de l'antiquité de la Chine"* (the revelation of the ancient China) in his *Pensées* with these suggestive words:

> Which is more credible of the two, Moses or China?
> It is not a question of seeing it as a whole.
> I tell you,
> there is something that can blind and something that can
>   enlighten.
> By this one word, I destroy all your arguments.
> "But China obscures," you say;
> and I say, "China obscures, but there is clarity to be found;
>   seek it."
> One needs to see this in detail; one needs to place the
>   papers on the table. . . .
> The difference between a book accepted by one nation,
>   and one which makes a nation.[34]

Believing the Chinese "natural theology" to be superior to that of the Europeans, Leibniz, an enthusiastic supporter of the Ricci-Prémarian approach, even ventured to suggest an exchange of missionaries between China and Europe. He says: "I am afraid that soon in our relations we are inferior to Chinese, so that it will be almost necessary to receive their missionaries to teach us the usage and practice of the natural theology, while we dispatch ours to them to teach the usage and practice of the revealed theology."[35]

The Catholic Riccian missionary testimonies in China resonate in the testimonies offered by the Protestant missionaries in Korea. We quote here in its entirety a representative Protestant testimony, well summarized by Wasson,[36] which refers to the pre-Christian Korean Confucian materials translated by Gale.[37]

Many passages occur in Korean literature that seem rephrasings of passages from the Christian scriptures.

God is represented as one who requires and will reward sincerity and righteousness. In 982 A.D. Ch'oe Sung-No wrote to the King:

"I pray that Your Majesty will do away with all the useless sacrifices and prayers, and show instead a righteous life and a repentant spirit, with a soul offered up to God. If this be done, trouble will naturally take its departure and blessings come down upon you."

In 1123 A.D. Im Wan wrote to the King:

"God can be approached by sincerity of heart alone and not by any outward form. Sacrifice offers no fragrance to him but a righteous life only."

Many passages teach that God sees the heart and will punish evil. In 1389 A.D. Cho Choon wrote to the last king to rule in Songdo:

"My prayer is that Your Majesty will remember that God reads the heart as in a mirror. When you reward anyone think first if he is one whom God would reward; and when you punish, think first if he is one whom God would punish."

In 1675 Song Si-yul wrote:

"He who bears tales that separate friends and cause strife is a bad man, and will be rewarded accordingly. I have seen it again and again through long years of experience. God, who sees as in a mirror, will certainly punish."

In the sixteenth century Lee Chun-kyung wrote:

"There is a union of the two spirits, God and man, seen in the meting out of blessing and misfortune. In form, God differs from man, yet, according to the law of the dual principles, which interweaves us as warp and woof, God and man work together . . . Man, however, being a material creature, with a tangible body, easily concentrates his thoughts upon himself and so misses the thought of God altogether. He foolishly leaves Him out of his reckonings saying, 'What can you blue heaven have to do with me?' or 'What concern can a crawling creature like man have with God?' So he gives free reign to self-will and yields himself up to loose and lascivious ways; in the end calling down disaster and making God, who ever lives, dispense calamity instead of blessing."

Other writers find it more difficult to construct a theodicy. They are perplexed by the problem of evil and the mysteries of providence. For instance, Choe Chi-won, the father of Korean literature, writes:

"I wonder why God feeds the vultures and owls, why the earth supports the caterpillars of destruction, and why the forces of evil fight and find peace and contentment, while brave soldiers are broken and defeated."

And Yul-kok (1536–1584), revered as the greatest sage of the Yi dynasty, wrote:

"Who has charge of the thunder and the sharp strokes of lightning, the blinding flashes that accompany them and the rearings that shake the earth: What does it mean? Sometimes they strike men dead and sometimes other creatures. What law holds this in hand? Frost kills the tender leaves while the dew makes all fresh and new again. Can you guess the law by which frosts and dews are given? Rain comes forth from the clouds but again some clouds bear no rain. What causes this: In the days of Sillong (Shen-Lung) rains came at people's call, and ceased when their wishes were fulfilled. In the Golden Age it was so. Was it because God in his dealings was specially favourable to those people? . . . Is there any law by which we could do away with eclipses altogether and have the stars keep their wonted courses, so that the thunder shall not startle the world, nor frosts blight the hopes of summer; that snow may not affect us, nor hailstones deal out death and famine; that no wild typhoons may rage; that there may be no floods; that all nature run straight and smooth; and that heaven and earth work in sweet accord for the blessings of mankind? When shall we find such a religion? All you great scholar chiefs, who are so deeply learned, I should think some of you would know. Open your hearts now and I will listen."

Kang Pil-ho, a famous scholar who lived from 1764 to 1846, wrote this concerning prayer to God:

"With the heart fully in control take your place before God, and put away all wandering thoughts. Religion is to be found here and nowhere else, and virtue can be discovered only in the heart. Work hard during the day and at night guard your thoughts with reverence and fear, lest you run counter to God's will and cast away your opportunity. In the middle of the night rise up with reverence and fear, and with a heart emptied of all selfish desire, with hands joined and dress decently arranged, burn your incense. If you do otherwise than I thus indicate can you expect to be blessed of God? My dear children, think well over these things. If you truly search with all the heart, God will answer your desires and will honour you in ways you know not. Do not lose heart or grow weary. As I write this, I myself make new resolves. Great God thou art light."

These "Saints" of Old Korea, as the writers just quoted are appropriately called, and the missionaries both taught that righteous living wins God's favour. Both groups emphasised the social efficacy of uprightness and upright personal conduct. They believed together that the practice of personal virtues would save the individual and would save the state as well . . . It was [a] common ground.

This "common ground" or analogy was of tremendous value on the Christian side as a bridgehead in the battlefield of evangelism. But at the same time one finds that this bridgehead was also zealously guarded and defended by the Confucians for the very same reason. As a matter of fact, this "common ground" gave the defenders reason to reject and fight against Christianity.

It was an absolute necessity for them to guard this strategic point, which was actually the heart of their religion, from the danger of "defilement." Otherwise, they felt the entire society would go to the "seducing heretics" if they should lose control of this important point. Christianity was not a "new" faith for them, but only perversions of doctrines of their very own. This was the attitude which the anti-Christian writers took, as has been reviewed.[38] This was also the attitude of the anti-Christian government, firmly held throughout the entire period of persecution which lasted more than a century.

Perhaps the following *Government Anti-Heresy Declaration* (*Hŏnjong kihae ch'ŏksa yunŭm*), issued in 1839 by the decree of King Hŏnjong, is typical.

Alas. According to the *Chung-yung* the Commandment of Heaven is called the "Nature." According to the *Shang-shu*, the Emperor on High, who is merciful to the people below and has given them moral sense is called the "Unchanging Nature" of mankind.

What is said in these discourses on Nature[39] is the monistic state of the ultimate being at the moment of creation. The words "Heaven" or the "Emperor on High" used here are terms to denote figuratively the Supremacy of the Being and the rulership and authority of the Supreme Being.

What is the Commandment? What is mercy? These words do not explicitly explain anything. But they imply an unmistakable truism.

Once the *li* (or Norm, or the attribute of the Ultimate Being, or the Being-in-Itself)[40] began to move it generated the two *ch'i* (or materials).[41] And when the four orders (or seasons) began to move as the result of the two *ch'i* everything was created and governed.

When man was allowed to partake in the "Nature" he also was given the virtues consisting of the four elements: altruism, justice in human relations, religious sentiments, and knowledge of good and evil. At the same time he is placed in ethical relations consisting of the five orders: father-son, king-subject, husband-wife, elder-younger, friend-friend.

Everything should be as it ought to be (as is shown in this Confucian doctrine). There is no necessity for further elaboration or manipulation. Otherwise, how can one say untroubled that Heaven gave birth to all men. Whenever and wherever there are things Heaven created, there is the law under which everything is governed. To obey the Law is to obey Heaven. To disobey the Law is to rebel against Heaven.

The prospects concerning Heaven worship and serving *Shang-ti* are the essence of the four virtues and five ethical relations. Why should one look elsewhere (in Christian teachings) to find out this truism?

Alas. Ever since the saintly patriarchs and the noble kinds were enthroned in the glorious past of the world, succeeding the rule of Heaven, there has been no other than this principle that was kept in awe, inherited piously, taught carefully and practised zealously. This principle is: Heaven be worshipped, *Shang-ti* be served. Throughout the ages from the time when Confucius, succeeding the wisemen of the ancient, systematised their doctrines for the prosperity until the age of the Sung philosophers who clarified the

heavenly ways and purified human hearts, the only principle that guided all men was: Heaven be worshipped and
Shang-ti be served.

Even the slightest mistake in applying this principle
has been heresy. But now we have encountered the shady
and fantastic lies that came from the foreign religion . . .

Those who call themselves Catholics (or Christians) say
that their doctrines are no other than the way of worshipping and serving Heaven. But we do not need to wait for
them to teach us that. Because, fundamentally speaking,
Heaven is to be worshipped and served. There is no need to
tell it. The ways they propagate are no more than folksy
ways of acquiring remission of sins and receiving Heavenly
Grace. In fact, this is nothing but blasphemous self-
glorification and presumptuous foolishness of man before
Heaven.

What we believe to be the correct way of worshipping
and serving Heaven and *Shang-ti* is to understand correctly the Heavenly Commandment, obeying faithfully the
merciful providence from above as is set forth in the teachings of the four virtues and five ethical relations . . .

In this heavily *Chu-hsian* document one finds the vivid
reflections on the *li* and the *ch'i* (in Korean pronunciation, *i* and *ki*,
respectively) disputation which was carried on bitterly among
Korean neo-Confucians during a period of more than a century.
Each sentence is crammed with complicated arguments in disguise.
It tries to harmonise the Li school with the Ch'i school, to unite
their efforts to combat their common enemy, Christianity. Nevertheless, it clearly shows the anti-Christian contentions of the ruling class of the day.

The value of this literature, however, is found in its argument
to equalize *T'ien* or *Shang-ti* with *li* through the media of *hsing*,
ming, and *chiang-chung*. Thus it makes clear for us what the pre-
Christian neo-Confucians in Korea really believed. We believe it to
be purely coincidence, but we find a strange correspondence between Korean Chu-Hsiism and the Chu-Hsiism interpreted by the
philosopher Leibniz, as shall be reviewed.

As for the overexaggerated Longobardian view on the "materialistic" or "atheistic" side of neo-Confucianism[42] and Chu-Hsiism in
particular, we find it rather difficult to agree. Fundamentally speaking, Chu Hsi was by no means "atheist" in the sense of modern

Western philosophy. He believed in all sorts of devils and spiritual beings as his literature abundantly shows.[43] It is true that he applied the "Buddhist" philosophy (comparable to Hellenism in the Orient) to the ancient beliefs of China (comparable to Hebraism to a certain extent), attributing the strongly rational character *li* to the Ultimate Being *T'ai-chi* or *Wu-chi* which was traditionally believed to be a personal Being *T'ien* or *Shang-ti*. But it is equally true that if there is no animistic belief at the basis, the whole elaborate system of Chu-Hsian ceremonialism in filial piety collapses.[44]

Furthermore we believe that there still is certainly room for reinterpreting Longobardian Chu-Hsiism, as was suggested long ago by Leibniz, who tried to understand the Sung philosophers from his own philosophical standpoint in the Western tradition. Reconciliation between the scholastic remnants and the new Renaissance rationalism was the object of his philosophy. He applied this formula to Chu-Hsiism which he believed to correspond surprisingly well to his own philosophical position.[45] We feel that the Chu Hsi scholars still have a great deal to learn from Leibniz. Leibniz wrote of Chu-Hsiism:

> The Chinese called it *Li* (par excellence), being, substance, and entity. This substance, according to them, infinite, eternal, uncreated, incorruptible, without beginning and without end. It is not only the "physical principle" of Heaven, Earth and other corporeal things, but also "the moral principle" of virtues, habits and other spiritual things. It is invisible; it is perfect in its being to the sovereign degree; it is the epitomy of perfection. They call it also "the consummate unity" or supreme, because as with numbers the unity is the principle; also with substance, in the essence of the universe, there is the One which is sovereign and which cannot be divided in its entity and which is the principle of all essences that are and can be in the world. . . .
>
> The *Li* is the "great void" or emptiness, the immense capacity, because in this essence all the particular essences are included. But they name it also the "sovereign plenitude," because it fills everything and leaves nothing empty. It spreads inside and outside of the universe. . . .
>
> It is this that we explain the immensity of God, who is everywhere and all things in Him. . . . They call *Li* the "nature" of things, and I believe it is as we call God the "*natura naturante.*"[46]

What the religious philosophy of Chu Hsi or Chu-Hsiism actually was is beside the point. It is sufficient to note that the Korean official document cited above, written by an avowed Chu-Hsiist, adopted by the Chu-Hsian cabinet and published by the regent with the royal seal,[47] strangely corresponded to the Leibnizian understanding of Chu Hsi on an important issue. For both, Chu Hsi was not an "atheist."

If Leibnizian Chu Hsi was a deviation from the authentic Chu Hsi, as some of the Longobardian sinologues in the West and some of the Eastern scholars may undoubtedly think, this Korean version of Chu-Hsiism expressed in the declaration is also a deviation. If so, what was the cause? If Leibniz was under Christian influence when he reinterpreted Chu Hsi in his own way, we strongly suspect that Korean neo-Confucians may have done so under the influence of their own strongly monotheistic indigenous religious ideas.[48]

The most vehement opposition to Christian doctrines from the Korean neo-Confucians is found rather in their criticism of the doctrines of Incarnation. In the Anti-Heresy Declaration above we read:

> Even everyday affairs ought to be in good accord with reason. We therefore must always find out with reason what is correct and what is wrong. The man whom they call Jesus is neither man nor god. No one knows for sure whether the story about him is true or false. The adherents of this faith propagate that he had come to the world from the Lord of Heaven and returned to the Lord of Heaven after his death and became one with God, the father of all men.
>
> How can there be more perplexed and perverse heresy than this one. "Heaven has neither voice nor smell." "Man has body and shell." The possibility of mixing of these two spheres was absolutely excluded from our belief. What a ridiculous thing to say that Heaven comes down to become a man and man ascends to heaven to become Heaven!

In fact this argument, based on the *Shih-ching* dictum[49] was used already on several occasions by several anti-Christian writers such as Pak Chiwŏn[50] and An Chŏngbok (1712–1791).[51] But their stand in this regard was a painfully weak one. Indeed, this accusation was to be brushed off as easily and efficiently by the Korean Christians as the same Confucian doctrines of *Sheng-jen* (sage) so profusely used in Confucian texts, as de Prémare demonstrated in his book. Though elementary, Confucianism had incarnation doctrines of its own.

The real trouble for the new converts in Korea was to place Jesus, the Western *Sheng-jen*, in the position of the ultimate Sheng-jen-ship, thereby seriously challenging the established sainthood of Confucius and his wise men in the spiritual hierarchy.[52]

CHAPTER NINE

Buddhism and Christianity: Paradise in the Great Beyond

It would appear odd indeed to attempt to approximate Christianity with Buddhism in the present-day Korean scene. Both sides, as organized religions, would claim that they have absolutely nothing to do with each other. Both were minority groups oppressed and persecuted by Confucianism in the Chosŏn dynasty and were equally liberated when the power of that ideology broke down. But they were never serious rivals in the past though both religions have been engaged in active proselytism. This is mainly because the social strata of adherents of the respective religions have been different.

Christian evangelism appears to be directed to people more or less under the influence of Confucianism. The first Christian converts, Catholic as well as Protestant, were made among the disinherited *yangban*s who were predisposed to progressive ideas.[1] On the other hand, Buddhism exerted its influence among the humbler people ever since the early Chosŏn dynasty when the Buddhist monks were ostracized by the Confucian *yangban* class. It has been the religion of the commoners ever since.

This social dichotomy seems to have persisted even after the Confucian social structure began to disintegrate in the changing society. It became more apparent when Korea was annexed to Japan, where Buddhism flourished and remained the most powerful religion in the modern period despite the Shinto discrimination. Korean Buddhists must have had mixed feelings, for the Japanese appeared to be despotic in political and economic affairs, but friendly and understanding insofar as their common religious life was concerned. On the other hand, resentment toward Japanese rule seems to have been greater among the Christian converts, especially those who came from a Confucian background. Traditionally the Korean Confucians were more or less contemptuous of everything that was Japanese and were particularly hostile to the enforced modernization that was occurring under Japanese rule.[2]

The "adherents to the Religion of the West" was the derogatory title given to Christians by Buddhists, while from the Christian point of view Buddhists were old-fashioned "idolators." This exchange of words was hostile, but there was no direct conflict between the two religions. They did not meet on the same plane because the predispositions of members of the religious bodies toward progressive ideas were considerably different.

Nevertheless, one must not forget that Buddhism had been an integral part of religious life in Korea ever since its introduction into the country in the fourth century.[3] Even during the long period of tribulation that began in the fifteenth century,[4] Buddhism never ceased to be influential among the populace, though it ceased to be the state religion.

Confucianism was certainly powerful, and it controlled the social system. But as a religion of the literati *yangban* class, it excluded from its benefits commoners as well as women, including those of the *yangban* class. The excluded majority of the society was left to Buddhism and shamanic beliefs. In this way, even though Confucianism was the superstructure of the social ideology and therefore vocal, there was another solid and firm layer underneath. Under the pressure of the government's anti-Buddhist policies, Buddhism was not permitted to monopolize this layer by itself. But its influence upon the public remained extensive. The most avowed Confucians themselves were not entirely free from these influences, because of the sheer fact that their first religious education was to a great extent Buddhist. This was because the mother, although excluded from Confucianism, was still the predominant religious influence in the home.

Furthermore, Confucianism lacked a theory of salvation that would meet the religious needs of individuals in their times of crises. Buddhism filled this gap superbly. Therefore, in such times of need, the latent Buddhism in a Confucian individual reasserted its existence over and over again. We suspect that this latent Buddhism is very much alive in the Korean society even today.

We must understand this latent Buddhism. The Mahayana Buddhism that reached the peninsula after being channelled through Chinese civilization was already acclimatized to the Chinese society with which Korea was affiliated. It was heavily Taoist in outlook[5] and was extremely adaptable to popular beliefs such as shamanism and animism, in more general and broader terms.[6] The *Ch'ilsŏnggak*, the Shrine of the Constellation of the Great Bear, and the *Sansindang*, the Shrine of the Mountain Spirits, gradually found their way into the architecture of the Korean Buddhist temples. The stone-pile altars of the local deities *Sŏnghwangdang* were added in front of the entrances to these temples, to more strongly protect the domain of the deities worshipped therein from the trespasses of other evil deities.[7] One may see in these new additions further "degeneration" of Mahayana Buddhism. But Buddhism paid the price willingly to win its integral position in the nation's religious life.

First of all, as with the first Chinese converts to Buddhism,[8] the *Pul* or Buddha, in whatever aspect and with whatever attributes of his manifestation, was a "Deity" to the first Korean converts. *Samguk sagi* lists the arrival of the first Buddhist missionaries Sundo to Koguryŏ in 372 C.E. and Marananda to Paekche in 384 C.E. in a matter-of-fact fashion among the events of special interest of those years, such as a big shooting star that darted toward the southeast one night, burning brightly, and a hailstorm one day that killed numerous birds and brought serious crop damage to one area. Such natural phenomena were thought to be divine manifestations. In fact, the establishment of the immediately prosperous Buddhist temples in those kingdoms seems to have been no more than a continuation and extension of the "national religion"[9] well instituted by then. Prior to the introduction of Buddhism, it was repeatedly reported that the kings worshipped "Heaven and Earth" at the "south altar" or some other religiously significant place to solicit supernatural protection for the nation. Buddhism assumed this role on the strength of its superior system, which substituted for the indigenous faith. Thus, Buddhism succeeded in becoming the *hoguk pulgyo*, or the "Buddhism that keeps the nation safe."

Samguk sagi records the introduction of Buddhism to the Silla Kingdom in more detail.

> In the fifteenth year of the era of King Pophŭng Buddhism began to prosper. Early in the era of King Nulchi, a Sramana

by the name of Mukhoja, or "Black Westerner," came to
Morye, a citizen of Silla's Ilsu Prefect.

He made a cave in Morye's house and placed an altar
therein. Some time before an ambassador from Liang, China,
brought to the King of Silla some gifts, including a royal
robe and some incense. Neither the minister nor the court
officials knew the name or the use of the incense.

Therefore, the court sent men all over the country with
samples in hopes of gathering some information about it.

Mukhoja (the Black Westerner) saw it and told them
that it was Mokwal. He said that when the incense is burned
it produces a fragrance that brings the supplication of the
burner to the Holy Divinity. They said the Holy Divinity
has three treasures: the first, Buddha, the second, Dharma,
and the third, Sangha. If one burns this and brings his
desires up to these three treasures, there will certainly be
spiritual benefits to follow.

Meanwhile, the princess' illness became worse. The king
sent for Mukhoja and asked him to burn the mysterious
incense and pray for her. And the princess regained her
health. The king was glad and gave him many gifts to
express his appreciation. Mukhoja came out (of the court)
to see Morye, gave him the gifts he had received and told
him that he was to return and bade farewell. Suddenly he
disappeared and nobody knew where he went . . .[10]

The predisposition of the people toward the supernatural made
it easy for them to accept this mysterious power which Buddha was
believed to have embodied in himself. Buddhism soon occupied the
religious life of the people with great success.

Temples financed by the kings were soon erected. Large and
small temples and monasteries were built everywhere in the country in an amazingly short period of time. Architecturally it was a
period of efflorescence. Plastic arts in general were greatly encouraged to produce the graceful stone statues, wood carvings, or iron-
cast Buddha images, some of which would become world renowned
masterpieces. With the delicate bas-relief on the surface, sound
produced by "secret ingredients," and its distinctive shape, the
Korean bells or *pŏmjongs* in particular won an eminent position in
the history of bell manufacturing in the world. Thus Buddhism
produced the most glorious period of Korean arts in the Silla
dynasty.

Supporting this efflorescence, there was the devotion of the nation, practiced equally by members of the royal family and humble farmers. The fundamental motive of this devotion was to solicit the blessing of Buddha for the benefit of the nation as well as the individuals in supplication. The motivation was frankly admitted and described by the devotees in written prayers and inscriptions on the dedicated objects.

Samguk yusa relates a legend about the construction of the nine-story pagoda of Hwangnyong-sa, or Emperor Dragon Temple, at Kyŏngju, the capital city of Silla.

One day in the tenth year of Chen-kuan [in China] and the fifth year of the reign of Queen Sŏndŏk, the twenty-seventh sovereign of Silla [635 C.E.], Munsu-posal [Bodhisattva Manjusri] revealed himself to the (Silla) monk Chajang who was studying abroad at Wu-t'ai-san, China.

Manjusri said: "Your queen, a member of the Kshatriya caste of India, already has possession of the Scriptures of Buddha. This is a special benefit with which she has been endowed by her precious life. Therefore your people are very different from the rest of the Eastern barbarian devils. But the personality of your people is as unruly and rebellious as the mountains and rivers of the land are steep and torrential. They believe in evil doctrines. Hence the disasters are sent down time and again from the Heavenly Deity. But fortunately you have many monks in the country. That is why your queen and the nobility and the commoners could enjoy peace." After he said this he disappeared. Chajang knew immediately that it was the manifestation of the great saint and wept tears of blood in thanksgiving and arose.

When he came by Lake T'ai-ho in China, a God-man suddenly appeared to him and asked what was his purpose for visiting that country. Chajang answered that he was seeking *bodhi*. Thereupon the God-man worshipped him and asked once again, "Is there any difficult problem in your country that troubles you?" Chajang said, "Our country is bordered by Moho [Malgal] to the north and we are close to Japan in the south. In addition, Koguryŏ and Paekche [the other two kingdoms in the peninsula] invade our country alternately. The land suffers from the intrusions of its neighbours from all sides. This is the very reason why the people have a hardened and rough character." The God-man said, "You have a queen. Therefore the nation has virtues but no prestige. Consequently the neighbours are scheming. You must return home quickly."

Chajang lamented and asked, "What good is there that I can do if I return home?" The God-man said, "The Dragon, the protecting divinity of the Hwangnyong-sa Temple [at Kyŏngju, the capital of Silla] is my eldest son. Under the command of Sikhin (the king of Mahabrahman), he has gone there to protect the temple. Return home and construct a nine-story pagoda on the grounds of the temple. Neighboring countries will come to surrender and barbarians will pay their tribute to you. The throne will be safe. After the construction is complete, commence the annual celebration of *P'algwanhoe*, releasing prisoners on these occasions. Then there will be no more invasions. I will be extremely grateful if you could also build a monastery in my honour on the southern bank of the capital and bless me. Then I will repay you for your devotion."

Having said these words, he gave a jade ball to Chajang and concealed himself mysteriously.

On the sixteenth day of Kyemyo in the seventeenth year of Chen-kuan [643 c.e.] Chajang returned [to Silla] bringing with him the gifts from the emperor of T'ang to the queen. The gifts included the Buddhist Scriptures [*Tripitakas* in four hundred boxes], Buddha images and some cassocks, in addition to silk and money. Chajang asked the queen for the construction of the pagoda and his request was granted . . .

When the pagoda was completed, a historic change took place. The three kingdoms were united under the sovereignty of Silla. Was it not due solely to the spiritual benefit from the construction of the pagoda?

It is told that when the pagoda was constructed, the king of Koguryŏ had to abandon his plan of invading Silla. The king said, "Silla now has three treasures. Therefore I cannot invade." What were those treasures? They were the *changryŏk* [which is supposedly the size of the actual stature of Shakyamuni, who was twice as big as an ordinary man] of the Hwangnyong-sa Temple, the nine-story pagoda of the same Hwangnyong-sa Temple, and the sacred jade royal band which the Silla people received from Heaven."

This has a parallel in the history of Chou [China]. Chou had the Nine Divine Kettles that prevented Chao from invading her.

One sang the praise of the nine-story pagoda:

The spirit and gods gave their help
To locate the blessed site no mortal could find.

The golden splendour of sunlight
Leaps and bounds on the roof wings

Whosoever climbed up the tower
Could not hold his tongue but praise

The glory of the nation over barbarian nations,
And breathe the peace that filled the universe . . .

It is recorded in the *Tongdo sŏngnip ki* (an account of the establishment of the Eastern Capital). Anhong, the writer of Silla, wrote as follows: "When the queen, the twenty-seventh sovereign of Silla, ascended to the throne, the nation had virtues but no prestige. The babarians, therefore, came to invade the country time and again. It was suggested then that a nine-story pagoda be built on the south side of the Dragon Palace to defend the nation from the disasters of the invasions. The first story was for Japan, the second for China, the third for Wu-yüeh (China), the fourth for T'angna, the fifth for Ŭngyu, the sixth for Moho, the seventh for Tanguk, the eighth for Yŏjŏk, and the ninth for Yemaek."[11]

This pagoda must have been a splendid one architecturally.[12] But it had a strange fate. It is reported in *Samguk yusa* that this pagoda suffered an earthquake while it was under construction, and seven lightning strikes after its completion. The damage was repaired each time but it was completely destroyed in a war in the sixteenth year of Koryŏ's Kojong era (1229 C.E.).[13]

In an old Japanese historical document, *Nihon shoki*, reference is made to a letter of King Sŏngmyŏng, the king of the Paekche Kingdom, as the first introduction of Buddhism from Korea to Japan. The letter was attached to the *Changryŏk* or *Chio-roku* (in Japanese), a Buddha image which the king of Paekche sent to the Japanese emperor Kin-mei in 552 C.E., and reads as follows: "It is said that the blessing of the *Changryŏk* Buddha image is exceedingly great. Therefore, I have performed the work of casting the image in reverence, beseeching the blessing upon you the emperor, to keep you in the virtue of highest good and the blessing upon the nation to prosper under your rule. *Moksha* be the blessing to all peoples in the world."

In another letter the King of Paekche writes: "This Dharma is the most meritorious one. It is difficult to understand and difficult to enter into. Even the prince of Chou or Confucius did not know about it. But it will bring to you limitless bliss, virtue and abundant rewards and *bodhi* most of all. If one has a special treasure which produces whatever the owner wishes, he can do everything with it. This treasure of the meritorious Dharma will be the same. If one prays with it, everything will be carried out as he wishes . . ."[14]

It is evident in these documents that in Paekche also the supernatural power of Buddha was the greatest attraction of popular Buddhism. In fact, we find this motive has been a dominant one throughout the history of Buddhism in Korean society. It was a form of laymen's Buddha all the time.

Near the end of his life and rule (918–943 C.E.) over the new kingdom of Koryŏ, Wanggŏn, the T'aejo (first king), declared a ten-article policy as his will.[15]

The first article reads: "[As have always been] . . . All the national affairs [hereafter] shall be managed and prosecuted under the (divine) protection, with the [spiritual] resources provided by Buddha. Therefore, the temples and monasteries of the Sŏn (or Zen or Ch'an) and Kyo sects shall be established and maintained. Abbots [as government officials] and administrative staff [appointed by the king] shall be dispatched to prevent the evil politicians as well as the false monks who may find chances to fight over the possession and property. . ."[16]

This religious policy of the founder was zealously kept by his successors. It is of special interest for us to note that many of the religiously important projects were carried out in the time of national crises, with the utmost devotion and dedication, to solicit the supernatural power of Buddha for the national welfare. This is exemplified in the manufacturing of new wooden block printing plates, part of a massive national project carried out during a period of disaster to replace the former set, which was destroyed during the Manchu invasion in 1011 C.E. and the Mongol invasion in 1236 C.E. It took sixteen years to accomplish the work, initiated in 1237 C.E. as an act of devotion. Blocks for printing 6,791 volumes of 1,512 sets (81,258 pages per square foot) were cut. The whole set is preserved at Haein-sa Temple in South Korea. It is the oldest and one of the best collections of its kind in the world.

Thus Buddhism flourished during the Koryŏ dynasty, which lasted five centuries until the neo-Confucian revolution came in the fifteenth century.

It is said that:

> Songdo, the capital of Koryŏ, was full of temples and monasteries... The temples were just next door to the palaces and government halls. Kings and queens paid regular visits to the temples and never lapsed a single month into neglecting their incense burnings. The big festivals of Yŏndŭnghoe and P'algwanhoe were celebrated in honour of Buddha. If the king had two sons, the eldest became the crown prince and the second became a monk, shaving off his hair...[17]
>
> [The people of Koryŏ] do excessive things in fanatic devotion to Buddha. The Buddhist exercises are too demanding. There are enough periodical festivals already established. But, in addition to these, numerous little festivals and "little" religious duties are also imposed upon the public. What they are seeking is a happy long life. In praying for that happiness they are throwing away their possessions... From the humble ones to the king himself all people take the shallow security which they possess in the face of the unseen yet imminent dangers, to be the work of the mysterious protecting power of Dharma.[18]

We find this type of Buddhism to be virtually the same as the one practiced at the beginning of the Chosŏn dynasty, some five hundred years after Wanggŏn and one thousand years after the introduction of this religion to Koguryŏ and Paekche.

The Chosŏn dynasty adopted a stern anti-Buddhist policy under the impetus of the newly invigorated neo-Confucianism.[19] Anti-Buddhism as social reformation culminated during the reign of T'aejong early in the fifteenth century. T'aejong (Yi Pangwŏn by his civilian name) himself was an avowed Confucian when he was a subject of the old Koryŏ dynasty. He had even passed a government examination in Confucianism and was an official in the government when his father, Yi Sŏnggye, a general in the army, led a successful revolution and became the first king of the new dynasty. When T'aejong ascended to the throne, the neo-Confucian reformers naturally found him the best monarch to carry through the thoroughgoing reform program that ultimately ostracized the Buddhists.[20]

But in his private life the story was a little different. In policy making T'aejong was an anti-Buddhist. On ascending to the throne as the third king he declared to his ministers: "I do not claim to know the doctrines of Buddha. But the spiritual powerlessness of this religion is now evident. What good did Buddhism do for the welfare of the nation? My father and my brother, the first and second kings, believed in Buddha. Therefore, they could not launch any positive action to exterminate Buddhism. But now I am willing to hear from you, my ministers. What are the appropriate measures to be taken?"[21]

But in 1408 C.E., as his father lay on his deathbed, T'aejong consulted with his trusted minister Hwang Hi, the famous Confucian, and said: "My father, the first king, is fatally ill. I know well that a prayer to Buddha for his health will not do any good. Yet I could not help but do so. I will call the monks [into the palace] to pray for him. What do you think about it?"[22]

To this Hwang Hi replied: "There is no harm in it, because it is for the health of the father."[23]

It is reported that more than one hundred monks participated in the exercises of Yaksa yŏrae worship. The king placed his royal robe on the altar in his devotion and kept vigils on his knees before the Buddha image. When his father died, the funeral was conducted in accordance with the neo-Confucian protocol but with the rich combination of Buddhist rituals.[24]

After the elaborate funeral, the king, reflecting on what he had done, told his minister Hwang Hi again: "How can I be so ignorant about the harmfulness of Buddhism. But I did so because it was for my father and I had no choice. As for me you must write the details of the things I did under the obligation [as a son] so that the posterity may know why I did [this foolishness]."[25]

During the five hundred years from T'aejong to present day, we find that the layman's Buddhism has remained virtually the same. From the beginning and along the course of its vicissitudes, the Korean layman's Buddhism became a thoroughly theistic religion in contrast to the "atheistic" Buddhism of the experts. The Buddhas were deities to whom devotion and supplication should be offered. *"Pul,"* or Buddha has always been associated with *"Sin,"* or god, since the period of the inception of Buddhism in the society, and these two soon became unified to make the single word, *"Sin-*

pul." How closely *Sin* and *Pul* were associated is exemplified in the
Buddhist celebrations of Yŏndŭnghoe and P'algwanhoe festivals,[26]
of which the loyal Buddhist King T'aejo of Koryŏ has written in
article six of his will, to which we have referred above. It is stated:
"Article six: The king wishes that Buddha be worshipped at the
Yŏndŭng Festival. And the Heavenly Deity and the deities of the
Five Mounts and the dragon deities in the big rivers be worshipped
at the P'algwanhoe celebration. We prohibit all subjects [of this
kingdom] to attempt to add to or take away from [what has been
instituted]."[27]

Nevertheless, at present, we find the contents of the two festivals to have been completely amalgamated during the course of the
last thousand years. The first festival Yŏndŭng, which was specially set aside by King T'aejo for the worship of Buddha, is no
longer a Buddhist celebration. The name of the festival is now
written in various ways with Chinese characters, according to different loyalties.[28] They are intended undoubtedly to produce the
approximate pronunciation of the original name, Yŏndŭng, or burning lantern. "*Yŏn*" (burning) is here associated with "*yong*" (dragon)
or "*yŏng*" (spirit). Actually, the present-day festivals are more or
less related to the worship of the deity of water and wind in fishing
villages around the southern tip of the peninsula; and it also is
related to the worship of the rainmaking deities in the interior
farming villages. Thus the Sin-pul syncretism was accomplished.

This syncretism went far. Once the Mahayana pantheon was
introduced, the equation between the corresponding deities in the
pantheon and the native mythology was carried out with striking
naiveté. No exactitude was necessary to place the "corresponding"
deities in the category of "equivalence." It seems to have been enough
for the Korean Buddhists to do their ingenious work of equation if
there were merely some suggestion of contextual parallels[29] or some
linguistic similitude between the corresponding deities.

The artificial equation of the monotheistic Korean deity
Hanŭnim with the Hindu-Mahayanic deity Indra in the monk Iryŏn's
version of the Tangun legend is a prime example.[30] On the merit of
his adopted Chinese name or "Hwanin" (in abbreviation) Indra
became identified with the Korean *Hanŭnim*, because the word
"*Hanŭnim*" also could be easily transliterated into Hwanin.[31] Indra,
who was given the title of *T'ien-chu*,[32] is the king of the *Tao-li-t'ien*,
the Hindu thirty-three heavens. Therefore, the *Tao-li-t'ien* was also
easily equated with the Korean *Hanŭl* or the Kingdom of Heaven.[33]
This is a perfect case of our "Sens c)" type of syncretism.[34]

However, no one could have even thought of such an artificial identification between two deities and two realms so far apart from each other, if there were no historical or cultural necessity for it. Indra, rather a subordinate deity in Mahayana pantheon, could not possibly be compared with the supreme *Hanŭnim* under normal conditions. The *Tao-li-t'ien* consisted of thirty-three heavens while the Korean *Hanŭl* seems to have been only one story up above the earth. Such an attempt of the overzealous Korean Buddhists may have been intended to be nothing but an effort to ascertain the supreme theistic quality of Buddha at the expense of national pride.

The first Buddhist "deity" that was given the highest honor in the Silla dynasty seems to have been Mirŭk, or Maitreya Bodhisattva. The reason for this is not very clearly given to us in the records. It may have been only the result of Silla's direct contact with the Maitreya-worshipping Chinese Buddhism that flourished since the period of the North and South dynasties through the Sui and T'ang dynasties. But we may also speculate that the Koreans of the day may have found in that religion some congenial elements to their indigenous belief. They seem to have had a kind of indigenous messianic hope.[35] If this were actually the case, the Maitreya, or a Future Buddha or "Buddhism's Messiah,"[36] would have caught the fancy of the people very quickly.

Salvation in the Tushita Heaven where Maitreya resides must surely have been a part of the motivation of their belief.[37] But a messianic hope in a future manifestation of Mirŭk as a "savior" of men and women from the national predicament must have been the more important portion of the motivation. Mirŭk was expected to appear as a knight of Silla, a *Hwarang* or "Flower Youth." The *Hwarang* knights' missions were to fight for justice, protect the weak and poor, and live a godly life free from self-love.

Samguk yusa reports how a pious monk Chinja (or Chŏngja) prayed to the image of Maitreya at the Hŭngryun-sa Temple in the era of the King Chinji for the coming of the Mirŭk *Hwarang*, incarnated as a knight, and how Chukchirang, a *Hwarang* knight, was admired as the incarnation of Mirŭk.[38]

According to the *Samguk sagi*, Kungye, the degenerate revolutionary of the Silla dynasty, too, was self-styled as an incarnation of Maitreya:

Sŏnjong (another name for Kungye) called himself Mirŭk Buddha. He put a golden crown on his head and dressed himself in the robe of an emperor. He named his first son

Ch'ŏnggwang Posal, or Blue Light Bodhisattva, and the second Singwang Posal, or Divine Light Bodhisattva. When he went out, he always rode on a white horse decorated on the mane and tail with colourful ribbons. Boys and maids followed him carrying a canopy for him and led the way carrying flowers. And he also made some two hundred monks follow the processions while reciting sutras. He himself also dictated some twenty sutras, of which not a single sentence was free from evil and wickedness. He even preached with the dignity of a high priest. But a monk by the name of Sŏkch'ong said that not a sentence of the preaching was free from heresy, and that in his instructions there was nothing worthwhile to listen to. When Sŏnjong, or Kungye, heard about this (criticism), he was angry. The monk was beaten to death with an iron bar . . .[39]

Parallel to this belief in Yonghwasamhoe, however, a more powerful belief in Amitabha Buddha and his realm in "Western Paradise" soon took roots in the Korean mind. Of special interest to us is the reason why the Pure-land school of Mahayana Buddhism as represented by the tradition of Asvaghosha, Nagarjuna, Tao-cho, Shan-tao, and Tzu-min that propagated the particular "Western Paradise" under the jurisdiction of Amitabha or Amita became so decisively influential among the Korean Buddhists.

As a historical explanation one may stress the fact that it so happened that the Pure-land school prospered in T'ang dynasty China. A Korean monk with a special gift for persuasive power and a pleasant personality in addition to ardent mystical devotion had gone there to study Buddhism. His name was Chajang, to whom we have referred with lengthy quotations above. He was an Amitabha worshipper when he returned in 641 C.E. to begin a period of thriving Buddhism in the Silla dynasty.[40] During the reign of Queen Sŏndŏk, the trinity of Amitabha, Ta-shih-chih, and Kuan-yin were enthroned on the main altar of Hŭngnyun-sa Temple undoubtedly under his influence.[41] Before long the Amitabha faith was the dominant trend among the Buddhists, among whom was Prime Minister Kim Yangdo.[42] He is said to have dedicated his two daughters to the temple as maids.[43] Thus the Amitabha faith became prosperous.

As for the second explanation, a psychological interpretation is due. In view of the monotheistic inclination of the indigenous belief of the people,[44] it is not surprising to see that Koreans found

Sukhavativyuha Buddhism to be intensively congenial. In the *Amitayusa-Vyuha* itself there are many paradises promised in all "ten directions" under the jurisdiction of a host of Buddhas. But instead of such bewildering confusion the Koreans rather felt more at home with Asvaghosha's exaltation of the "one Buddha" Amitabha and his salvation in the Western Paradise.

Korea produced many prominent scholar-priests for the world of Buddhism, among whom the greatest in their literary contributions are Kyugi (K'uei-chi),[45] Wŏnhyo,[46] and Kyŏnghŭng (Ching Hsing).[47] And it is rather a remarkable thing to see that all three great men have written extensive commentaries on the three Pureland texts, regardless of their sectarian affiliations.[48]

The way of achieving the Amitabha salvation was "faith and faithfulness." The modern Korean and Japanese Buddhists like to use in their Buddhist language a phrase, "absolute submission," to express their *"Gefühl"* as Mahayana Buddhists faithful to their Asvaghosha tradition. Strangely enough the same vocabulary was adopted by modern Christian theologians in those countries and has been put to good use as the translation of the Schleiermacherian term *"das Abhängichkeitsgefühl."* The Mahayana "Luthers" of Rodolf Otto[49] and Reichelt[50] stood on faith, as elaborated in Asvaghosha's *Awakening of the Faith*, in which four faiths, or four aspects of faith, are explained. That was in fact the universal attitude of the pious Buddhists in Korean society as a whole. They strove to live by faith and faithfulness.

It would be a grave injustice if we failed to describe the special interest in Theravada Buddhism within the Mahayana context that recently awakened in Korean Buddhism. But we need not drift into the sea of Buddhist scholasticism. We feel that insofar as the layman's Buddhism, or especially the "latent" Buddhism among non-Buddhist Koreans is concerned, *jñana marga* (way of knowledge), in Hindu terms, was out of the question all together. Regardless of their sectarian affiliations, *bhakti marga* (way of devotion) was the only way for their salvation either through self-attaining faithfulness (*jiriki*) or totally abandoning faith (*tariki*) to the mercy of Buddha.

Looking back on what we have delineated above, we feel that neither the doctrinal nor the practical side of the layman's Buddhism is wholly incomparable to the corresponding sides of popular Christianity in Korea. Did this "latent Buddhism," then, have something to do with the explosive growth of the Korean church? An orientalist answers this question in the definite affirmative. E. A. Gordon, in her brilliant paper "Some Recent Discoveries in Korean

Temples and Their Relationships to Early Eastern Christianity"[51] writes: "It is impossible [by far to deny] that the zeal with which the natives have embraced Christianity since Korea was opened to the world in modern days is proof of some latent spiritual life in which the germs of the Ancient Faith survive [through Buddhism], and are therefore responsive to a quickening touch."[52] Though she makes her points above with subtle, negative adverbs, she is quite firm and even arrogant about her "discoveries."[53]

According to her, the first Buddhist missionaries to come to Korea from China were Nestorian Christians.[54] One of the earliest Buddhist temples built in Korea was called "Ibullan" Temple, and she believed it to be a transliteration of "Ephraim." She seeks her support in the architecture of the stone cave-temple Sŏkkuram,[55] which has an unparalleled style in East Asia. She tries to compare it with the corresponding type of architecture in Christendom, and she writes: "Its cryptic character puts its relationship with the underground churches and basilicas found everywhere in Southern and Western Europe."[56]

She sees in Maitreya the image of the Judeo-Christian Messiah.[57] To prove this point she also published a book entitled, *Messiah, the Ancestral Hope of All Nations.* Likewise, Kwanŭm, or Avalokitesvara, is compared with the Holy Ghost[58] and Amitabha to the Godhead.[59] She even "ventures to think"[60] that Bodhidharma is no other than Saint Thomas, the "Apostle of the Hindus and Chinese," according to the Malabar Breviary.[61] Numerous Buddhist symbols are painstakingly identified with those of Christianity. She builds her diffusionistic interpretation on the basis of the successful Nestorian missionary work which was carried on in the T'ang dynasty, especially during the reign of the great Emperor T'ai-tsung in the seventh century.

We admit that she goes too far and too hastily. But her "discoveries" are not entirely unsupported by Western scholars, among whom there is Reichelt, who also perceives in the development of Mahayana Buddhism in China an influence from Nestorianism. He writes: "When one recalls the fact that Shan-tao lived near the Nestorian sphere of activity and just at that time when the Nestorian church was proclaiming its "good news" with its primitive power and strength, it is very easy to see evidence of a clear influence from the Christian mission at this point. It is also an incontestable fact that just at this period, a quiet but sure inner process began to work within Chinese Mahayana, pointing to a more monotheistic Amitabha-concept."[62]

Taking one step further, Reichelt suggests a possibility of Asvaghosha's direct contact with the "Western system of salvation."[63]

In fact, the communication between Nestorianism in China and T'ang Buddhism may have been more than an imagined one. Nestorianism had actually adopted Buddhist terms: "Buddha" for God, "Arhat" for saints, *"fen-shen"* for incarnation, *"ti-yü"* for hell. Furthermore, the Nestorian Messiah (or Meshikha) may have been confused with Maitreya because of the common character they share in their Chinese titles. A missionary named Adam was reported to have collaborated with an Indian monk in translating Prajñaparamita into Chinese. The Buddhist scholar Takakusu relates this in his lecture on the "Impurity of Chinese Buddhism."[64]

Whatever the case may have been, diffusion or convergence, one thing is made very clear for us here. The type of Mahayana Buddhism that became the most influential among the Koreans had some unmistakable similarities with Christian concepts. Therefore, it will not be an error to say that the eschatological silence of Confucianism[65] was supplemented by Mahayana Buddhism to make the forthcoming Christian impact an explosive one.

It is very interesting to note that all of the anti-Christian Confucian writers in Korea agreed that the Christian concepts of Heaven and Hell were nothing but the same doctrines of Buddhism which they had already condemned. Pak Chiwŏn, one of the representatives, writes: "Li Ma-tou [Matteo Ricci] believed in the same [Buddhist] doctrines of Heaven and Hell. Then why should he reject Buddhism and attack it as if it were his enemy?"[66]

CHAPTER TEN

Taoism and Christianity:
Unio Mystica

Johannes Bettray, in discussing Matteo Ricci's firm attitude against Taoism, suggests: "Ricci could have emphasized more strongly the possible historical connections between [Taoism] and Christianity and thus could doubtless have come up with arguments for a conversion to Christianity. As it is, he sees practically nothing but negative in Taoism and rejects this system just as he rejects Buddhism."[1]

Research into these "possible historical connections"(*die möglichen historischen Zusammenhänge*) must be an exciting and rewarding one for a student in the field of history of religions. But what we are more concerned with in the present study is to find out what phase or phases of what we call "religious Taoism" *(Tao-chiao)* are suggestive of the *Zusammenhänge* to Christianity. If such possible points of contact should be located, then we will be able to describe more easily and effectively the scene of the contact between these two religions in a society.

The first phase of this kind in Taoism is its theism. Taoist theism is thoroughly anthropomorphic in its character, which makes the Taoist pantheon even more coherent than that of Mahayana Buddhism. Buddha or Buddhas are made deities in Mahayana belief. Buddha assumes a theistic character more extensively, perhaps, in China under the influence of Taoism.[2] But still they preserve a quality that is somewhat different and detached from a purely theistic character. One may call it "Buddha-ness," a remnant of "fundamental" Buddhism.

141

In strong contrast to this, the gods of Taoism have realistic personalities, perhaps too much so to be transcendent "deities." It is true that in Confucian theism, *T'ien* or *Shang-ti* remains a personal God, regardless of the efforts of neo-Confucian "materialistic" interpretations. This Confucian theism, however, has not been able to achieve full development as a religion. Perhaps it is hindered by too much sophistication on the part of the wise men of China. Some seriously doubt that Confucianism has ever been a "religion." *T'ien* is made so transcendental that no one, except some of the saints or *sheng-jen*, can make intimate communication with it. It is mentioned in Emperor K'ang-hsi's declaration of 1700: "And from both fear and respect that they have for him [*T'ien*], they do not dare to call upon him directly by his own name, yet they have the custom of invoking him under the name of Supreme Heaven, Merciful Heaven, Universal Heaven."[3]

But Taoism has the privilege of possessing realistic deities and the means of direct communication with them. The Taoists may even "indulge" in the "drunkenness of god(s)," or *Gottesversessenheit*. In other words, Taoism was a full-fledged theistic religion in the literary sense when it encountered Christianity in Eastern societies.

Furthermore, Taoism has a monotheistic hierarchy in its pantheon. As if it were a well-organized government under an absolute ruler on earth, the fundamentally polytheistic pantheon is systematized in a tight hierarchy under the sovereignty of the Supreme Deity, Shang-huo-chiu-huang-tao-chün, or Yüan-shih-t'ien-tzun.

According to the Chart of Hierarchy or *Chen-ling-wei-yeh-t'u* (Positions and Occupations of the True Spiritual Beings) prepared by T'ao Hung-ching of the Liang dynasty, there are seven classes of true spiritual beings, or *shen-tzun*. And in each class there is a ruling *chu-tzun* deity. Each *chu-tzun* has his own office and duty to perform. Each office, which looks like a government by itself in its scale and size, consists of various numbers of *chün*, or very important persons; *shen*, or immortals or holy persons; *fu-jen*, or women; *yü-nü*, or jade women (virgins); huang-hou, or kings and feudal lords; *hsien-che*, or worthies; *chiang-chün*, or generals; *shih-che*, or messengers; and *li-shih*, or warriors. In other words, there are seven sets of governments under the absolute ruler Yüan-shih-t'ien-tzun. The seven ruling deities and their offices are as follows:

I.   Supreme Ruler
II.   Lord of All Tao-Creation
III. Lao-tzu, Revealer of Tao

IV. Lord of T'ai-Ch'ing Tao-Instructor of Truth, Mysteries; The Savior
V. Chang Tao-Ling, Lord of Secretariats
VI. Lord of the Scriptures and Charms
VII. Emperor of Death and Punishment

An interesting feature of this arrangement is that it appoints all important legendary or historical personalities in Chinese history, including females, into offices in accordance with their individual capacities. Confucian saints and Confucius himself are appointed suitable positions.[4] Lao-tzu is given three separate lordships.

Though it was apparent that this hierarchy matured under the influence of interaction with Buddhism,[5] there is no spirit of reconciliation shown toward that religion here. Not a single Buddhist deity or *religioso* is given the honor of participation. It is true that Lao-tzu is elevated and even sometimes identified with Yüan-shih-t'ien-tzun. But the ultimate supremacy appropriated to Yüan-shih-t'ien-tzun has given him a transcendental quality, so that he may rule the universe through his vicars and deputies from behind the mystery. It is clearly stated that all the lords and subordinate deities are subject to his command, and they all should "learn" Tao in order to lead the faithful, or ch'ün-chen, to immortality.

The supremacy of Yüan-shih-t'ien-tzun is clearly shown in his spiritual rule over the spiritual universe. One finds in the fantasy delineated in the scripture *Tu-jen-shang-pin-miao-ching*, an ideal picture of a saintly Chinese emperor at work. He is the Yüan-shih-t'ien-tzun. Yüan-shih-t'ien-tzun himself is eternal and has no beginning or end. But his government must go through complete revolution periodically, after each *chieh* or *kalpa*. The length of one *chieh* is 4.1 billion years. And at each revolution the kingdom adopts a new name for the new era in a Chinese fashion, such as Yen-k'ang, Ch'ih-ming, Lung-han, Kai-huang. His capital is called Yü-ching or the Jade Capital (or simply the king's capital), situated in Ch'iung-sang's field.

The second phase of Taoism that reminds observers of some kind of *Zusammenhänge* with Christianity is found in its ethical teachings. The essence of the Taoist scriptures may be summarized in the four characters, *jen-ai-ch'ing-ching*, or altruism (universal), love (individual), clarity (moral), and purity (ritual). It is true that these religions and ethical ideals are set as utilitarian goals to help the faithful attain their individual immortality, or

hua-hsien. But as ethical exhortation, they stand very close to
Christian teachings.

It is specially noteworthy for us that Mo Tzu (Mo-ti), the fifth
century B.C.E. "heretic" to Confucianism, was accommodated into
the lordship of Taoism in the fourth class of the above hierarchy.
Consequently, his teachings on "universal love" are integrated into
the ethical ideals of Taoism. Now this Mo-ti is "un Jesus-Christ
d'Extrême Orient."[6]

> One can compare the teaching of Mo-ti to that of Jesus
> Christ without too much exaggeration: both of them cer-
> tainly proclaimed the love of God and and neighbors. But
> for Mo-ti the love of neighbors is primary. It is certain that
> his doctrine, founded on the theistic tradition of the lite-
> rati, resembles the occidental theism and spiritualism.[7]
>
> However, his philosophical system was fundamentally
> the logical development of that of Confucius, to whom he
> clung tenaciously despite the divergencies that might have
> existed between them. The principal difference is that Mo-
> ti did not seek to justify his theory solely through the au-
> thority of the ancient sages, but rather through the use of
> reason and dialectic. The old concepts of the scribes and the
> sooth-sayers on the Saint, Superior Man and their virtues
> that Confucius had previously conserved were completely
> abandoned by Mo-ti. He did not borrow those concepts but
> instead created the notion of altruism or *Jen*, which he
> developed and advanced to the extreme of universal love.
> According to Mo-ti, love should not be spread to others in
> accordance to their rank or class, and thus diminish to the
> degree that one was removed from the center of his exist-
> ence, that is to say, from himself and his family. With
> universal love, all recepients of love, distant and close, are
> equally merged, and only love which makes no distinction
> among others can save the world. This principle should be
> applied even to the point of sacrificing oneself.[8]

Therefore, it is not surprising if one should find a very Christian
tenor in Taoist scriptures such as *Pao-p'o-tzu*, *T'ai-shang-kan-ying-
p'ien*, or *Kung-kua-ko*.

It is apparent that the Korean Taoists were very much attracted
to this ethical edification, because they produced excellent Korean
colloquial translations from these texts and they occupy the most

important part of the Taoist publications in Korea. One very interesting feature in this relation is that these Korean writings brought in some of the appropriate illustrations from Korean sources.[9]

The third and most important phase of Taoism that resembles Christianity is found in its "*unio mystica*" as religious motivation. The Taoists were intensively interested in attaining immortality through *unio mystica* with Divinity, as the Christian mystics were. The Taoist ways for this attainment run the whole gamut of religious efforts possible to humanity from spiritual sublimity to sheer magic.

On the highest level there is the religiously pious, philosophically speculative way explored by Lao-tzu and Chuang-tzu, and pursued by the intellectually oriented faithful through negative efforts (inaction) to harmonize themselves with Nature and Tao. On the second level, there is the ethical way referred to above. In an early Taoist piece of literature *Pao-p'o-tzu*, the author Ko Hung mentions:

> If you are seeking immortality you must accumulate virtues by endeavouring to be loyal (to the king), pious (to parents), harmonious (with friends), obedient (to elders), kind (to subordinates) and faithful (to all others). Otherwise, you will forfeit the blessing of your long life. If you commit a crime of considerable consequence, the deity of your life will cut one *chi* (300 days) from your life. If you make a small mistake, the deity may also cut a *suan* (three days) from your life. The length of a man's life is decided before he is born. Consequently, one lives long if he makes little offence, and he meets early death if he commits a lot of crime. Therefore, you will not be able to enjoy your long life even if you drink a lot of medicine of immortality and master the spiritual techniques, unless you start from now to accumulate your virtues.[10]

In spite of the warning of Ko Hung above, there is the third level: ritualism and spiritual techniques. In Taoist terminology, the techniques are abstinence, letter charms,[11] worship, and prayer. The techniques and ritualism require exactitude, and thus stern legalism has come to take an important place in Taoist life.

On the fourth level, there are the physical techniques. Abstinence from ordinary diet, "medicine" with magical effect (such as *chin-tan*),[12] breath control (yoga in Chinese dress), and massage and sexual techniques (to economize vitality). There are a lot of "bizarre practices and superstitions" (as Doré names them) in these Taoist activities. But one must admit that the popular Christianity in the West has not been entirely free from the similar practices described even on the lower levels mentioned above. It is very true that the greater number of the Taoists were victimized by their superstitious beliefs and evil leaders. But we must not forget that there are also noble teachings and doctrines brought to them by those who arrive at religious sublimity through their painful experiences and persistent speculations in the Taoist ways.

We agree with the great sinologue de Groot who takes Taoism as the very core of *"Universismus,"* which is the basic religion of China.[13] In fact, the organized Taoist church is nothing but an institutionalized small portion of the entire population which embraces Taoist beliefs.

The real strength of Taoism seems to lie therefore beneath the surface, as with the floating iceberg. We have here humorous and yet true examples that well illustrate the situation for us. The famous anti-Buddhist writer Han Yü of T'ang was an ardent Confucianist. But he is the author of the prayer *Chi-hsiang-chün-fu-jen-wen*, which he dedicated to the Taoist goddess of the Shang River. Of course, it is a literary work. But it was composed for the actual purpose of prayer.[14] Ts'eng Kuo-fan of the Ch'ing dynasty was a fiery anti-Buddhist, anti-Taoist scholar as well as a great statesmen. But we find in his collected letters a note that he sent to his helper saying that he was suffering from a bad boil on his head. He mentions: "I am sure I am suffering because I neglected to keep clean my ancestral home. Will you please sweep the grave for me carefully and see that the dirt is not stirred (lest the ancestral spirits should be disturbed)?"[15]

In present-day Korean society, Taoism as an organized religion is almost invisible. There were only two or more Taoist temples in Seoul (destroyed during the Korean War). But it is an entirely different story insofar as its influence upon the society is concerned. The real strength of Korean Taoism also seems to have been concealed under the surface. It still is strongly imbedded in the popular beliefs and is very real to the society. We must now narrate the vicissitude of this religion on the peninsula in order to describe the historical scene in which Christianity came into contact with this belief.

As for the official date of introduction of Taoism into Koguryŏ, one of the three kingdoms and the closest to China, the historical documents *Samguk sagi,*[16] *Samguk yusa,*[17] *Old T'ang-shu* and *T'ang-shu*[18] seem to agree on the seventh year in the King Yŏngnyu era (624 C.E.). A Taoist priest was sent to Koguryŏ that year by the Emperor Kao Tsu of the T'ang dynasty as a one-man goodwill mission. He is said to have brought with him the image of Yüan-shih-t'ien-tzun and some Taoist scriptures and taught Lao-tzu to the people. The next year, it was reported that the king of Koguryŏ sent Koreans to T'ang to bring back more instructions on the doctrines of "Buddhism and Taoism." T'ang desired to propagate among her neighbors the faith which she adopted as her state religion.

But in all probability Taoism had already been well established in Koguryŏ previous to that date, because if we can trust reports from the Chinese side, when the T'ang priest on the goodwill mission preached Lao-tzu, "the king himself and several thousand Tao priests and laymen turned out to hear him."[19] It is probable that there already existed some kind of distinction between the Tao priests and laymen. The report also reflects the tremendous response of the people to the message which he brought with him. This may also indicate that Taoism was already known well enough among the people to create such a spontaneous response on that occasion. Furthermore, the unmistakable Taoist influences upon the society are evidenced in the gorgeous mural paintings of the Koguryŏ (royal) tombs of the supposedly pre-Taoist period, located in the wide area within the Koguryŏ territory in P'yŏngan province as well as T'ung-kou, Manchuria.[20]

Sekino suggests that the Koguryŏ *taemyo* is the royal tomb of either King Yŏngyang (590-618 C.E.) or King Yŏngnyu (618-642 C.E.).[21] Either case is improbable, however, because the documents *Samguk sagi, Kaesomun chŏn, T'ang-shu Kaoli ch'uan,* and *Tzu-ch'ih-t'ung-chien* Vol. 196, all agree that King Yŏngnyu was killed by his rebellious minister Kaesomun and his remains were abandoned. Meanwhile, *Samguk sagi, Silla pongi,* and *King Munmu's Eighth Year Paragraph* suggests the location of the tomb of Yŏngyang to be somewhere in the west, in the vicinity of P'yŏngyang. Yi Pyŏngdo believes that the *taemyo* is the tomb of King P'yŏngwŏn (circa 586 C.E.).[22] Though not conclusive, we believe that Yi's evidence is superior to Sekino's. All the remaining tombs belong to the same period. The special features of these tombs are the full-blown Taoist symbols which are splendidly painted on the murals. But surprisingly there is very little Buddhist influence on them.[23]

The Hyŏnmu, or the Blue-Black Tortoise; Ch'angnyong, or the Blue Dragon; Paekho, or the White Tiger; and Chujak, or the Red

Bird or Griffin—the four Chinese divine animals—are generally represented on the murals, showing that the *feng-shui* (*p'ungsu* in Korean) belief had already been firmly established in that area by then. These animals are the symbols of the respective North, East, West, and South, astronomical directions or "diagrams of the earth," based on an arrangement of the twenty-eight principal constellations in four groups.[24]

To take an example from the *taemyo*, in addition to these four divine animals or *ssu-shen-t'u* (portraits of the four divinities) on the main walls there are many Taoist symbols painted superbly in the rich decorative design. Four angels (female), perhaps the Taoist *hsien-nüs*, or the jade maidens, take their graceful pose on the north wall. They are flying toward the west among wind-blown bits of clouds. One (the second angel) is carrying a medicine container in her left hand while picking the Taoist medicine plant *ling-chih*,[25] grown in the field of the blue heaven, with her right hand.

There are the legendary Three-peak Mountains or Three Mountains on which the immortal trees grow. The inevitable phoenix and giraffes also are represented. On the right-hand side wall from the entrance there is a picture of a flying bird on whose back a person, perhaps the occupant of the tomb, sits comfortably. These murals are definitely the forerunners of the Korean art *sipchang-saengdo*, or the "pictures of the ten immortals," a favored theme in Korean paintings, embroideries, and engravings. Therefore, we believe that the Taoist fantasy and longing for immortality had firmly taken its roots in the Kingdom of Koguryŏ even before the official date given above. That fantasy has been a part of Korean mentality ever since.

As for Paekche, the second of the three kingdoms, it is also probable that Taoism was introduced even before Buddhism arrived. According to the accounts of *Samguk sagi*, a Paekche general named Mukkohae advised the crown prince of King Kŭnch'ogo on the occasion of a victorious war against the neighboring Koguryŏ and said: "It is mentioned in the Taoist literature that one will not be ashamed if he knows how to be satisfied with what he already has in possession. There will be no danger if he knows when to stop before he goes to excess. We have won a lot. Why should we seek more?"[26] The war was fought before the official arrival of Taoism.

We find among recent excavations of Paekche some bricks with delicate bas-reliefed mountain figures. These are called "Mountain View Bricks," for they portray the symbolic decorations of the Three Peak Divine Mountain of Taoist origin.

In the case of Silla, the third of the three kingdoms, we do not have any direct record concerning the introduction of Taoism. But it is Silla where the impact of Taoism was felt most strongly. We are told that the "God-man" who advised Chajang, the most influential Buddhist monk, to build the important pagoda at the Silla capital was none other than the dragon spirit[27] of the lake. The protecting deity of the Emperor Dragon Temple or Hwangnyong-sa,[28] the centre of Silla Buddhism, was indeed the Yellow Dragon, the son of the T'ang Dragon who appeared to Chajang. Korea may also have had its own indigenous dragon,[29] but it certainly seems to be the T'ang dragons that played more important roles in protecting the kingdom. Some of the Silla Buddhist kings were believed to have become dragons when they died, and the Kamŭn-sa Temple or the Temple of Gratitude, was built in honor of them.[30] In fact, the dragons seem to have occupied a more important position than Buddha himself in Silla Buddhism.

Now what was this T'ang dragon and what was its religious affiliation? Of course, this dragon has something to do with the legendary Indian *naga* (or dragon) which was often personified. In a syncretic Chinese embodiment *naga* was adopted into the belief of the "good dragon" or *Shan-lung* who willingly rendered good services in protecting Buddhism.

But in our interpretation, this T'ang dragon had something more to do with the dragon of *I-ching* and the Blue Dragon of *feng-shui* or *kamyŏ*, as is evidenced in the celebration of the *P'algwanhoe*, one of the two main Buddhist festivals.[31] The festival was set aside for the worship of "the Heavenly Deity" *Ch'ŏllyŏng*, the deities of the Five Holy Mountains, and the dragon deities in the river.[32] These are Taoist deities rather than Buddhist. This suggests strongly that the celebration was something else than purely Buddhist. We feel that there must have been unmistakable Taoist influences involved.

The *feng-shui* was introduced to Silla largely by the Buddhist monks who studied in T'ang. Among them we have the greatest geomancer, Tosŏn, who rendered his services to King T'aejo of Koryŏ in helping him select the correct location and site of the future capital city of Koryŏ as well as the sites of the palaces, royal tombs, temples, pagodas, and monuments all over the peninsula, the newly unified territory. The purpose was to secure geomantic assurances for the welfare and prosperity of the nation.

Tosŏn studied *feng-shui* under the instructions of T'ang's famous Ch'an priest I-hsing. The alleged *feng-shui* scripture under the title *Tosŏn ŭlyong kyŏng* contains the following instruction: "Korean mountains and rivers are steep and torrential. Hence the wars, revolutions and disasters. When you go back to your country to propagate our Tao you must build *Fu-tou* or Urn-pagodas on strategic points to guard the vitality of the mountains and rivers from escape. You must not leave vacant lots on those important places. You must ward off the evil effect from without. Then you may pay attention to the comings and goings of the spirits of the waters."[33] One finds how strongly this text resonates and parallels the Chajang story that we have quoted above. In fact, this text supplements and explains the Chajang story from *Samguk yusa*.

Of course, *feng-shui* is not identical to Taoism. Confucianism claims a greater share in this heritage. Many of the eminent monks practiced it. It was, in fact, a pseudoscience for the animistic societies in the East as a whole, and everybody in those societies could take part in it without any scruples due to their religious affiliations. Nevertheless, the very fact that this common heritage, rather than purely Buddhist elements, provided the core of the events in that age in the Silla dynasty suggests that possible route which Taoism took to enter the kingdom. One may also recall that the Amitabha faith in China proper already had been in close contact with and deeply influenced by Taoism.[34]

Such syncretic tendencies[35] appeared very early in the history of the three religions in Korea. It is reported that in 643 C.E. a minister named Somun advised Koguryŏ's King Pojang: "The three religions are like the three legs of the [Chinese] iron pot. If one leg is lacking the pot is not stable. Confucianism and Buddhism are flourishing in our country but not Taoism. This is an unsatisfactory state of affairs [in view of the fact that a nation must] equip with all religions and merits thereof. Let [the students] be sent to T'ang to seek the doctrines of Tao and [bring back the learnings] to teach our people."[36]

We find in Silla's scholar Ch'oe Ch'iwŏn the same idea but with something more for us to note. In an address dedicating a tablet erected in honor of Nallang, a *Hwarang* knight, he mentions:

In our century there is a Tao, deep and mysterious, called *P'ungnyu*, the origins of which are recorded with details in the *Sŏnsa*. It embraces the three religions grafting them into its own body and nourishing the divergent understandings therefrom in harmony for the benefit of the whole nation. It teaches filial piety in family situations, and patriotism in the national concern, in harmony with the teachings of Minister of Crime of Lu [Confucius].

It teaches "inaction" in conduct and ultimate understanding in mysteries in harmony with the spirit of the Keeper of Archive of Chou [Lao-tzu]. And it teaches not to attempt evil things and encouraged good deeds in harmony with the virtues of the Prince of India [Buddha].[37]

In this rhetorical address he mentions an indigenous religion called *P'ungnyu*, which absorbed and integrated the influences of the three religions. One thing that interests us here is that there was the Taoist influence upon the religion called *P'ungnyudo* or *Hwarangdo*.[38]

Hwarangdo was a religious body of the knights of Silla. *Hwarang* was also called *Sŏllang* (*hsien-rang* in Chinese), *hsien* being the same word as the Taoist immortal, *hsien*. Ch'oe Ch'iwŏn mentioned the *Sŏnsa*, or *Hsien-sa*, a historical account of the origins of *Hwarangdo* which is now lost. Unfortunately the memory is lost with the document. Nevertheless, we can infer from the secondary evidence scattered all over the *Samguk sagi* and *Samguk yusa* that *Hwarangdo* was a body, composed of sons and daughters of noble families who were endowed with intellectual gifts as well as physical strength and beauty. The purpose of the organization was to train them as knights, to make them brave and fearless in battle and to be sincere and loyal in their behavior toward all men in time of peace. As is indicated with the title *Hwarang*, "Flower Youth," beauty was the supreme value in this movement. Justice was the principle in action.

It is no wonder that this body produced a great king like Kim Ch'unch'u, a general like Kim Yusin, and war heroes like Kwan Ch'ang, the lady-like warrior Wŏnsullang, who all contributed to the prosperity of the nation with no equal in Korea's entire history. In order to attain and sustain these noble ideals, artistic activities such as music and dancing, and religious piety such as spiritual training on the mountains were standard requirements together with Spartan military training. They were commanded to make excursions throughout the country to familiarize themselves with the topography of the country as well as civic problems of the entire population. The itinerary of these excursions always included the mountains and rivers, sacred places in Taoism. They were trained to live "with nature" and "in nature." It was also their religious exercise. Thus, their ideals were made approximate to Taoist immortality.

Of Taoist immortals, the Taoist Ko Hung writes: "An immortal can jump into the clouds and even fly without wings. He can ascend to the heaven riding on a dragon, floating upon the clouds and he is even able to climb up the staircase hung in the air. He can transform himself into a bird so that he can fly in the blue sky or into a fish so that he can swim in the deep seas. He is able to visit all the famous mountains according to his heart's desire. He can eat (absolve) energies from the air and live on the spiritual herb *chih-ts'ao*. He can make himself unnoticeable or even completely invisible to mortal eyes."[39]

One will find how this description of the Taoist immortal has similarities with the great Korean Buddhist Wŏnhyo's idealization of Maitreya. Wŏnhyo writes: "The personality of Maitreya Bodhisattva is as follows: His remoteness and closeness one cannot measure. No one can understand his depth or openness. He has no beginning and no end. His existence is not spiritual, nor material. Heaven and earth cannot bear its merits. The universe cannot contain his virtues. The eight saints of the world cannot apprehend his wisdom. The seven eloquences cannot explain away his ultimate truth. Deep and deep mystery, no one can say anything nor keep silent about him."[40]

This future Buddha Maitreya belief of the Silla monk Wŏnhyo and the immortal belief of the Taoist Ko Hung seem to have found common historical representatives in several of the Silla *Hwarangs*, such as the Silla heroes Mirŭk Sŏnhwa,[41] or Chuk Chirang, who were believed to be the incarnations of Mirŭk in the form of a Taoist *hsien*. Even the vulgar rebel Kungye or Sŏnjong could claim himself to be one of the Maitreya-Immortal-*Hwarang*.[42]

Sadly enough, however, the *Hwarangdo* penalized itself with its own pride and factionalism among the members as the sunset of the creative age pressed closer, and ugly degeneration set in to weaken the movement and allowed organized Buddhism to start destroying the competitive body with dangerous potential. Confucianism in later years succeeded Buddhism and contributed greatly in exterminating the movement.

But it is rather remarkable to see that the leaders of the rebellious movements of the oppressed people over the course of Korean history either sincerely believed themselves to be or at least pretended to be such *Hwarang* Immortals. Some of the tragic heroes, such as the Admiral Yi Sunsin who defended Korea from Japanese invasion in the last part of the sixteenth century, were made to be immortals or saints posthumously in later years, but some assumed the role while they were actively engaged in the revolts. Hero worship certainly has some latent tendency conditioned by this belief.[43]

This tendency was crystallized in the Tonghak movement from which Ch'ŏndogyo was born.[44] "*In nae ch'ŏn*" (Human being is the heaven), the principal doctrine of this religion, is no other expression than that of the longing for *unio mystica* with the Ultimate Power, Ultimate Principle, Ultimate Being of the universe, which they call *Hanŭnim*, or *Ch'ŏnju*. The Korean Protestant Church shares the term *Hanŭnim* with Ch'ŏndogyo. The Catholic Church in Korea also shares the term *Ch'ŏnju*, or *T'ien-chu*, with this "indigenous" religion.

One thing we should not fail to mention in this connection is that Ch'ŏndogyo "had to" adopt the Taoist "spiritual techniques" and charms, as well as scriptures in order to succeed the valuable tradition of *Hwarangdoism*, crystallized in the substrata of the society throughout its painful history. On the refined level of the *In nae ch'ŏn* doctrine, we feel that no Korean is entirely free from its influence.

CHAPTER ELEVEN

Christianity and Popular Belief in Korean Society: New Discovery of an Old Faith

Pre-Taoist, pre-Buddhist, and pre-Confucian ancient Korea had its own indigenous religion. It is evident in the historical documents. Let us start with Tangun, the legendary God-man who is believed to have founded the ancient kingdom of Korea, or Old Chosŏn, in the twenty-fourth century B.C.E. He is the central figure of this ancient belief.

Do not be alarmed if Tangun looks almost completely submerged in Taoist and Buddhist renderings in the legend about him. It is merely due to the fact that the two extant versions of the legend built around him happen to be ones which are colored deeply by the respective religious affiliations of the ages in which the story is told. But regardless of such historical alterations made in the painful vicissitude of Korea's history, we feel that we still can establish the identities of the personalities in the Tangun legend with some degree of certainty.

Tangun's name is recorded in historical documents in three different transliterations (of a Korean word in Chinese characters). They are: *Tangun* with the Chinese graph *"tan"* meaning "altar," *Tangun* with the Chinese graph *"tan"* meaning "sandalwood," and *Ch'ŏngun* meaning "Heavenly Lord." But we have good reason to believe that *Tangol* is also a transliteration of the same word, though this series is used only in oral traditions, as shall be reviewed.

155

The *tan* (altar) and the *tan* (sandalwood) appear with the full texts of the legend in the historical documents of the thirteenth century onward. But the actual date of the origin of the letter itself must be much older, since the said documents always refer to an *"Old Record,"* which unfortunately is now lost. The Chinese historical record *Wei-chih*, in which *T'ien-chün* appears, is some seven centuries older than the recorded legend mentioned above. But we believe that it was merely a Chinese translation, instead of a transliteration, of the Korean word *Tangun* or *Tangol*, as will be shown shortly. To our interpretation, the *Tangol* series seems to be more basic and fundamental, even if it never appears in the historical documents dominated by the Buddhists and Confucians. Nevertheless, the *Tangol* series has remained with the populace in oral traditions, though it is only used as a technical term with a specified meaning, perhaps as a result of a possible linguistic drift.

In short, though the belief that is associated with Tangun has never occupied any prominent position in Korean religious history ever since the introduction of the organized religions from China, it has remained intact, submerged deep in the popular belief, and it has played the role of sustaining and maintaining that belief which is an inclusive type of monotheism and which characterized all religious life of the people regardless of their religious affiliations.

Iryŏn's version of the Tangun legend as recorded in *Samguk yusa* is the earliest one now extant.[1] The historian Iryŏn was a Buddhist monk of the highest rank in the time of the Koryŏ dynasty, and it is he who appears to be responsible for having colored with Buddhist influence the legend which apparently was largely Taoist in character until it reached his hands. The text reads:

The *Old Record* relates: "In olden times there was Hwanin. His son Hwanung, born of his concubine, desired for himself an earthly life and wanted to be among human society. The father, knowing his son's intention, looked down upon the San-wei and T'aebaek [or the T'aebaek peak of Mount San-wei], and came to the conviction that his son might bring some benefits to human beings. The father gave his son three talismans and let him go. Hwanung descended to T'aebaek mountain (Iryŏn's own comment: 'Mount T'aebaek is Myohyang-san, as is it now called') under the trees of the sacred altar which place was called the Divine Place.

He had command over the Wind Noble, over the Lord of Rain and the Lord of Clouds. Therefore he had to attend to the planting of grain, the regulation of human life, of sickness, of punishment, and he had to judge good and evil; in short, he had more than three hundred and sixty affairs to direct.

In this world he regulated all metamorphosis. At this time there were a bear and a tiger who lived together in a cave. They often prayed to the god Hwanung (or "Male") and they wished to be transformed into human beings. Hwanung gave them a bundle of sacred mugworts and twenty cloves of garlic. He instructed them to eat this and not to see the sunlight for one hundred days—then they would really acquire human form. These (herbs) the bear and tiger took and ate. They [following the instructions] remained in seclusion for twenty-one days and the bear acquired the body of a woman; but the tiger had not been able to abstain [from looking at the daylight] and so it was not possible for him to obtain human form.

The bear-woman could find no one to marry, whereupon under the trees of the altar she prayed to become with child. Hwanung changed his form and married her. She became pregnant and bore a son and his name was Tangun Wanggŏm."[2]

We find in this text a tapestry of the Taoist and Buddhist accounts on the Tangun legend. But it is apparent that Taoism plays the leading role here by providing the entire framework of the story.

First, the scene of the court of the deity Hwanin in heaven here reminds us of the Taoist supreme deity, Yüan-shih-t'ien-tzun, or the Jade Emperor. Second, the names of the mountains which Hwanin and his son Hwanung looked down upon are derived from Taoist literature. They are the San-wei, or the Three Peril Mountains, mentioned in *Shu-ching* and *Shan-hai-ching*.[3]

Third, there are the Taoist "talismans." And fourth, there are the three supernatural beings: Wind Noble, the Lord of Rain, and the Lord of Clouds—all Taoist divinities.

Fifth, there are cosmic figures, such as more than three hundred and sixty affairs, twenty-one days, etc. They have Taoist significance. Sixth, there are animal stories, also familiar in Taoist tales. Seventh, the magical herbs, the inevitable medicines in Taoist mythology are present. And eighth, there is Tangun, whose name is recorded with the character Tan meaning "altar" which strongly reminds one of Taoist worship and prayer.

These are the reasons we believe that the text before its Buddhist corruption might have been largely Taoist, something as depicted in Kim Chewŏn's article on the Wu Liang Tzu stone slabs of the Han dynasty.[4]

Iryŏn, on the other hand, masterfully inserts two vital comments[5] to the text and puts the legend into a decisively Buddhist color. His first comment is on the name of the deity *Hwanin*. He interprets Hwanin to be the Buddhist *Chesŏk Hwanin*, or *"Hwanin"* in abridged form. Therefore, he simply adds a Buddhist honorific title: *Chesŏk* (or *T'i-shih* in Chinese pronunciation) to the name of the deity. And by doing so he simply identifies Hwanin with the Hindu-Buddhist deity *Indra*, the divine ruler of the Sumeru peak in the Thirty-three Heavens, or Taoli Heaven, whose honorific title was T'ien-ti-shih. His name has many other Chinese transliterations, notably with characters with the sound of *han* and *in*.

We do not believe that Iryŏn was necessarily the one who actually accepted the name Hwanin for the supreme deity in the text, because Hwanin, a syncretic word from Taoist-Buddhist background, was already undoubtedly part of a familiar religious vocabulary among the Koreans of the day. The *Leng-yen-ching chu-chieh*, a Chinese commentary to the Buddhist Scripture *Surangama Sutra* with heavily Taoist tones, was already much read in Korea. And in this literature we find the following sentence: "On the mountain peak of the Sumeru in the Taoli Heaven lives the Lord of Heaven whose personal name is Indra [Han-in and Hwanin in Chinese and Korean pronunciation respectively], and whose given name is Yü-huang Shang-ti [Jade Emperor] of Spirit Mountain."

We find in the text that Hwanin (or Indra) and Yü-huang (or Jade Emperor) are completely identified. And by this identification, Indra, a subordinate Mahayana deity, is elevated to the supreme position in the Taoist pantheon.[6] This made transplantation (maintaining the newly acquired status) to the soil of the Korean legend easy. For it already was in a Taoist setting. Therefore, we feel that somebody other than Iryŏn himself could have also easily done this, if he had some reasons to do it. (Probably the reasons were linguistic.)[7] Whoever the responsible person, we imagine that he was a man of Taoist rather than Buddhist inclination.

With his second comment, Iryŏn does a more marvellous job. He ingenuously identifies, with a simple comment, Mount T'aebaek in the text with Mount Myohyang-san, the centre of the Tangun cult. There are many mountains in Korea that bear the name *paek*, meaning "white," and *park* meaning "bright."[8] And we believe that this mountain was one of the *paek* mountains before the "new" name Myohyang-san was given. But the very name Myohyang-san happens to be similar to the Myo-kao-san, the Hindu-Buddhist Sumeru in Chinese linguistic attire. It seems that this was the very reason why monk Iryŏn emphasized the identity of T'aebaek and Myohyang-san. Thus Hwanin's position as Indra is decisively strengthened in this legend.

The next version of the Tangun legend is found in *Chewang ungi*, a historical epic composed in 1287 C.E. by Yi Sŭnghyu, a devout lay Buddhist. He wrote a short poem which he dedicated to Tangun and added a note himself as follows:

> The *Pongi* relates: Shangje Hwanin[9] had a son, born of a concubine, whose name was Hwanung. He asked his son: Are you willing to go down to Three-Peril Peak of Mount T'aebaek for the benefit of all human beings? Hwanung gave an affirmative answer. Thereupon, Hwanung received three heavenly talismans and led the three thousand spirits behind him and descended upon the summit of Mount T'aebaek under the divine Tan tree. This is the Heavenly King Tanung.
>
> He let a "granddaughter" drink medicine to become a human being and let her marry the spirit of the Tan tree. A boy was born and his name was Tangun. He occupied the territory of Chosŏn and became its king. Therefore, the people of the Silla kingdom, and Koryŏ, the tribes of South and North Okjŏ, East and North Puyŏ and the Ye and Maek are all descendants of Tangun.[10]

In this text we find considerable differences from the previous version above. We notice first that the Taoist influence has been considerably reduced here by cutting out, from the viewpoint of the writer, the unessential parts of the story. The bear-woman, *ungnyŏ*, is replaced by a granddaughter, *sonnyŏ*, perhaps as a consequence of the corruption from the original text. The writer or the copier of this version of the legend may have deemed it necessary to strike out the undignified term "bear" from his ancestry by substituting a *son*, which is apparently out of context. We will return to these terms.

The more important change that takes place here is found in the substitution of *Tan* as *sandalwood* for *Tan* as an *altar*. And the father of Tangun is made to be the spirit of the sandalwood.

According to Iryŏn's version, it is under the trees of the sacred altar where Hwanung, the son of Hwanin, descends. But now it is the spirit of the sandalwood who becomes the father of Tangun. This corruption may have also come from a Buddhist zeal, to deepen the Buddhist influence upon the legend. *Chŏntan* (sandalwood) is a medicine tree that has religious significance in Buddhism.[11]

This version brings us information about the geographical diffusion of this Tangun belief at the time when this version of the legend was born. The named kingdoms and territories of the comparatively unacculturated areas at that time covered virtually all of Korea and Manchuria, the former territory of Koguryŏ. There are two more texts besides those mentioned above. One is found in the article concerning the geography of P'yŏngyang, the alleged capital of Tangun, in the *Sejong sillok*, compiled by Yun Hoe, Sin Saek, and Maeng Sasŏng in 1442 C.E.

The other one is found in Kwŏn Nam's commentary on his grandfather Kwŏn Kŭn's poems called *Ŭngjesi*, or Poems Composed in Response.[12] It is interesting to note that Yun Hoe, Sin Saek, and Maeng Sasŏng's 1442 C.E. version is almost a literal copy of Yi Sŭnghyu's 1287 C.E. version. Both of these copies relate the legend to an old record, *Tangun pongi*.[13] On the other hand, Kwŏn Nam's 1461 C.E. version follows, with some modification, Iryŏn's 1270 C.E. version. These two copies, likewise, relate to a record called *Kogi*. So here we have two sets of identical legends based on two different "old" records.

In view of the differences existing between these two sets of records, in the wording as well as in the structure of the legend, we assume that: the *Tangun pongi* and the *Kogi* were two different writings on the same legend. In connection with the founding of Puyŏ Kingdom, Iryŏn's *Samguk yusa* also refers to a record called *Tangungi*.[14] We feel that this literature may be the same "Old Record" that Iryŏn and Kwŏn Nam refer to in regard to our legend.

Now if we compare the two documents *Kogi* and *Tangun pongi* as they are copied in the two sets above, respectively, we find the latter shows a further development from the former one, with a different character for the word "Tan" and in its substitution of the word "*ungnyŏ*" with "*sonnyŏ*," as has been observed. We notice that in this latter document, the Taoist influence decreases while the Buddhist influence increases. Furthermore, we see growth of the geographical perspective in the latter, which we take to be a later development. Therefore, we are inclined to take the former one,

Kogi, as the first document and the latter one, *Pongi*, as the more recent one.

As to the dates of the origins of these documents, we have no positive evidence. However, the newer second document provides an important clue for us. In recording that Tangun's domain extended over a broad region that included the whole peninsula as well as a good portion of Manchuria, the document carefully avoids the use of the letter *ch'i* meaning "to govern," which is apparently needed in the context.[15] But actually *ch'i* is substituted with *li*, a word supplementary to *ch'i* in ordinary usage. We speculate, therefore, that this substitution may have taken place for the reason that *ch'i* is the name of Koryŏ's King Sŏngjong (982–998 C.E.). It would have been desirable to avoid it during and immediately after the reign of the king with the name *ch'i*, as was common practice in East Asia. Had the substitution actually taken place on the original document itself for that reason, then we would be able to place the date sometime later than 982 C.E. If it had taken place by a copier's hand, then we can place the date prior to the Sŏngjong era. However, we do not have any conclusive evidence for either case.

Nevertheless, the emphasis on the geographical perspective in the second document seems to reflect the spirit of Koryŏ's expansionism of the King Sŏngjong era, newly awakened under the stimulation of the newly invigorated Manchurian Khitan, over which Korean once had suzerainty. Expansionism was the tenor of the Sŏngjong era. And in considering the archaic transliteration of the names of the dynasties in Korean history, as recorded in this second document, such as the use of different Chinese characters in the spellings of Silla and Koryŏ, it is advisable for one not to place the date of the document too close to *Samguk yusa* or *Samguk sagi*'s twelfth century C.E., in which the transliteration of the official names of these dynasties were standardized.

If our approximation of the date of this second document is not very far from the fact, we can safely place the first document to a date prior to it. How far the date can be pushed back, we don't know. If Kim Chewŏn's Wu Liang Tzu slabs are really a pictorial representation of the Korean legend, the date ought to be pushed back to somewhere in the Chinese Han era. The legend may have been completely Taoist then.

We feel that the *Sŏnsa* or *Hsien History* to which Ch'oe Ch'iwŏn refers[16] has also something to do with this rather more Taoist element of the legend. We believe that Kim Pusik's *Sŏninwanggŏm* (or *hsien-jen-wang-chien* in Chinese)[17] reflects the same legend only in a more Taoist inclination.[18] Kim Pusik's *hsien* cult and Iryŏn's Tangun cult seem to converge on the same locality in northwest Korea around P'yŏngyang, or Changdanggyŏng, and Kunghol-san, or Kuwŏl-san or Asadal.[19] Furthermore, all the texts as well as documents concerning the Tangun legend seem to agree in testifying that Tangun did not die. They all report that Tangun entered into the sacred mountain Asadal or Kuwŏl-san to become a mountain god or to immortalize himself. The *hsien* idea and the Tangun belief seem to amalgamate completely here. We believe that Tangun was a *hsien* in Kim Pusik's language.

In regard to the date problem of this legend a word about the rationalistic view on the legend expressed by the historians of old Korea is in order. First of all, the "Father of Korean History" Kim Pusik (1075–1151) of the Koryŏ dynasty neglected the legend altogether. This is why some modern historians attempt to place the date of the origin of this legend sometime later than Kim Pusik's time.[20] In all probability, however, the prototypically sinophile and Confucian Kim Pusik knew of it and suppressed it intentionally for political reasons. This legend would have lent prestige as well as strength to his political opponent, the revolutionary Taoist-Buddhist monk Myoch'ŏng. Myoch'ŏng endeavoured to remove Koryŏ's capital from Songdo, the capital at the time, to P'yŏngyang, the centre of the *hsien* and Tangun cult in northwest Korea, in order to annihilate Kim Pusik's work of building up a little China in Korea. Kim Pusik eventually led the army to crush this rebellion.[21] Myoch'ŏng was an expansionist who looked up to the north, dreaming of uniting all the territories as delineated in the second version of the Tangun legend, under the power of the kingdom of Koryŏ. But Kim Pusik wanted to keep the nation at peace with Ming in order not to interfere with Ming's interest in Manchuria. We believe that this kind of consideration may have led Kim Pusik to his silence.

The Confucian Kim Pusik's silence finds an explicitly rational expression in the anti-Buddhist, anti-Christian, and vehemently Confucian writer An Chŏngbok (1712–1791) of the eighteenth century who wrote a compendium of Korean history, *Tongsa kangmok*. He mentions Tangun, saying:

As I investigated the reports in the *"Old Record of Korea," Tongbang kogi* and a few more of the kind, I find all the stories about Tangun full of wild fantasies and heresy. As a person, Tangun must have been a man specially endowed with saintly virtues. That is why he was elevated to the kingship. In ancient days, the divine and holy birth of an extraordinary person was very different from the birth of ordinary people. But why should contradictions to such an extent be attached to the Tangun story? The title so-called Hwanin chesŏk came from the Buddhist scripture *Fa-hua-ching* [*Saddharma-pundarika Sutra*]. And the rest of the titles are from the tales of the monks.

Silla and Koryŏ supported a pagan religion [Buddhism] and harmful effects have culminated in the present predicament. This land of ours went through many times of war and fire, and precious historical documents time and again met destruction. But the writings of the monks were preserved in remote caves and could be safely handed down. But we lament that a historian cannot possibly use anything from this data. If one mistakenly collects them in his or her writings, then the fallacies may ultimately be taken as real facts as time goes by.

How can we devote a corner of the space in a book, which should be filled with the wisdom of wise men, to such strange tales . . .

As for the Temple of the Trinity, Samsŏng-sa, now standing on Kuwŏl-san Mountain, we know that they worshipped therein Hwanin, Hwanung and Tangun, from the previous Koryŏ dynasty until today. It is, in truth, quite appropriate to worship Tangun. But the worship of Hwanin and Hwanung will have to go quickly, because true Tangun worship could have nothing to do with the spirit worship of Hwanin and Hwanung [of Buddhist manipulations].[22]

The rationalist An Chŏngbok's approach to the legend displays a surprisingly sound commonsense view. But regardless of his liking it or not, he has to admit that it was an old tradition. Of course he knew that it was distorted by the Buddhist monks, but it was also preserved by them for a considerable length of time. He hints that the "monks" even had with them some written documents of some historical value, which he quickly condemned, as a faithful Confucian of his age should have.

Let us turn our attention to the trinitarian setting of the legend. The *Samsin* cult, or the trinitarian worship (not quite a Triune God in the Christian sense) which An Chŏngbok points to in the above document, appears to have been an essential part of the legend. It is apparent that this cult had both chronological depth as well as social and geographical breadth on an amazing scale.[23]

Nevertheless, the very structure of this trinity strongly suggests possible influences from either Taoism or Buddhism or both. The Tangun trinity resembles very much the Taoist *T'ai-ch'ing*, or Supreme Purity; *Shang-ch'ing*, or Superior Purity; and *Yü-ch'ing*, or Jade Purity, insofar as its hierarchy is concerned. In the opening scene, a Taoist heavenly court is presupposed. In this crude theology there is no preexistence of the Son or Grandson in heaven. They have to be born. Nevertheless, they are made deities just the same not only because of their divine birth but because of their beings which are made eternal. Hwanin thus is made the supreme deity, and Hwanung and Tangun are made the *Ch'ŏnwang*, or heavenly kings. In view of the entire Taoist setting, it is not inconceivable that this Tangun trinity was artificially arranged by some imaginative Korean Taoist.

Meanwhile, the Korean Buddhists may have had their share in this rendering by appropriating the Buddhist *Trikaya* (three bodies) belief to the Tangun trinity. The Tangun trinity may be a product of a myth patterned on *Dharmakaya*, *Sambhogakaya*, and *Nirmanakaya* of the Buddha.

But why should the son Hwanung be born of a concubine? Who was this consort of Hwanin who played the same role as the bear-woman in the birth of Tangun? It is a foolish thing to demand logic in mythology. But to us the shadowy and too artificial existence of this concubine seems to have been necessitated by the sheer fact that if a son, Hwanung, was going to be born at all, a mother was needed. This is why we suspect that the Taoist or Buddhist influences may have preceded the differentiation of the belief in a primordial divinity into a trinity.

The union between Hwanung and the bear-woman also seems to be necessary under the same conditions. But in this particular case, we find a linguistic clue that may lead us to a fuller understanding of the legend. We feel that it is advisable to start to unlock this legend with this term "bear-woman," because this lexical item, *kŏm* or *kam*, is the only one in the whole legend that has not been affected by either Taoist or Buddhist influences.

"*Kŏm*," or "*kam*," as a phonemic unit, plays an important part in the religious vocabulary of the Korean language. It signifies sacredness as well as mysterious power. As a transliteration, "*kŏm*," or "*kam*," is given a Chinese character, *chien*.[24] In combination with *"ryŏng," "kam"* is widely used in the Korean language to signify mysterious power or spiritual potential. Rope made of straw as a charm and hung on the doorway to stop the trespassing of evil spirits is *"kŏmjul."*[25] In Iryŏn's *Samguk yusa*, Tangun is given a title: *Wanggŏm.* And Ch'oe Namsŏn takes this title as the transliteration of *"Ul-kŏm,"* or *"Ung-kŏm,"*[26] which signifies a charismatic endowment of a king.

"Kŏm" is also transliterated to *"kam."* The holy chamber or idol case is called a *"kamsil"* (*"sil,"* meaning "room"). It is rather strange, but in fact the *kam* (or north) described in *I-ching* and the Korean *kam* (or sacred) have somehow been contracted with each other to form a strange belief. North, or *kam,* has always been associated with the spiritual or mental experience of *mysterium tremendum* and is, therefore, holy. The whole area in Manchuria immediately north of the Korean border has been called *Kando.* We suspect that it must be a corruption of *Kamt'o,* or the "sacred northern territory."[27] It must be also an ethnic nostalgia which is involved in this matter. The Koreans look to the north believing that their forefathers came down from there in time immemorial. North, or *kam,* is symbolized in *I-ching*-based geomancy with a tortoise called *Hyŏnmu.*[28] And the character, *"hyŏn,"* is also associated with *"kam"* in Korea, because *"hyŏn"* reads *"kamŭl-hyŏn"* in Korean.

All of the above mentioned words, we believe, are derivations from the original word *kŏm,* or bear. *"Ung,"* which means "bear," is extensively used in connection with the names of rivers, mountains, and towns around the peninsula. We believe that all of them were meant to be sacred places. At the same time these local names also reflect the name of the people who lived there.

In Chinese historical literature we find a tribe, an important part of present-day Korean ancestry, recorded as *Maek* people, *Yemaek. Maek* is an animal name that reminds one of a bear in association. It is probable that the proud Chinese employed these words to imply their contempt for one of the surrounding "barbarian tribes." Though arbitrary and ill-minded they appear, the names have been in fact an actual transliteration of Korean names, as suggested by Yi Pyŏngdo.[29]

The modern Chinese pronunciation of *Yemaek* is *Houei-mai.* But the "h" sound in *Houei* could have been easily contracted with "k," to make *Houei* into *Kouei.* Therefore, it is speculated that in ancient China, *Houei-mai* may have been pronounced actually *Koueimai,* instead of *Houei-mai,* which is *Yemaek* in Korean pronunciation. This speculation is supported by the fact that sometimes the

Chinese records also employed another transliteration, *Kaema*, as the name of the same tribe. *Kŏm* and *kam* are closely related in pronunciation, as are *Houei-mai* and *Kaema*.

The Koreans, of course, chose more dignified letters for the transliteration. The letters chosen are *Koguryŏ* and *Koryŏ*, which mean literally high and beauty. In any case, it is quite possible that *Kaema* or *kŏm* (*-ma*), or *kam*, was actually the national (tribal) name of the people. We have another piece evidence to support our interpretation. Regardless of the three Chinese characters with which *Koguryŏ* is written, the Japanese still read it as a two-syllable word, *Koma*, which strangely reminds us of the now lost ancient Korean pronunciation. In Korea itself, ironically, the actual pronunciation is lost. *Koguryŏ* is read as the Chinese characters are read. But it is the *Koguryŏ* and *Koryŏ* from which "Korea" was derived.

What can we make out of these linguistic phenomena? Was *Kŏm*[*-a*] a tribal name possibly with a totemic background? That is not entirely impossible in view of the fact that "bear ceremonialism" is a custom so widely diffused among the Ural-Altaic people, including the Siberian and Manchurian tribes as well as the Finno-Ugrain groups.[30] But as far as the present writer is aware, there is no trace of totemic behavior observable in present-day Korea. The hunter's life in prehistoric society has become an entirely forgotten memory. But the linguistic traces are still observable with some accuracy. The Ainu's *"kamui"* (bear, master, or God)[31] and the Japanese *"kami"* (above, or gods) may also be linguistic derivations from a common stock.[32]

It is doubtful that we could ever trace back in linguistic time the "bear-*kŏm*" term to reach the Ural-Altaic main stock itself. But it is extremely interesting to observe that according to many ethnographers (Potanin, Mikhailowski, et al.) the term *"kam"* is widely used to denote a charismatic person among the Altaic Tartars and the Abakan Tartars (Turco-tartars). In Mongolian, the term is *"kami."*[33] Whatever the case may have been, we now know that the Tangun legend is not entirely a "fabrication of the monks." In reality, it does reflect a forgotten past, as is shown in the bear-woman tale.

The next item to be analyzed is the second deity, Hwanung. It is apparent that at Iryŏn's time, there were several variations of the Tangun legend already, which Iryŏn himself or his disciple Mugŭk were unable to harmonize. We feel that these conflicting accounts show rather the antiquity as well as the authenticity of the legend itself.

It is apparent that there were independent accounts of the divine origins of their respective tribal ancestors among the prehistoric tribal communities located in North Korea and Manchuria, but they seem to have converged into a prototype mythology. The mysterious birth of Haeburu, the forefather of North Puyŏ, is accounted for as the result of a marriage between Haemosu, Son of the Emperor of Heaven, or Ch'ŏnje, and a local woman.[34] This North Puyŏ was the ethnic resource of the kingdom of Koguryŏ. The birth of Koguryŏ founder Chumong was also accounted for with the same type of mysterious marriage.[35] Chumong's divine father was Haemosu, who married a woman named Yuhwa.

In both of the cases above, the mysterious father is the same personality, Haemosu, Son of the Emperor of Heaven. And the most interesting feature is that the women Haemosu married, on both occasions, have been suggested to be daughters of the *Kŏm* communities. The mother of Chumong is reported to be the daughter of a Habaek. And we feel that "*baek*" here has something to do with "*maek*," which is associated with "*ung*," or bear. Therefore, we believe that Hwanung's marriage to the bear-woman in the Tangun legend also shares this mythological structure with these variations.

Furthermore, here we find a parallel between Haemosu and Hwanung. Linguistically speaking, Haemosu's "*su*" is equivalent to Hwanung's "*ung*." The Chinese character for "*ung*" means "male," while "*su*," or "*sut*," in Korean means "male." We believe that the former "*ung*" is a translation of this "*su*," meaning male in Korean, and the latter "*su*" is the transliteration of the Korean word, "*su*."

Can we approximate *Hwan* with *Haemo*, too? *Hwan* and *Haemo* are phonetically similar, because the vowel "a" often contracts with "ae" in the Korean language. "*N*" and "*m*," or "*mo*," also often contract with each other, especially in such clumsy transliterations.

Now, what is *haemo*? In this case, we also find "*ae*"-"*a*," and "*mo*"-"*m*" contractions. Furthermore, in the Korean language, "h" is pronounced with a sound similar to the German "ch," and it often contracts with the "k" sound as in the case of the "h" in Russian pronunciation. If this is the case, "*haemo*" may well also have been "*kŏm*." In Japanese historical records, Korean immigrants in that country are recorded as *koma-su*. "The people (or males) of the sacred land" or "the people of the land of *kŏm*" may be the intended meaning of it.

What is Tangun, the third of the trinity? We find in Kwŏn Nam's text of the legend referred to above a very interesting

comment in which the following words are inserted: *"hwan"* is generally taken as *"tan."* We can interpret this in two ways. We can
think that what Kwŏn wrote about is the linguistic similitude between *"h(an)"* and *"t(an)."* On the other hand, he also could have
referred to the semantic similitude between *"han-ŭl"* or *"hanŭl"*
(heaven), and *"tan"* (heaven). The "han-hanŭl-heaven" combination
is found in the Hwanin case also, as shall be reviewed.

The *"tan"*-heaven combination is inferred from the following
two sources. Firstly, in Chinese history *Wei-chih* (Volume on Korea, passages on Mahan), one finds the following description of the
religious activities of the Korean communities: "Each Korean country, or community, has a chief priest called *ch'ŏngun* (or *t'ien-chün*
in Chinese) who serves the Heavenly Deity. And every country has
a special city of asylum called *sodo* (or *su-t'u* in Chinese) where a
big tree is erected, on which bells and tambourines are hung. In
this way they worship God." This description was copied at least
four more times in other Chinese records.[36] According to this record,
there is a chief priest called *ch'ŏngun,* or "heavenly gun," whose
role seems to correspond with that of Tangun.[37] Tangun was the
king as well as the chief priest.[38] If this is the case, we can safely
approximate the semantic features of *ch'ŏn* (*t'ien* in Chinese pronunciation) and *tan.*

Secondly, this role of *ch'ŏngun* as described in these records
seems to have been preserved in the degenerated, more specific
role of local shamans, whose title is "tangol" or "tangul" in present-
day Korean society. They are the franchised shamans for the particular adherents of the localities. Meanwhile, linguistically *tangol*
or *tangul* is traceable back to Mongolian shamanist traditions and
ultimately to the word *"tengri,"* which means "sky" or "heaven."[39]

Now, then, can we approximate the *gun* to *gul*? We feel that it
is not entirely impossible because we find the vowel *"u"* is stable in
both cases. Furthermore, the Korean *"l"* is more often silent than
"l" in English or French. It occurs frequently at the end of the last
syllable. Therefore, *"gul"* or *"gu"* is quite possible. From *"gu"* to
"gun" is also possible, because in the Korean language there is also
a movable *"n"* as in Greek.

If our identification of Tangun to *ch'ŏngun* is right, then, the Tan
Tree, or sandalwood, in the legend could also be interpreted to be the
"big tree" at the asylum in the sacred place called *sodo.*[40] We feel
that this makes more sense than the Taoist or Buddhist interpretations of the tree in question. The shamanist bells and tambourines

are also reported in this connection in the *Wei-chih*. It is also a valuable source of information in understanding Korean shamanism.[41]

What is *Hwanin*, the name of the first deity in our linguistic considerations? As has been repeatedly referred to in the present paper, it should be read as "*Hanŭnim*," because, first of all, it is probable that the penult "*nŭn*" may have been neglected or dropped by the alleged Buddhist or Taoist writer of the legend when he masterminded the unification of "*Hanŭnim*" with Hwanin, or the Hindu-Buddhist Indra, or the King of the Taoli Heaven. The phonetic similarity between *Hanŭnim* and Hwanin may have led him to this bizarre syncretism.

But the semantic similarity of *Hanŭnim* as the sovereign Sky-God to Indra, the King of the Taoli Heaven, may also have led these simpleminded men to carry out their mission. "*Hanŭnim*" as the Sky-God must have been originally "*Hanŭl-nim*," "*Hanŭl*" being sky and "*nim*" being an honorific personal suffix of social distinction. Phonetically speaking "*l*" of *Hanŭl* becomes silent before the "n" of *nim*. Therefore, the original form of *Hanŭnim* may well have been "*Hanŭl-nim*."

Did *Hanŭnim* belief, which still is so vividly alive in the Korean mind, exist in pre-Confucian, pre-Buddhist, pre-Taoist Korea? It *did* exist, most emphatically. The Chinese historical records describe profusely the religious life of the Korean people at the dawn of civilization. The Ye people had a heaven-worshipping festival called *much'ŏn*, or "heaven-worship in dancing."[42] And the Puyŏ's heaven-worship called *yŏnggo* or "heaven-worship in drum songs," the Mahan's heaven-worship as *ch'ŏnsin* or "the festival of the heavenly deity"[43] are reported together with numerous descriptions of heaven festivals of the Three Kingdoms of Koguryŏ, Paekche, and Silla.[44]

Korean society is not an exception among those in the Asiatic region, including the Arctic peoples and the nomads of northern and central Asia, where the supreme sky-god is worshipped.[45] Let us quote from the excellent study of Eliade in which he summarizes the findings of the ethnographers who worked in the region from the middle of the nineteenth century. These descriptions give us a splendid framework as well as background of the Korean religious life.

We may begin our brief sketch with the supreme sky gods adored by the Arctic peoples, and the nomads of North and

Central Asia. The Samoyeds worship Num, a divinity who dwells in the sky (or the seventh heaven) and whose name means "heaven." But he cannot be physically identified with the sky, for, as Schmidt points out, the Samoyeds also consider Num to be the sea and the earth, that is to say the whole universe. Among the Koryaks, the supreme divinity is called "the one on high," "force," "the world." The Ainu know him as "the divine master of the sky," "the heavenly god," "the divine Creator of the worlds," "the Protector," and so on; but also as Kamui, which means "sky".... But I need hardly say these names and attributions do not exhaust the personality of the Supreme God of the Arctic peoples. He is, above all, an omnipotent god, often the only one, and master of the universe....

Other titles and epithets of the sky god complete our definition of his nature and functions. The Beltirs address their prayers to the "most merciful Khan" (Kaira-Kan) and to the "Master" (*cajan*). The Tartars of Minusinsk call their supreme god "Creator of the Earth" (*car cajany*); the Yakuts "the wise master creator" (*urun ajy tojon*) or "the most high master" (*ar tojon*), the Tatars of the Altai "the great" (*ulgan, ulgen*) or "the very great" (*bai ulgen*) and in their invocation he is even "white light" (*ak ajas*; cf. Ostyak *senke*, and "most luminous Khan" (*ajas kan*). The Ostyks and Vuguls add to the name Turem the qualifications "great," "numinous," "golden," "white," "most high," "Lord Master my father," "good golden light from on high," and so on. In prayers and written texts the sky god is often called "father."

Simply to list these names and titles shows the celestial, sovereign and creative character of the Uralo-Altaic supreme god. He dwells in the sky.... His throne is to be found in the highest place in the sky, or on top of the cosmic mountain. The Abakhan Tatars even speak of "the vault" of the sky god, the Buriats of "the house blazing with gold and silver," and the Altai peoples of a "palace" (*orgo*) with a "golden door" and a "golden throne." The god has sons and daughters, and is surrounded by servants and messengers whom the shaman meets on his ecstatic ascent into heaven.[46]

In view of the fact that Koreans are closely related to the Ural-Altaic stock ethnologically, it is not very difficult to infer that they also shared the characteristic belief of these societies above.

Did the prehistoric and historic *Hanŭnim* belief exist, then, in the seventeenth century also when the Christian impact was felt in Korea? We can answer this question in the affirmative, because not only seventeenth-century but also present-day Korea is still immersed in this belief through and through. We can trace the living evidence easily and abundantly in Korea today.

In his excellent article, "Die Himmelsverehrung der Koreaner,"[47] Thomas Ohm observes: "The belief in Heaven [Hananim, Hanulnim or Hanŭnim](the language use varies according to region) is still held all over Korea, as it has always been. There may be some young people who no longer believe him or even joke about him; but in general, Koreans are convinced of his existence. It is something self-evident to them."[48]

To support his rather astonishing statement Ohm interviewed a number of Koreans as well as missionaries who resided in the peninsula over a long period of time. They all confirmed Ohm's testimony.

But this "something self-evident" is not so self-evident.

All Koreans perceive in Hanŭnim the highest being. If one questions them, however, about the specific nature and the characteristics of this being, one is bound to be disappointed. The ideas about this being are nebulous and imprecise. The concept of "heaven" lacks precision and concreteness, a fact which may be linked to the lack of reverence the Koreans show toward Hanŭnim which in turn leads to a lack of interest in theorizing about it. In addition, Koreans do not feel the need to comprehend everything fully and clearly.

The people are not even capable of saying whether Hanŭnim is a personal or impersonal, a spiritual or a material entity, or, in other words, whether Hanŭnim is to be understood as heaven in the spiritual sense, or sky in the physical sense. One comes across contradictory opinions in this respect.

According to Andreas Eckhardt, Koreans perceive Hanŭnim as a kind of "heavenly force, world soul and nature spirit."[49] Johannes Kim is of a similar opinion saying that in the past Koreans have simply revered heaven as a spiritual force. Only later, he believes, did the concept of God evolve out of it.

Another Korean, however, explained to me—this happened in Hamhŭng on the 16th of September, 1936—that the people definitely perceive Hanŭnim as a personal God. By Hanŭnim, he said, they did not mean the blue sky but the creator (*Chomulju*). Hulbert interprets the beliefs of the Koreans in a similar fashion. He even believes that the Koreans, as far as their reverence for Hanŭnim is concerned, are strict monotheists. The attributes accorded to Hanŭnim correspond, in his opinion, to those attributed to Jahweh. Some of the more ignorant Koreans denied that Hanŭnim is incorporeal, pointing to the visible sky to reinforce their point of view, while at the same time attributing to Hanŭnim fatherly concern for humankind and retributive power over evil.[50]

Ohm brings us thus far so that we can see the possible range of the different opinions that can be expressed concerning the *Hanŭnim* concept of Koreans. But, to be sure, the varieties of opinions and disagreements among them do not necessarily mean that the *Hanŭnim* belief is nothing but a vague notion. On the contrary the belief is surprisingly real to them.

All of these reports seem to make it clear that we will not get anywhere by directly questioning the Koreans about what Hanŭnim is, but that better results might be achieved by concentrating on what Hanŭnim does. Koreans attribute to Hanŭnim the power to rule the world. Hanŭnim is the heavenly lord and the ruler of the universe. He is said to know everything. Everybody is familiar with proverbs such as "The high heaven hears (knows) what happens on earth."

All that is good comes from Hanŭnim, but no evil comes from there. Great misfortunes and bitter suffering can be traced back to his grace or his will.

The Koreans believe, furthermore, that Hanŭnim rewards those who are good and punishes those who are evil. As I was told by teacher Kim in Tokwon, bad people are still warned: "*Hanŭri musŏpchi annya?*" (Do you not fear heaven?) Somebody who wants to proclaim his innocence might say: "*Hanŭri kubŏ posinda!*" (Heaven is looking down).[51]

Furthermore, the *Hanŭnim* cult has nothing to do with nature worship. "As far as Hanŭnim's relationship to nature spirits is concerned, one may, with all appropriate caution, say the following: Hanŭnim is not a nature spirit in the same sense as are the many nature spirits worshipped in Korea. This is evidenced by many statements about him and about the characteristics and actions attributed to him. Hanŭnim is on an entirely different plane from the nature spirits."[52]

The fact that *Hanŭnim* "stands on a totally different plane" from other deities explains why *Hanŭnim* is so transcendental to Korean minds. In fact, Korean *Hanŭnim* is a perfect example of the *"Deus Otiosus."*[53] He is a transcendental, but not aloof, deity. He is remote, but not blind to human destiny. Prayer is offered to him in time of need. Therefore, together with his attributes of grace and justice, as are shown in the *"Hanŭri musŏpchi annya?"* (Aren't you afraid of Heaven?) and *"Hanŭri kubŏ posinda"* (Heaven is watching down) ideas, *Hanŭnim* is associated with holiness and *"kam."* Whence, the piety on the part of *Hanŭnim* worshippers is strictly required.[54]

Ohm is not standing alone on his interpretation of the *Hanŭnim* cult. Many others share his view, among them Hulbert, "one of the best experts on Korea" (*einer der besten Kenner Koreas*), who also expresses basically the same view when he says: ". . . the purest religious notion which the Korean today possesses is the belief in *Hanŭnim*, a being entirely unconnected with either of the imported cults and as far removed from the crude nature worship."[55]

How could then the belief in *Hanŭnim* be "kept" in such an acceptable condition from a Christian point of view? There is a tangible reason for this, and we find it in the role of shamanism, which still is powerful in Korean social life today.

Shamanism has long been treated somewhat unjustly by many ethnographers, perhaps due to the degenerative activities as well as the very ignorance of the shamans themselves. Furthermore, the ethnographers themselves may have been prejudiced by their own religious background. Shamanism has been always associated with magic and sorcery. But fortunately recent scholarship[56] has brought into the light for us some of the basic structures of this peculiar yet universal religious phenomenon. Narrowing down our attention to the North Asiatic region, including Korea, we find shamanism has successfully sustained its role in keeping monotheism pure and strong, while, at the same time, maintaining its own specified functions in the respective societies. Shamanism works as a buffer to keep the monotheistic belief safe from the impact of crises in many Asiatic societies. And we believe that this was the case with Korea, too.

Let us paraphrase the carefully chosen words of Eliade once again in this connection.

The arctic, Siberian, and Central Asian peoples are made up chiefly of hunters-fishers or herdsmen-breeders. A degree of nomadism is typical of them all. And despite their ethnic and linguistic differences, in general their religions coincide. Chukchee, Tungus, Samoyed, or Turko-Tatars, to mention only some of the most important groups, know and revere a celestial Great God, and all-powerful Creator but on the way to becoming a *deus otiosus*. Sometimes the Great God's name even means "Sky" or "Heaven". . . .

This celestial God, who dwells in the highest sky, has several "sons" or "messengers" who are subordinate to him and who occupy lower heavens. Their names and number vary from tribe to tribe. . . . These sons, messengers, or servants of the celestial god are charged with watching over and helping human beings. The pantheon is sometimes far more numerous, as, for example, among the Buryat, the Yakut, and the Mongols. . . . But, as we shall show later, there is reason to believe that both this multiplication of gods and their mutual hostility may be comparatively recent innovations. . . .

As for the Arctic, Siberian, and Central Asian religions, in which shamanism has reached its most advanced degree of integration, we may say that they are characterized on the one hand by the scarcely felt presence of a celestial Great God, and on the other by hunting rites and an ancestor cult that imply a wholly different religious orientation. . . . Replacing the descripton of some shamanic performance in the frame of the general religious life of the people concerned (we are thinking, for example, of the celestial Great God and the myths about him), we sometimes find ourselves amazed; we have the impression of two wholly different religious universes. But the impression is false; the difference lies not in the structure of the religious universes but in the intensity of the religious exerience induced by the shamanic performance.[57]

We have almost nothing to add from the Korean materials to this splendid delineation of shamanism, because Korean shamanism is so closely related to this stereotype. We share the opinion of Clark, who testifies after his careful study of Korean shamanism that: (after referring to an article in the *Encyclopaedia of Religions and Ethics*) "the author of that article was writing from the standpoint of Siberian shamanism, and knew absolutely nothing of Korean shamanism, but with just a few tiny exceptions, this is an exact picture of what is found in Korea today."[58] Linguistically, first of all, Korean shamanism is securely affiliated to this Siberian shamanism. *Mudang*, the Korean term for a female shaman, clearly indicates its affiliation to the common linguistic stock of the Mongol *"udagan,"* Buriat *"udayan"* and Yakut *"udoyan."*[59] *Paksu*, or *pŏksu*, the term for the male shaman, also may have linguistic connections to the Kazak-Kirghis *"baqca."*[60]

The role of the Korean *mudang* is identical with that of the Siberian stereotype. She is a medium, a diviner, but not a magician or a priest. And most of all she is an ardent and honest believer herself. Her trade also coincides with that of the stereotype, including general divination, diagnosis of sickness, and ghost chasing. She is in perfect accord with the Siberian tradition when she is in action in seance. She summons spirits in the dark, sings and dances and channels. *Mudang* is also normally hereditary. Furthermore, she shows the same hermaphroditic tendencies. Her paraphernalia as well as the decorations on her tunic show clearly the traditions from the north. True to the tradition, *paksus*, or male shamans, play rather an insignificant role in Korean shamanism.

It is true that the *mudang*s adopt the three sets of pantheons (Taoist, Buddhist, Confucian) as far as possible so that the numerous deities can be invoked at appropriate occasions. But as is expected, they also preserve the *Hanŭnim* belief quite clearly. They hold firmly their mythological orientation in the *Hanŭnim* cult. Although *Hanŭnim* has been *Deus Otiosus*, they even dare to evoke the deity on many occasions, if not frequently, if the situation calls for it.[61] *Hanŭnim* is the supreme deity for them, and the three pantheons are called on for practical services.

A keen-eyed observer witnesses:

> Korea presents a unique opportunity for a comparison of Christianity, the most highly developed, with spirit-worship, the least systematic of all religions. Probably nowhere else in the world has the Christian missionary effort met with such immediate success as in the Hermit Kingdom . . .
>
> This fact is due no doubt to the sudden awakening on the part of the people to the value of Western civilisation . . . But to a still greater extent the warm reception accorded to

the great Western religion grew out of the numerous points of contact between the Korean faith and that of most missionaries . . .

It is a great victory at the very start to have to deal with a spiritually rather than a materialistically inclined people, and whatever may be said as to the peculiar developments of the animistic faith, this essential conviction as to the reality of spiritual things is identical in both religions.

Add to this consideration and as an outgrowth from its belief in prayer and the tremendous earnestness manifested in its practice on the part of these spirit worshippers, and another important point of contact emerges.

But of even more importance in this connection is the relatively lofty conception of God which characterizes not only the original faith of the Koreans, but even the Buddhism and Confucianism of the peninsula.

In spite of the mass of superstitions and the myriad of bad spirits that control the life of the people, they have preserved in a most striking fashion a doctrine of the unity of God, and, moreover, there runs through the crude notions as to his nature and relationship to mankind a series of most worthy conceptions.[62]

His observation is rather a hasty one, but does not miss the point. He clearly senses that numerous points of contact between the indigenous Korean faith and Christianity existed when the Christian evangelism reached Korean shores. What are these points of contact? Were the contacts actually made between the two beliefs? How was the bridge built between them?

First of all, the monotheistic *Hanŭnim* concept may have created the first point of contact with the oncoming Christian herald for the Koreans. To be sure, in the Riccian Christian documents that came into Korea in the seventeenth century, the Christian concept of God was explained in Confucian terms and language. But, in view of the fact that the Korean society of that century must have been as monotheistic as the society of today, it is not too difficult to infer that the new converts, who so quickly made themselves Christians, were also under the influence of the *Hanŭnim* belief, though they were avowed Confucians. The dividing line between the concept of the Confucian *T'ien* or *Shang-ti* and the Korean *Hanŭnim* is extremely hard to draw, not only because the

Confucian writers of the seventeenth century wrote only with Chinese characters and in Confucian terminology, but also because the similarity between the two concepts prevents us from clearly distinguishing the dividing line.

Nevertheless, as has been suggested,[63] one may assume that even the alleged neo-Confucian scholars in Korea, who followed Chinese writings, according to which they were supposed to be nontheists, introduced into neo-Confucianism something from their personal resources which transformed this nontheistic outlook into an outlook that was deeply theistic. We have noted that of the Protestant philosopher Leibniz, who endeavored with the help of his version of Chu-hsiism to harmonize Renaissance rationalism and Christian faith. This heavier inclination to theistic or mono-theistic tendency of the Korean Confucians can be interpreted, without risking too much, to be the consequence of their indigenous belief. As reported by a missionary, it is most probable that in Korea even a Buddhist monk, who was reciting the name of the Buddha Amitabha, would shout "*Hanŭnim* !" for help when he was in a sudden moment of crisis such as breaking through the ice on a thinly frozen river.[64] A similar statement can be said about a neo-Confucian as well.[65]

Under such circumstances the Riccian *Shang-ti*, or *T'ien-tzu*, was soon translated into *Hanŭnim*, but when and who did it first, we do not know. We do know that the Catholic Church in Korea, under the edification of the Société des Missions Étrangères, which officially denounced the Riccian approach,[66] had strictly adhered to the name *Ch'ŏnju* (the Korean pronunciation of *T'ien-tzu*), or Lord of the Heaven, in order to guard against the supposedly dangerous influence of the *Hanŭnim* cult. But the results seem to be the same. When P. Sebastian Schnell, a German Catholic priest was explaining *Hanŭnim*, he said: "Thus, *Hanŭnim* is *coeli dominus* [Lord of Heaven], the literal translation of the Chinese word *T'ien-chu* [*Ch'ŏnju*]."[67] To him, as to many other Catholics, *T'ien-chu*, or *Ch'ŏnju*, is synonymous with *Hanŭnim*.

With the Protestants, God was *Hanŭnim* from the very early days of Korean church history, though we do not know the exact date of the beginning of the use. The first Christian literature in Korean used *Shang-ti* or *Sangje* (in the Korean pronunciation), for *Hanŭnim*, perhaps due to the fact that they were direct transla-tions from Chinese. But even then, in conversation or preaching, *Hanŭnim* may have been used more widely. Because this usage ultimately became an issue of controversy, and after a "heated discussion," the term *Hanŭnim,* or *Hananim,* was adopted as official in 1912.[68] It is apparent that the missionaries did not start to use it. They must have only followed the public demand.

Official adoption or accommodation of the *Hanŭnim* term was an important step taken by the Protestant churches to secure their permanent place in Korean society. And we suspect that this important step also gave rise to the "dangers" of inviting some of the essentially connected religious elements to the indigenous *Hanŭnim* belief, namely, the spiritual world structure which resembles very much that of the Mahayana-tinted shamanist heaven and hell; the souls, spirits, devils, as well as angels of syncretic lesser deities in the shamanist pantheon therein; the shamanist ecstasy with a cunning equation to the experience of the Holy Spirit and the ensuing healing power to the New Testament-like miracle. The shamanist asceticism together with the accompanying "arctic hysteria" seems to have succeeded in changing their original costumes into that of the Christian ones which give a false impression to the casual visitors to the Korean churches who take them as the modern version of the New Testament churches.

It seems quite clear that shamanism in Korean society today has been of assistance rather than an obstacle to Christian evangelism by providing the preconditions for a special type of Christianity to prosper, which has congenial elements to that arctic hysteria. The perennial revival meetings held in the cities and on the mountains, where the secluded "prayer halls" (*kidowŏn*) are located, remind us of the shamanic performance practiced only in a massive and refined way. The too rapid growth of the Korean church along this line constitutes the main concern of the thoughtful Christian leaders of the land today.

Conclusion

In the above chapters we attempted to look into the context in which the contact between the Christian message and the pre-Christian religious heritages of the Korean society took place. And we indicated that the popular belief of the society had elements very congenial to Christian doctrines. How decisive a role this congeniality played in touching off the explosive growth of the Christian church in the land is yet to be proved. It can be proved only with an extensive documentary or factual evidence assembled from Korean data from the post-Christian society. And research of this nature is beyond the scope of the present study.

However, we may express our conviction that there is a strong possibility of arriving at a full explanation of the "unique" event along the direction we have taken and pursued thus far. We have observed that the religious tradition of Korea had in a substantial way such congenial elements as the monotheistic concept of God, longing for salvation, messianic hope, eternal life in the Great Beyond, and so on. We now can safely assume that the religious precondition for a successful Christian evangelism was thus well prepared on the historical stage of Korean society at the moment when the Christian impact came.

The historical and social environments were most favorable. And the churches successfully met the need of the society, religiously and culturally, by providing the new but well-tested systems, institutions, organizations, as well as effective methods and good leadership. And we believe that the miracle was thus wrought.

It seems that the Korean religious heritages were conducive, rather than detrimental, to the rapid progress of evangelism. Likewise they may serve to mold the characteristics of young Korean Christianity all in good time when it becomes mature, provided that an intelligent and positive approach is made from the part of the Christian churches in Korea.

Notes

Chapter One

1. Korea was called a "Hermit Nation," because until 1881 she kept her doors shut against the expanding West. Cf. chapts. 3 and 4.

2. Adrien Launay, Martyrs Français et Coréens 1838–1846, Béatifiés en 1925, Paris, 1925, p. 9. L'Église de Corée a des origines très particuliéres, marquées d'un caractère special de sagesse humaine guidée par la sagesse divine. Elle n'a pas été créée par le zèle des missionaires, comme les Églises de l'Annam, du Japon or de la Chine.

3. Cf. Hwang Sayŏng Silk Letter, Description on Yi Sŭnghun in Ch. Dallet, *Histoire de L'Eglise de Corée*, Paris, vol. 1. 1874, p. 16f.

4. Launay, op. cit., p. 9. Elle [l'Église de Corée] a donné un exemple peut-être unique dans les annales des missions modernes, en prenant naissance à la fin du XVIIIe siecle, en quelque sorte spontanément, sans évangélisation directe, par la seule action de la grace divine sur des âmes avides de vérité religieuse. Tels les rois Mages, au fond de l'Orient, scrutant les anciennes prophéties, soupiraient en attendant l'étoile qui devait les conduire à Bethléem, tels les docteurs de Corée dans l'isolement de leur royaume solitaire, étudiant les livres où ils espéraient trouver l'esplication du monds. Aeux aussi apparut une lumiére mysterieuse qu'ils virent briller dans des écris tombes provindentiellement sous leurs yeux.

5. Alexandre de Gouvea: Extractum epostolae excellentissimi, admodumque reverendi episcopi Pekinensis, ad illustrissimum admodumque reverendum episcopum caradrensem. *DE STATU CHRSTIANISMI IN REGNUM COREAE MIRABILITER INGRESSI* (emphasis is mine). This precious little document was translated into Portuguese and French from the Latin text and published respectively in Lisbon (Sobre a introduccao, e progressos de Christianismo en Peninsula de Corea, desde o anne de 1784- ate ao de 1797, Lisboa, Anno MDCCCVIII) and in Paris ("Relation de l'établissement du Christianisme dans la Royaume de Corée," *Choix des Lettres Édifiantes, Écrites des Missions Étrangères, Missions de la Chine*, Tome Troisiéme, Parris, MDCCCVIII, pp. 249–277. With an Introduction of the land and the people

under separate title: État du Christianisme dans la Royaume de la Corée, pp. 245–248).

The French version was produced several times (Nouvelles Lettres Édifiantes des Missions de la Chine et des Indes Orientales, Tome Cinquieme, Paris, 1820, pp. 259–294; Vevue L'Histoire des Mission. Nuitieme Annee No. 3, September 1931, pp. 387–415). Hitenaka Tanaka's Japanese translation has been published twice on *Kirisuto-kyo Kenkyu*, vol. 17, 1940, Doshisha University Press; and on *Chosen Gakuho*, No. 10, December 1956, Nara, pp. 194–216.

6. De Gouvea, op. cit., p. 46 and p. 48. "Intra breve tempris spatium quamphirimi fuerint in christum credentes. . . . Intra quinque annorum spatium christianorum numerum ad quatuor circiter millia pervenisse constet."

7. Mgr. Duvred, *Catholic Church in Korea* (English Version), Hong Kong, 1924, p. 50.

8. Ibid., "By September of 1868 two thousand of them had already fallen under the blows of the persecutors. In 1870 public rumor placed the number of Christians who had suffered death at eight thousand—not counting those who died of hunger and exposure where they had taken refuge."

9. Dallet, op. cit., vol. 1, p. 11. "Les Jésuites fixés à la cour impériale, quelque gênés qu'ils fussert dans l'exercice de leur zèle, n'ont certainment pas laissé échapper de pareilles occasions d'entrer en rapport avec les representaits d'un royaume apien non encore évangelise."

10. Cf. d'Elia, op. cit., vol. 3, pp. 329–334, 363–372, 378. Ricci and Pantoja, his companion, came to visit the capital city, and were detained by Chinese officials in the "Castle," in which all foreign visitors took their lodging. They met many nationals there including Vietnamese, Burmises, . . . Arabians as well as Koreans. The Korean Peninsula was added on the world map by Ricci, in his second revised edition of "Mappamondo," *Shan-hai-yu-ti-t'u*.

11. Peter Hwang, *Chen-chiao-feng-pao*, Shanghai, 1904.

12. Cf. chapt. 4.

13. As is quoted by Yi Nŭnghwa, *Chosŏn Kidokkyo kŭp Oegyo sa* (History of Korean Church and Diplomacy), Seoul, 1928, p. 51.

14. Dallet, op. cit., p. 11f.

15. Cf. Dallet, op. cit., pp. 57–68.

16. Ibid., p. 69.

17. Cf. chapts. 5 and 7.

18. Mutel Gustav, *Lettre d'Alexandre Hoang à Mgr. De Gouvéa, Évênque de Pékin*. Hong Kong, 1925; Yamaguch, Masayuki, "Secret Dispatch Written on Silk Cloth by Hwang Sayŏng," *Chosen Gakuho*, No. 2, Oct. 1951.

19. Hwang was arrested by the police on September 15, 1801. The government was eager to find out where the well-known Christian leader and scholar had hidden himself. By a cruel torture the police were able to extract a clue from Thomas Hwang Sim, the prized prisoner, and this clue ultimately led the police to the mountain village where Hwang had just completed the document.

20. Execution by cutting off of head as well as both hands and feet.

21. *Chosŏn wangjo sillok* (The Royal History of Yi Dynasty), vol. on Sunjo.

22. The true copy was written on silk with black ink, while this false one was written with alum, so that it could be read only when the silk is wet in water. The extraction was made by the anti-Christian scholar Yi Mansu.

23. K. S. Latourette, *Expansion of Christianity*, vol. 6, pp. 415–416.

24. Launay, op. cit., p. 11. "Cette pieuse et touchante supplique ne saurait être passée sous silence."

25. Ibid., 11–12. François et les autres chrétiens de Corée prosternés en terre, nous frappant la poitrine, offrons cette lettre au Chef de toute l'Église, Père tres haut et très grand.

C'est avec la plus grande instance, la plus vive ardeur que nous supplions Votre Sainteté d'avoir compassion de nous, de nous conner des preuves de la miséricorde qui remplit son coeur et de nours accorder le plus promptement possible les bienfaits de la rédemption.

Nous habitons un petit royaume, et avons eu le bonheur de recevoir la sainte doctrine d'abord par les livres, et dix ans plus tard ar la prédication et la participation aux sept sacrements.   -

Sept ans aprés, il s'éleve une persecution. Le missionnaire [Chu] qui nous était arrive fut mis à mort avec un grand nombre de chrétiens; et tous les autres, accables d'affliction at de crainte, se sont despersés peu à peu. Ils ne peuvent se réunir pour les exercices de religion, chacun se cache.

Il ne nous reste d'espérance que dans la très grande miséricorde divine, et la plus grande compassion de Votre Sainteté, qui voudra bien nous secourir et nous delivrer sans retard; c'est l'objet de nos priéres et de nos gémissements.

Pepuis dix ans, nous sommes accablés de peines et d'afflictions; beaucoup sont morts de vieillesse ou de diverses maladies, nous n'en savons pas le nombre; ceux qui restent ignorent quand ils pourront recevoir la sainte instrucion. Ils desirent cette grâce, comme dans une soif brulante on desire se dessiterér; ils l'appellent, comme dans un temps de secheresse on appelle la pluie. Mais le ciel est tres élevé, on ne peut l'attaindre; la mer est très vaste et il n'y a pas de pont qui nous permette d'aller chercher du secours. Nous, pauvres pécheurs, ne pouvons exprimer à Votre Sainteté avec quelle sincerite, avec quelle ardeur, nous desirons reçevoir son assistance. Mais notre royaume est petit, éloigne, situe dans un coin de la mer; il ne vient ne vaisseaux, ne voitures, au moyen desquels nous puissions reçevoir vos instructions et vos ordres. Et quelle est la cause d'une telle privation, sinon notre peu de ferveur et l'énormité de nos péchés? C'est pourquoi maintenant, nous frappant la poitrine avec une crainte profonde et une douleur sincere, nous prions humblement le grand Dieu qui est mort en croix, qui a plus de sollicitude pour les pécheurs que pour les justes, et Votre Sainteté qui tient la place de Dieu, qui soin de tout le monde, et delivre veritablement les pécheurs.

Nous avons ête rachetés, nous avons quitte les ténèbres; mais le monde afflige nos corps; le péché et la malice appriment nos âmes. Nos larmes, nos gémissements, nos afflictions sont de peu de valeur; mais nous considérons que la miséricorde de Votre Saninteté est sans bornes et sans mesures; elle aure donc compassion des breis de ce royaume qui ont perdue leur pasteur, et elle nous anverra des missionaires le plus tôt possible, afin que les bienfaits et les merites du Sauveur Jesus soient annonces, que nos ames soient secourues et délivrées, et que le saint nom de Dieu soit glorifié partout et toujours.

26. Dallet, op. cit., vol. 2, Livre III., pp. 236–321; and Launay, op. cit., pp. 209–250.

27. Hwang, op. cit. Kyŏngsin (1800) April Myŏng-hoe Description; Description on Chairman Augustine Chŏng Yakchong.

28. Cf. Alexandre de Gouvéa, op. cit., p. 58.

29. Hwang, op. cit., Description on Chairman Augustine Chŏng Yakchong.

30. Cf. ibid., Description on Yi Kahwan, Chong Yagyong, Yi Sŭnghun, Hong Nakmin.

31. Cf. ibid., Description on Peter Cho.

32. Cf. ibid., Description on Martin Yi Chungbae.

33. Cf. ibid., Description on John Ch'oe Ch'anghyŏn.

Chapter Two

1. Cf. *Minutes of Ecumenical Council of New York*, 1900, pp. 308–311.

2. Harry A. Rhodes, ed., *History of the Korea Mission, Presbyterian Church USA, 1884–1934*, Seoul, 1943, p. 76.

3. Ibid.

4. T. Stanley Saltau, *Korea, The Hermit Nation and Its Response to Christianity*, London and New York, 1932, p. vii.

5. Cf. *Annual Report of the British and Foreign Bible Society for 1885*, pp. 215–216; see also L. George Paik, *The History of Protestant Missions in Korea 1832–1910*, P'yŏngyang, 1929, p. 48.

6. Rhodes, op. cit., p. 76.

7. Ibid.

8. Paik, op. cit., pp. 47f.

9. Cf. Part II, chapt. 4.

10. Saltau, op. cit., p. vii.

11. For comprehensive statistics of the Presbyterian Church of Korea between 1884–1927, see C. A. Clark, *The Korean Church and the Nevius Methods*, Appendix II, pp. 263–272.

12. A. W. Wasson, *Church Growth in Korea*, New York, 1934; cf. chapt. 4.

13. K. S. Latourette, *A History of the Expansion of Christianity*, vol. 1, p. xv.

14. Cf. chapt. 4.

15. Rhodes, op. cit., p. 387.

16. Verbatim proceedings of the "First Korean Congress" held in the Little Theatre, 17th and Delancey Streets, Philadelphia, April 14–16, 1919, pp. 50f.

17. Cf. chapts. 4 and 5.

18. At a later date, Communists changed the word "*Hanŭnim*" to "People" only to violate the grammatical structure. The Korean verb is conjugated with rigid social distinction in form. If it is God who protects the nation, the verb stands on the highest form, while if it is the "people," then the form should be the lower one. The Communists had failed to squeeze the lower form into the song because of its metric difficulties.

19. *The Korean Mission Field*, vol. 4 (May 1908), p. 65; *Annual Report of the Board of Missions M. E. Church South* (1908), p.10; cf. Paik, op .cit., p. 353.

20. *North Presbyterian Report for 1907*, pp. 283f.

21. A. J. Brown, *Report on a Second Visit to China, Japan and Korea*, 1909, p. 85.

22. According to the Korean government statistics, as of July 1, 1994, Christians are 24.1 percent, with Protestants 18.2 percent, and Catholics 5.9 percent.

23. James H. Grayson, *Korea: A Religious History*, 1989, p. 206.

Chapter Three

1. Rudolf Sohm, *Kirchengeschichte in Grundriss,* Zweite Aufl. Leipzig, 1888, p. 3.

2. Cf. Yi Sangbaek, *Hanguk Munhwasa Yŏngu Nongo* (Studies on Cultural History of Korea), Seoul, 1948, p. 67.

3. Cf. Kim Wŏnyong, *Hanguk Kohwalja Kaeyo* (A Short History of Movable Type Printing of Old Korea, with English resume), Seoul, 1955.

4. Maurice Courant, *Bibliographie Coréene, Tableau Litteraire de la Corée, Contennant la nomenclature des Ouvrages publiés dans ce pays jusqu'en 1890,* Paris, 1894, Tome I, Introduction, cxlf.

5. Cf. C. W. Rufus, "Astronomy in Korea," *Transactions, Korea branch of the Royal Asiatic Society,* vol. XXVI, 1936, pp. 1–48.

6. Literary works of these men were collected in the *Ssu-ku Ch'uan-shu* (Concordance of Chinese Literature assembled under imperial orders 1772–1774), Beijing.

7. Cf. chapt. 7.

8. *Koryŏ sa,* Biography of Chŏng Tojŏn.

9. His treatise *Pulssi chappyŏn* (Discourses on Buddha) consists of radical criticisms in nineteen chapters. For further information, see Youn Eul Sou, *Le Confucianism en Corée,* Paris, 1939, pp. 130–133.

10. *Sambong chip,* Chŏng Tojŏn volume *passim.*

11. Cf. K. S. Latourette, *The Chinese and Their Culture,* revised ed., New York, 1946, p. 244.

12. Cf. Henri Bernard Maitre, *Sagesse Chinoise et Philosophie Chrétienne,* Paris, 1935, pp. 89f.

13. It is believed that the entire literary works written by the prolific Chu Hsi were reprinted and published in Korea. Only two are absent from the list of Korean editions of Chu Hsi's works. There are twenty-nine entries included in this list. Evidence shows that Hayashi Razan, the noted Japanese Confucian of the seventeenth century, who read Korean books extensively, studied neo-Confucianism mainly from Korean sources

which include at least sixteen books. Cf. Y. Abe, "Hayashi Razan's Confucianism and Korea," *Chosen Gakuho,* No. 10, December 1956, pp. 1–45.

14. Cf. George Peter Murdock, *Social Structure,* New York, 1949.

15. Hiaku Nanun [Paek Namun], *Chosen Shakai Keizai-shi* (Social Economic History of Korea), vol. 1, Tokyo, 1933.

16. Cf. Nicolas Berdyaev, *The Meaning of History,* English tr., New York, 1936, p. 212.

17. Yi Ik, *Sŏngho sasŏl.*

18. Ibid., on calendar.

19. Ibid.

20. Cf. Latourette, *A History of Christian Missions in China,* New York, 1929, pp. 102f.: "The calendar occupied an important place in China. Its acceptance by a conquered nation was recognition of the suzerainty of Peking and in other ways it was of political significance. It was used, too, throughout the Empire to determine lucky and unlucky days for weddings, funerals and various events and transactions of social and business life. [Matteo] Ricci had noticed its importance. He therefore urged [the Jesuit Society] to send out an expert astronomer. . . ."

21. Hu Shih, *The Chinese Renaissance,* pp. 31–33; cf. Bernard-Maître, Sagesse Chinoise, pp. 194f.

22. To be faithful to the relationship to the Ming dynasty with whom she had entered alliance, Korea was reluctant to cooperate with the Manchus, the conquerors of the Ming. The prince, the heir to the throne, was taken hostage to Beijing by the angry Manchus who came to invade the country. In Beijing he was approached by the Jesuit missionary and the director of the observatory of the Ch'ing at that time, Adam Schall von Bell. We have described their meeting and friendship (cf. chapt. 1). The prince died some three months after returning home from his captivity. It is apparent that he was deeply influenced by Christian doctrines. If he had lived long enough to exert influence in the government, the entire course of Korean history thereafter may have been a very different one.

23. For a detailed account, see *Yijo sillok* (The Royal History of Yi dynasty) vols. on Injo and Hyojong; cf. Hyŏn Sangyun, *Chosŏn Yuhak sa* (History of Korean Confucianism), Seoul, 1947, pp. 197–213.

Chapter Four

1. Cf. A. J. Toynbee, op. cit., Abridgment II, p. 182.

2. Henri Bernard-Maître, op. cit., p. 94.

3. Paul Dudon, *Saint Ignace de Loyola*, Paris, 1934, pp. 173ff.; cf. Bernard-Maître, op.cit. *"le sincère amour des lettres et du savoir de la Renaissance se joint avec la plus jalouse integrité de la doctrine."*

4. Hsü-kwang-chi's *Euclid Geometry Textbook*. It was actually translated orally by Ricci and recorded by the Chinese scholar by whose name it was generally known. Cf. *Fonti Ricciane*, vol. II, Rome, 1949, pp. 357f., footnotes.

5. *Royal History*, Injo 23rd Year; 27th Year; Hyojong 4th Year; *Kukcho pogam* (The Handbook of Royal Court of Yi dynasty).

6. *Sŏngho sasŏl, Sŏguk ŭi jo* (On the Western Medicine)

7. *Sŏngho sasŏl, Tamch'ŏn jo* (On the Western Astronomy).

8. *Yi Imyŏng Ip Yŏngyŏng sŏyanginsŏ* (On Yi Imyŏng's Meeting with Westerners in Peking). *Kukcho pogam*, Injo 9th Year.

9. *Kukcho pogam*, Injo 9th Year.

10. Translation by Vincent Gronin in his *The Wise Man from the West*, London, 1955, p. 219.

11. Johannes Betrray, *Die Akkommodationsmethode*. p. 167; cf. chapt. 5.

12. With the French fleet under the command of Admiral Roze in 1866; with American Pacific Fleet under the command of Rear Admiral Rodgers in 1871.

13. *Choix des Lettres Édifiantes*, vol. 3, Paris, 1808, p. 247.

14. This booklet was translated into French, German, and English not long after its publication in Dutch. Four editions in Dutch are known. It appeared in English in at least two of the famous old English collections of travel, viz., that of Churchill and that of Astlay & Pinderton. Cf. foreword by M. N. Trollope of the modern publication in *Transactions of the Korea Branch of Royal Asiatic Society*, vol. IX, p. 19.

15. English tr. from French text, *Transactions of Korea Branch of Royal Asiatic Society*, vol. IX, p. 106.

16. Ibid., vol. II, p. 106. Also *The Royal History, Hyojong vol.*

17. William Elliot Griffis, *Corea, the Hermit Nation*, 7th ed., 1904, p. 168.

18. *The Royal History, Hyojong vol.*

19. John McLeod, *Voyage of His Majesty's Ship Alceste to China, Corea and the Island of Lew Chew; with an Account of Her Shipwreck*, London, 3rd ed., 1820, pp. 43–47.

20. Carl Friedrich Augustus Gutzlaff, *Journal of Three Voyages Along the Coast of China in 1831, 1832, with Notices of Siam, Corea, and the Loochoo Islands*, London, 1834.

21. Ibid., pp. 323–324.

22. Dallet, op. cit., vol. 1, p. 376. Pendant l'été de cette même année, le pavillon britannique se montrait sur les côtes de la Corée. Un navire marchand, expédie probablement par quelques agents des sociétés blbliques, aborda près de l'ile appelée Quen-san, presque à l'entrée de la formée par la Côte Ouest de la province de Tsing-tsieng. L'éetonnement fut general, et les chrétiens surtout étaient en grand emoi, car ce navire portait écret sur son pavillon, en gros caractères chinois: Religion de Jesus-Christ. Quelques chrétiens, pensant recontrer des frères, s'empressèrent d'aller a bard, sans s'inquiter des mauvaises affaires qu'ils pouvaient s'attirer de la part du gouvernement; mais ils furent bien surpris quand, à leur arrivée, un ministre protestant les salua avec ces paroles qui sont sacrementelles parmi les païnes; "Que l'esprit de la terre vous benisse!" A ces mots les neophytes voyant qu'ils s'étaient trompés, et deviant qu'un peige était tendu a leur bonne foi, se retirèrent en toute hâte, sans même reponde au salut, et ne reparurent plus.

23. Gutzlaff, op. cit., vol. 1, pp. 325–326.

24. Ibid., p. 356.

25. *The Royal History, Chŏngjong vol.*

26. Ibid., Sunjo vol. on the 1st Year of Sunjo.

27. Ibid., Sunjo 1st Year, August.

28. Ibid., Kojong 2nd Year.

29. Ibid., Hŏnjong, Chŏngmi.

30. Two of the American vessels that made expeditions along the Western coast of the Korean Peninsula suffered shipwrecks in 1866. It was May 12th when a steamship "surprise" met tragedy off the Chŏlsan coast. The crew was sent back home via China and the Korean officials in the nearby town Chŏlsan rendered their services as were required. But another vessel, the *General Sherman,* met a different fate some months later in September (July in the Korean lunar calendar which was still being used). She was burned on July 27th by the Koreans when she forced her way deep into the peninsula from the Yellow Sea on the Taedong River. There was an armed conflict, and all the crew on board were killed. The fate of this American vessel is well publicized and remembered by Koreans because it had a direct relation to Korean church history. Thomas, a Scottish Protestant missionary whose goal was to reach the "hermit nation," was on board and died with the crew.

31. *P'yŏngan Kamsa Pak Kyusu Changgye* (Report of Pak Kyusu, the Governor of the P'yŏngan Province).

32. Ibid.

33. Ibid.

34. "Ch'oe Nanhŏn" is thought to be a transliteration of the name of the ill-fated vessel, *General Sherman,* from which apparently Thomas, with a flare of humor, got his inspiration for his three-syllable Chinese name.

35. *Hwanghae Kamsa Pak Sŭnghwi Ch'igye* (Report of Pak Sŭnghwi, Governor of Hwanghae Province).

36. *P'yŏngan Kamsa Yi Yongsang Ch'igye* (Report of Yi Yongsang, Governor of P'yŏngan Province).

37. Ibid.

38. The Catholic persecution which was started right after the establishment of Christianity in Korea in the 1770s, persisted during the whole period until 1882. It reached its zenith with Taewŏngun's persecution (1866–1870), in which no fewer than ten thousand Catholics were martyred. In fact, Thomas's tragic visit coincided with the early phase of this persecution.

39. Korea made treaties with the United States in 1882; with Great Britain in 1883; with Russia and Italy in 1884; with France 1886; with Austria-Hungary in 1892; with Belgium in 1901; and with Denmark in 1902.

40. Cf. chapts. 5 and 7. Neo-Shintoism prevailed in Japan during the period of her acculturation. Buddhism was curtailed by the newly awakened Shinto zeal. Shintoism played the leading role in controlling the former long-time partner in syncretism: Buddhism-Ryobu Shinto, and promoted its position to that of a state religion.

41. L. G. Paik, op. cit., pp. 393f.

42. Cf. Chŏng Inbo, *Tamwŏn Kukhak sango* (Tamwŏn's Manuscripts in Korean Studies), Seoul, 1955, pp. 70–102.

43. Cf. chapts. 7 and 9.

44. John R. Mott.

45. A. W. Wasson, *Church Growth in Korea*, New York, 1934.

46. Cf. Ernst Troeltsch, *The Social Teaching of the Christian Churches*, 2 vols., English tr., New York, 1931; H. Richard Niebuhr, *The Social Sources of Denominationalism*, New York, 1929, reprint, 1954.

47. R. E. Speer, and H. T. Kerr, *Report on Japan and China*, New York, 1927, p. 52. Cf. also Wasson op. cit., p. 127.

48. George M. McCune, *Korea Today*, Harvard University Press, 1950, pp. 31–32; cf. Andrew J. Grajdanzev, *Modern Korea*, New York, 1944, p. 84.

49. Liston Pope, *Millhands and Preachers*, Yale University Press, 1942.

Chapter Five

1. Cf. A. J. Toynbee, *A Study of History*, "Challenge and Response," vol. I, pp. 271–335, vol. II, passim.

2. The term "accommodation" is used in connection with a special missionary method. Cf. Josef Schmidlin, *Katholische Missiongeschichte*, Steyr, 1925; Johannes Thauren, *Die Akkommodation in Katholischen Heidenapostolat*, Münster, 1927; Johannes Bettray, *Die Akkommodationsmethode des P. Matteo Ricci, S.J. in China*, Rome, 1955.

3. Der Missionar in "Volksanschauungen und Volksgewohnheiten alles bekämpfen und eliminierren [muss], das aus dem eigentlichen Heidentum stammend dem Christentum direkt entgegengesetzt ist, allerdings ebenfalls mit möglichstem Masshalten und klugen Takt unter Berücksichtigung aller erlaubten Volksgebräuche," Schmidlin, op. cit., p. 220. Cf. Bettray, op. cit., p. xxviii.

4. Anton Huonder, *Der heilige Ignatius von Loyola und der Missionsberuf der Gesellschaft Jesu*, Aachen, 1922, p. 117. Deutlich ist überall zu erkennen, dass die sogennannte Jesuitische Akkommodationmethode tätsächlich auf Ignatius zurückgeht. Er ist ein überzeugter Anhänger derselben, freilich in seinem Sinne. Bei ihm ergab sie sich folgerichtig aus dem grossen Grundgedanken, den er an die Spitze seiner Exerzitien stellt. Danach gibt es nur einen absoluten Wert: Die grössere Ehre Gottes. Alles andere, es mag sein, was es will, hat nur relativen Wert. Es ist gut, wenn es zur Ehre Gottes dient, es ist umso besser, je mehr es dieselbe fordert. Von allen geschöpflichen Dingen, Werkzeugen, Mitteln, Wegen gilt der Grundsatz: tantum quantum. Sie sind zu gebrauchen, inwiefern und soweit sie zum Ziele, d.h. zur Verherrlichung Gottes und zum Heil der Seelen dienen. Cf. Bettray, op. cit., pp. xxiv–xxv.

5. Schmidlin, op. cit., pp. 38f.

6. Ibid., pp. 24f.

7. Cf. chapts. 6 and 7.

8. For an excellent summary, see Latourette, op. cit., pp. 102–155.

9. I Cor. 9:22. American translation by Good Speed.

10. Jone, *Gesetzbuch des kanonischen Rechtes*, p. 145: "Alle Kleriker sollen ein für ihren Stand passendes Klerikales Gewand tragen, wie es den rechtmässigen partikulären Gevohnheiten und den Vorschriften des Ortsordinarius entspricht." Quoted in Bettray, op. cit., p. 1.

11. Bettray, op. cit., p. 2.

12. Ibid., p. 4.

13. Ibid., p. 16.

14. Ibid., p. 25.

15. Ibid., p. 35

16. Ponti Ricciane, I, p. 197; cf. chapt. 7.

17. Thauren, op. cit., p. 56. Quoted in Bettray, op. cit., p. 43.

18. Cf. Bettray, op. cit., p. 67.

19. Cf. chapt. 8 and present chapter below.

20. *Brief Riccis vom 10. Mai 1605 an P. Costa*; cf. Bettray, op. cit., p. 256.

21. *Una grande dispute che il P. Matteo Ricci Hebbe con un Ministro degli idoli molto famoso sopre le cose della santa fede.* Cf. *Fonti Ricciane*, II, pp. 72.

22. Cf. ibid.

23. A recent English biographer pictured the scene of the encounter lucidly in a very convincing way. Cf. Cronin, pp. 143.

24. Fonti Ricciane, II, p. 72.

25. *Briefwechsel* f. 4b, quoted in Bettray, op. cit., p. 257.

26. *Briefwechsel mit dem Bonzen Shen Lien-chih*, Peking nach 1607, f. 20a–f., 21a., f. 8a.

27. "Im Kampfe gegen den Buddhismus kan es Ricci nicht wenig zustatten, nachweisen zu können, das der Buddhismus keine eigentliche Nationalreligion Chinas war." Bettray, p. 258.

28. *Sotria dell' introduzione del Cristianesimo in Cina scritta da Matteo Ricci, S. J.*, New edition by Pasquale Me. D'Elia, Rome, 1942, quoted in Bettray, p. 269.

29. Cf. chapts. 7 and 10.

30. Cf. Bettray, op. cit., p. 270 footnote.

31. Ricci made a strict distinction between the usage of *"sheng"* in Confucianism and Christianity. In his *T'ien-chu-shih-i,* the Chinese literatus, the partner of the dialogue, thinks aloud that the Christian *"sheng-jen,"* that is, Christ, must have been an extraordinary man, like Confucius, not God. To this the Western literatus tries to elaborate the Christian usage of *"sheng"* and explains that though great and *sheng* he was, Confucius was no longer a *"sheng"* in the Christian sense, because he was a son of man. Cf. *T'ien-chu shih-i,* chapt. VIII.

32. Matteo Ricci, op. cit., chapt. II.

33. Cf. Bernard-Maître, op. cit., p. 107.

34. Ibid.

35. Opere Storieche, tome I, p. 265, quoted in ibid., pp. 106f. *"accommodaient au génie de la Chine tout ce qu'il pouvait se rappeler de nos philosophes, de nos saints et des auteurs anciens ou modernes."*

36. Bernard-Maître, op. cit., p. 103. *"un écrit où les raisons d'ordre naturel seraient appuyées au moyen des arguments tirés des livres chinois."*

37. Opere Storiche, tome II, p. 207, quoted in ibid., p. 103. *"J'ai noté beaucoup de passages qui sont en faveur des choses de notre foi, comme l'unité de Dieu, l'immortalité de l'âme, la gloire des bienheureux, etc."*

38. Ibid., p. 102.

39. Bettray, op. cit., p. 242.

40. Bernard-Maître, op. cit., p. 111.

41. Ch. Kortholt, *Leibnitii Epistolae,* II, 249ff., quoted in Franz Rudolf Merkel, *G. W. von Leibniz und die China-Mission,* Leipzig, 1920, p. 106, footnote 1. *"Pour moi, avec la permission de ce bon père [Ricci], et de ceux de nos pères qui le suivent, je suis d'un sentiment contraire, et je croy que les Anciens ont été aussi Athées."*

42. Anton Huonder, *Der Chinesische Ritenstreit,* Aachen, 1921, p. 11ff.

43. Op. cit., p. 107. *"Il devait donc d'une certaine manière dépasser le confucianisme."*

44. Thauren, op. cit., p. 85f.; cf. Bettray, op. cit., p. 163.

45. "The revolt in the seventeenth century against the rational philosophy of the Sung and Ming dynasties, and the development of a new technique in classical scholarship in the last three hundred years with its philosophical and historical approach and its strict emphasis on the importance of the documentary evidence—these, too, may be called the Fourth

Renaissance." Hu Shih, *The Chinese Renaissance*, Chicago, 1934, p. 45.
See Bernard-Maître, op. cit., p. 177.

46. Cf. chapt. 1.

47. Yi Ik, *Collection of Works of Sŏngho*, vol. 55, *Comment on T'ien-chu chih-i.*

48. Ibid.

49. *gye chip.*

50. *Yŏrha ilgi, Hokchŏng p'iltam.*

51. Cf. Muraoka Noritsugu, *Shinto-shi (Nihon Shiso Shi Kenkyu*, vol. 1), Tokyo, 1956.

52. Hirata Atzutane, *Ko-shi sei-bun*, Section I.

53. Ibid., Sections I and X.

54. *Hon-kyo Kai-hen, Complete Works of Hirata Atzutane*, vol. II.

55. Found in Ricci's *Chi-jen-shih-pien.*

56. *Hon-kyo kai-hen*, vol. II, p. 13.

57. Charles Allen Clark, *The Korean Church and the Nevius Methods*, New York, 1930; Peter Beyerhaus, *Die Selbständigkeit der Jungen Kirchen als Missionarisches Problem*, Barmen, 1956, pp. 216–255.

58. Mateer, *A Review of Methods of Mission Work*, Shanghai, 1900, p. 32; cf. Clark, op. cit., p. 13.

59. Reprinted in book form by the Presbyterian Press, Shanghai in 1886; 2nd ed. by Foreign Missions Library of the Foreign Mission Board, Presbyterian Church USA, in 1899.

60. Underwood, *The Call of Korea*, 1908, p. 190.

61. Beyerhaus, op. cit., p. 17.

62. Ibid., pp. 31–44.

63. Ibid., p. 45.

64. "Outline of Missionary Policy," in *Report of the Select Committee*, p. 44, quoted in Beyerhaus, p. 55.

65. *Allegemeine Missions-Nachrichten*, 50, quoted in Beyerhaus, p. 41.

66. Clark, op. cit., p. 12.

67. Ibid., p. 13

68. *The Call of Korea*, op. cit., pp. 109f.

69. Samuel Moffat, *Quarter Centennial Report,* Korea Mission, Presbyterian Church USA, 1919, p. 18.

70. Cf. *Minutes 1921 Chosen Mission, Presbyterian Church USA, 1921,* pp. 83, 85; 1922, p. 89. Cf. Rhodes, ed., op. cit., pp. 488f.

71. Charles Allen Clark, *The Korean Church and the Nevius Methods,* op. cit., 1930.

72. Ibid., pp. 21f.

73. Ibid., pp. 23f.

74. Ibid., pp. 24f.

75. Ibid., p. 27.

76. Ibid., pp. 29f.

77. Ibid., p. 30.

78. Ibid.

79. Ibid., "Misapprehensions of the Methods," pp. 37–53.

80. Yi Kwang Su, "Defects of the Korean Church Today," *The Korea Mission Field,* vol. 19, No. 12, 1918, p. 254, quoted in L. G. Paik, op. cit., p. 206.

81. Clark, op. cit., p. 74. Cf. R. E. Speer, *Report of a Visit to Korea,* 1897, p. 10.

82. "Only a faintest glow of yellow light seeps through an occasional paper covered door. From within a snug little home come the muffled strains: 'Yessu, Yessu, Kweehan Yessu (Jesus, Jesus, Precious Jesus).' A little family of plainest people, like thousands of others, are having their family worship before stretching out for their well-earned rest. . . ." Arch Campbell, *The Christ of the Korean Heart,* 1954, p. 8.

83. Paik, op. cit., p. 302.

84. Ibid.

85. Yi Kwang Su, op. cit., p. 254, quoted in Paik, op. cit., p. 206.

86. Clark, op. cit., p. 45.

87. Ibid., pp. 125f.

88. Ibid., p. 220.

89. A missionary nickname given to the Korean leaders who came back home upon completion of their theological training abroad.

90. Karl Hartenstein, *Die Mission als Theologisches Problem,* Berlin, 1933, passim.

Chapter Six

1. The term is extensively employed by David Pareus, who called the Lutherans and the Reformed to the *Irenicum sive de unione evangelicorum concilianda* (Heidelberg 1614–1615); and Georg Calixtus, who was the author of the abortive "syncretic" controversy in the seventeenth century, in the face of the perpetual division of Protestantism.

2. His article on "syncretism" in the *New Schaff-Herzog Encyclopedia of Religious Knowledge.*

3. M. Pinard de la Boullaye, *L'Étude Comparée des Religions*, II, Ses Methods, 2e ed., Paris, 1925, p. 518. Table des Norms de Choses.

4. Toynbee, op. cit., vol. V, p. 534.

5. Cf. ibid., vol. V, pp. 530f.

6. Ibid.

7. Adolf Harnack, *The Mission and Expansion of Christianity in the First Three Centuries*, 7 vols., English tr., New York, 1908.

8. According to Harnack, "Christianity was not originally syncretic itself, for Jesus did not belong to this circle of ideas, and it was his disciples who were responsible for the primitive shaping of Christianity" (p. 38). Christianity became syncretic (II. p. 391). That was the price which Christianity had to pay to win the pagan world in which it established its church. "After the middle of the third century A.D., Christianity fails to be considered as syncretic religion in the fullest sense"(II, p. 393), and became a "syncretic religion par excellence"(II, p. 394).

9. Ibid., I, pp. 121f.

10. Ibid., p. 127.

11. Ibid., p. 131.

12. Ibid., p. 145f.

13. Hendrik Kraemer, *The Christian Message in a Non-Christian World*, New York, reprint, 1946, p. 200.

14. Toynbee, op. cit., IV, p. 225.

15. Roland Bainton, *The Reformation of the Sixteenth Century*, Boston, 1952, pp. 128–129.

16. Cf. chapt. 8.

17. E. Troeltsch, *Die Absolutheit des Christientums und die Religions-geschichte*, Tübingen, 3. Aufl., 1929, p. 20.

18. Toynbee's prayer in the gandiose finale to his ten volume work, *A Study of History* (X. pp. 143):

Christe, audi nos.
Christ Tammuz, Christ Adonis, Christ Asiris, Christ
    Balder,
hear us,
by whatsoever name we bless thee for suffering death for
    our salvation.
Christe Jesu, exaudi nos.
Buddha Gautama, show us the path that will lead us out
    of our afflictions.
Sancta Dei Genetrix, intercede pronobis.
Mother May, Mother Isis, Mother Cybele, Mother Ishtar,
    Mother Kwanyin,
have compassion on us,
by whatsoever name we bless thee for bringing our Savior
    into the world . . .

19. Toynbee, ibid., V, pp. 439ff.

20. In his book *Vishnu Narayana*, Rudolf Otto observes that "the majority of the adherents of different religions are hardly aware of the authentic content of their own religion and de facto live in religions of second degree. He calls it *Religio Publica*." H. Kraemer, *Religion and the Christian Faith*, Philadelphia, 1956, p. 43.

21. D. T. Suzuki, *Outlines of Mahayana Buddhism*, Chicago, 1908, p. 13.

22. Cf. chapt. 7.

23. Cf. James Moody Gustafson, *Community and Time: A Study of Church from a Sociological and Social, Philosophical Perspective* (a doctoral dissertation submitted to Yale University), 1955.

24. Cf. chapt. 7.

25. Romans 10:14.

26. Eugene A. Nida, *God's Word in Man's Language*, New York, 1952, passim.

27. Wilhelm von Humbolt, quoted in E. Cassirer, *Language and Myth*, English tr., New York, 1946, p. 9.

28. Walbert Buhlmann, *Die Christliche Terminologie als Mission-methodologisches Problem*, Schöneck-Beckenried, Switzerland, 1950, p. 9.

29. Ibid., 24ff.

30. Ibid., pp. 28ff.

31. Ibid., pp. 12f. Wer erfahren hat, wie die Naturvölker durch und durch von der eigenen Religion erfasst sind, wie aber umgekehrt diese Religion auf vagen, verschwommennen Vorstellungen beruht, der weiss, dass das Christentum als siegreiche Gegenkraft war unbedingt das Erlebnismässige mitbringen muss, aber ebenso sehr ein klares, scharf umrissenes Wissen. Nur so kann dem Missionar die Enttäuschung erspart bleiben, den krassesten heidenchristlichen Syncretismus gebraut zu haben, der ganze Gruppen unvermerkt dem Prediger einer chrislichen Häresie anheimfallen zu lassen.

32. Comparatively well-studied examples within the field of missionary enterprise in the simpler societies can be seen in D. W. T. Shropshire, *The Church and Primitive Peoples: The Religious Institution and Beliefs of the Southern Bantu and Their Bearing on the Problems of the Missionary*, (with a foreword by R. R. Marrett), London, 1938, especially Part II, pp. 333–454; H. Ian Hogbin, *Experiments in Civilization: The Effects of European Culture on the Native Community of the Solomon Islands*, London, 1933, pp. 173–219.

Chapter Seven

1. Harry A. Rhodes, ed., *History of the Korea Mission, Presbyterian Church USA 1884–1934*, Seoul, 1934, p. 47.

2. G. H. Jones, "The Spirit Worship of the Koreans," *Transactions, Korea Branch of the Royal Asiatic Society*, vol. II, Part II, 1901, p. 39.

3. H. B. Hulbert, *The Passing of Korea*, New York, 1906, p. 403.

4. J. S. Gale, *Korea in Transition*, New York, 1909, p. 70.

5. H. G. Underwood, *The Religions of Eastern Asia*, New York, 1910, p. 94.

6. Cf. H. G. Underwood, "A Partial Bibliography of Occidental Literature on Korea from Early Times to 1930," *Transactions, Korea Branch of the Royal Asiatic Society*, vol. XXIV, Seoul, 1935.

7. Cf. C. A. Clark, *Religions of Old Korea*, New York, 1932, pp. 210.

8. Cf. chapt. 8.

9. Cf. chapt. 10.

10. Cf. Julins Jakob Schaarb, *Geschichte und Begriff, eine Kiritische Studie zur Geschichtemethodologie von E. Troeltsch und Max Weber*, 1945.

11. Peter Beyerhaus, *Die Selbständigkeit der Jungen Kirchen*, p. 216.

12. His "Preface to the Nanllang Inscription" recorded in *Samguk sagi*, vol. 4.

13. Cf. chapt. 11 and conclusion.

14. Kim Chewŏn, "Han Dynasty Mythology and the Korean Legend of Tan Gun," Archives of the Chinese Art Society of America, III, 1948–49, pp. 43–48. Kim, the former collaborator with Carl Hentze at the Museum of Antwerp, Belgium, provided an interpretation to the hitherto unidentified scenes depicted on two of the stone slabs of Wu Liang Tzu of the Han dynasty. Kim identified the figures and the dramatic scenes depicted with the Tangun legend of Korean origin.

15. Imanishi Ryu, *Chosen Koshi no Kenkyu*, Seoul, 1937.

16. For further information on Wu Liang Tzu, see E. Chavannes, *Mission Archaeologique dans la Chine Septentrionale*, Paris, 1909; W. Fairbank, "The Offering Shrines of Wu Liang Tzu," *Harvard Journal of Asiatic Studies*, V (1941), 1, pp. 103f.; C. Hentze, *Die Sakralbronzen und ihre Bedeutung in den frühchinesischen Kulturen*, Antwerp, 1947; C. Hentze, *Altchinesische Bronzen und Kultdarstellungen*, Antwerp, 1947.

17. Cf. W. Schmidt, *Handbuch der Vergleichenden Religionsgeschichte*, Münster, 1930, XIV, pp. 213; W. Schmidt, *Der Ursprung der Gottesidee*, I, Freiburg, 1949, pp. 752–766.

18. Etymologically speaking, Korean *kom* (bear) may have been derived from the common linguistic stock from which the Ainu *kamui* (bear-god) or Japanese *kami* (god) also originated. Cf. chapt. 2.

19. A. I. Hallowell, *Bear Ceremonialism in the Northern Hemisphere*, Philadelphia, 1926.

20. Hendrik Kraemer, *The Christian Message in a Non-Christian World*, op. cit., p. 156 et passim.

21. Ibid., pp. 201f.

22. J. J. M. De Groot, *Universismus, Die Grundlage der Religion und Ethik, des Staatswesens und der Wissenschaften Chinas*, Berlin, 1918, p. 2. In Wirklichkeit sind die . . . drei Religionen Äste eines gemeinsamen Stammes, der seit uralten Zeiten bestanden hat; dieser Stamm ist die Religion des Universismus . . . Universismus, wie ich sie von jetzt ab bezeichnen will, ist die eine Religion Chinas; die drei Religionen aber bilden nur ihre integrierenden Bestandteile. Deshalb fühlt sich auch der Chinese gleichmässig heimisch in ihnen, ohne durch widerstrebende und einander unvertragliche Dogmen beschwert zu sein.

23. Carsun Chang, *The Development of Neo-Confucian Thought*, New York, 1958, p. 48.

24. *Hung-ming-chi Hou-hsu, Kuang-hung-ming-chi*, vol. I. In a book popularly attributed to Lie-tzu, one finds a high official Pi asking Confucius: "Who is the Saint?" "Fu-tzu [Confucius] solemnized his expression and kept reverent silence a while and spoke: 'Ch'iu [Confucius], that is, I heard that there is in the West a Saint who does not rule, but the world is not rebellious. He does not inculcate but the people believe in him. He does not propagate, yet the people gladly follow him." However, conclusive evidence shows that the said document, *Lieh-tzu,* was a latter day fabrication of a Confucian-Buddhist in either Wei or Chin dynasties. Cf. T'ang, Yung-t'ung, *Han Wei Liang-chin Nan-pei Ch'ao Fo-chiao Shih*, vol. 1, 2nd ed., Peking, 1955, pp. 4f.

25. Cf. ibid., p. 16.

26. In chapter 20, *Li-huo-lun,* Mou-tzu graded his contemporary documents according to the degrees of exaggerations.

27. T'ang, op. cit., pp. 16–46.

28. In its original form, it contained some 170 books, among which there are only 67 books remaining. It is supposed to be the earliest work on Taoism. Cf. Chang, op. cit., p. 42, footnote.

29. *Hua-hu-ching.*

30. *Hou-han-shu* 72, Biography of Prince Ying of Ch'u.

31. Yang Hsuan-chih, *Lo-yang Chia-lan-chi*, IV.

32. Cf. Tokiwa Daijo, *Shina ni okeru Bukkyo to Jukyo, Dokyo,* Tokyo, 1930, pp. 512f.

33. *Wen-shih-ch'uan.*

34. Paul Radin, *Primitive Religion: Its Nature and Origin*, New York, 1937, passim.

35. Rudolf Otto, *Vishnu Narayana.* See chapt. 6.

36. Quoted in *Hung-ming-chi*, III.

37. *Li-chi*, on Music.

38. Chou Yu-t'ung, *Chu Hsi*, Shanghai, 2nd ed., 1934, p. 5.

39. See chapters 5 and 8.

40. Tokiwa, op. cit., pp. 374–376.

41. Cf. K. S. Latourette, *The Chinese: Their History and Culture*, New York (3rd Rev. ed., 1947), pp. 353–358.

Notes   201

42. Lo Erh-kang, *T'ai-p'ing-t'ien-kuo Shi-hua*, Nanking, 1956.

43. Latourette, *The Chinese*, op. cit., pp. 355 and 356.

44. Latourette, *A History of Christian Missions in China*, op. cit., p. 190.

45. E. P. Broadman, *Christian Influence upon the Ideology of the T'aiping Rebellion 1851–1864* (A Doctoral Dissertation, University of Wisconsin), Madison, 1952, p. 114.

46. Latourette, *A History of Christian Missions in China*, op. cit., pp. 285–286.

47. Toynbee underestimated the syncretism between Shintoism and Buddhism, initiated by Gyo-gi Bosatsu (Bodhisattva), a grandson of a Korean immigrant to Japan, and developed by Kobo Daishi (cf. chapt. 9). To fit this Japanese example to his own preplanned scheme Toynbee rendered it to be "almost exact parallel to the process of the introduction of a Greek divinity, *de toutes pieces*, into a Latin vacuum." According to him, the *Ryobu* Shinto was "not a case of syncretism at all," but an arbitrary "matter of nomenclature" which is involved in "a uniform cultural process." Cf. Toynbee, op. cit., V, p. 528, esp. footnote 2.

On the contrary, we argue that *Ryobu* Shinto was an exemplary case of syncretism. The "arbitrary" identification of Shinto and Buddhist deities was rather an inevitable process for the Japanese society to make itself a real adherent to Buddhism. It is true that it was only the Shingon sect that explicitly attempted to bring out these essential features of the native religious "responses." But one cannot confine it to the Shingon sect only, by any means, because, as Reischauer perceived correctly, it was a universal phenomenon, especially on the level of the *religio publica* in that society. See A. K. Reischauer, *Studies in Japanese Buddhism*, New York, 1917, p. 98 and p. 338, footnote 17. The average Buddhist or Shintoist in Japan does not hesitate to pay due respect to the *Hotoke* or *Kami* in the temples or shrines regardless of their religious distinctions.

48. Cf. chapt. 5.

49. Georg Schurhammer, *Das kirchliche Sprachproblem in der Japanischen Jesuitmission des 16 u. 17 Jahrhunderts*, Tokyo 1928, pp. 25–33, as is paraphrased and translated by Bernard-Maître, in his *Sagesse Chinoise et Philosophie Chrétienne*, p. 96. "Il crut pouvoir employer le terme "Dainichi" pour désigner Dieu en japonais ... Ce terme était absolument déplacé puisque entre divers sens, il significait la "materia prima," le grand soleil ou la divinité du grand soleil ... Même les organes sexuels du genre humain! ... Dès que des gens scandalises l'en eurent averti, il se remit à parcourir les divers endroits où il avait prêche en disant: Ne priez pas Dainichi."

50. Transliteration has been employed for a long time by the translators of the Buddhist texts into Chinese. So there was no need for the Jesuits to invent any new system. They simply adopted the Buddhist models. From *"Dios"* (*Deus* in Portugese) came the *"De-u-shi,"* which was intended for the pronunciation of *"De-u-s(u)."* However, in Buddhist semitransliteration in China proper the *bodhi* seeds were rendered into *"Bo-de-shi"* which resembles the Japanese Jesuit *"De-u-shi."* In any rate, the general flavor of the entire Kirishitan vocabulary, as a whole, was unmistakably Buddhist. They must have sounded like some Buddhist words to the Japanese ears, except they were strange words of which they could make no meaning whatsoever until they learned from someone who knew. This terminology was put into a good use in Kirishitan literature for the purpose of keeping secrecy when they were driven underground by the persecution. But the transliteration was already in progress when the persecution came.

51. Cf. Koya Tagita, "Transformation of Christianity in a Japanese Farming Village," *Min-jok-gaku Kenkyu* (The Japanese Journal of Ethnology), vol. 18, no. 3, 1953, pp. 1–32 (with English summary). The remnants, circ. 30,000 as of 1953, are called the "Hanare" or Separatists by those former Kirishitans who were reconverted to Catholicism. The Hanare group is subdivided into three subgroups: "Furu-Kirishitan" or Old Kirishitan, "Furu-Chio" or Old Calendar, and "Moto-Chio" or the Original Calendar. The Catholic Calendar, transmitted in 1634 C.E. and revised on many occasions since, is kept with "great care" among them.

52. Cf. chapt. 5.

53. Soun Kŏsa Yi Kyugyŏng, *Oju yŏn mun.*

54. Cf. chapt. 10.

Chapter Eight

1. P. Brou, "Les Jésuites sinologuoes de Pékin et leur Éditeurs de Paris," *Revue l'Histoire des Missions,* 1934, II, p. 552. "accusé d'avoir prêché l'indifférence en religion, pursuivi des chiméres d'une Église dans la China avant Jesus-Christ, substitué à Israël comme nation choisie le peuple chinois. Et ainsi de suit." Cf. Bernard-Maître, *Sagesse Chinoise,* op. cit., p. 144.

2. Cf. chapt. 5; J. Bettray, op. cit., p. 235.

3. Le Comte, *Nouveaux memoires sur l'état présent de la Chine,* II, Paris, 1696, pp. 108–109. Paraphrased by M. Pinot, *La Chine et la formation de l'esprit philosophique en France,* p. 91–92, and quoted by Bernard-Maître, op. cit., pp. 132–133. [L]a religion chinoise semble avoir conservé

intactes et pures au course des ages les premieres verités révélées par Dieu aux premiers hommes. "La Chine, plus hereuse dans ses commencements que nul autre peuple du monde a puisé presque dans la source les saintes et les premières vérités de son ancienne religion." Le Premièrs empereurs bâtirenet des temples à Dieu, et ce n'est pas une petite gloire à la Chine d'avoir sacrifié au Créateur dans le plus ancien temple de l'Univers." La piété primitive se conserva dans le peuple grâce aux empereurs qui prirent soin de l'entretenir, si bien que l'idolâtrie n'arriva pas à se glisser en Chine. "Avant les superstitions dont l'impiété du dieu Fo (Bouddha) infecta la Chine, on n'avait jemais vu d'idoles ou de statues parmi le peuple . . . de sorte que ce peuple a conservé près de deux mille ans la connaissance du véritable Dieu, et l'a honoré d'une maniere qui peut servir d'exemple et d'instruction même aux Chrétiens.

La religion chinoise a ce privilege unique de nous montrer ce que pouvait être la vie humaine à ces âges fortunés où regnaient à la Chine "la paix, la bonne foi et la justice," et en même temps, elle nous explique la facilité que les jésuites éprouvent à convertir la Chine. Les Chinois ne font, en somme, que retrouver dans le christianisme, mais avec plus de clarté et d'évidence, cette religion primitive dont le souvenir n'est pas entièrement oublié chez eux malgré les progrès qu'ont faits par la suite l'idolâtrie et l'atheisme.

4. For information on his life, work, and writings, see J. H. de Prémare, *Dogmes Chrétiens Tirés des Anciens Livres Chinois*, Paris, 1873, p. 13f.

5. Cf. ibid., pp. 14f.

6. Cf. ibid., pp. 16f.

7. Cf. "Lettre [de P. Bayard] au P. Souciet [received on July 28, 1723]," *La Revue d'Extrême-Orient*, 1887, vol. 3, pp. 15–22 as is quoted in Bernard-Maître, op. cit., p. 149.

8. Korthold, ed., *Leibnizii Epistolae*, 3, pp. 15–22, quoted in Bernard-Maître, op. cit., p. 149. Ayant continué cette anné avec la même application l'étude des anciens livers de la Chine, j'au eu le bonheur d'y faire de nouvelles découvertes . . . , le systeme presque entièr de la vraie religion s'y trouve renfermé . . . , les principaux mystères de l'Incarnation du Verbe, de la vie, de la mort du Sauveur, et les principales fonctions de son saint ministère sont contenues comme d'une manière prophétique dans ces precieux monuments de l'antiquité chinoise. Vous seriez étonné aussi bien que moi, de voir que ce n'est que comme un tissu continuel d'ombres, de figures, ou de prophéties des vérités de la loi nouvelle . . . J'ajouterai ce que je crois qu'on doit supposer comme une chose très certaine, savoir que les livers canoniques et les caracteres chinois sont beaucoup plus anciens que les chinois eux-mêmes, et que ce sont des monuments fideles de la tradition la plus ancienne, que les Peres communs de toutes les nations ont

laissés a leurs descendants, et que les Chinois ont conservés plus
soigneusement que les autres.

9. de Prémare, op. cit., p. 20. *"étants fausses, tréméraires et
scandaleuses."*

10. Ibid., p. xiv.

11. There may have been two separate publications of the Ms. I used
the edition of 1878 published by the Bureau des Annales de Philosophie
Chrétienne, Paris. In this edition there is no *Bref Laudatif* to which Bernard-Maître refers. According to Bernard-Maître, this book was published
by the Traditionlistes Catholique du XIXe Siecle, with a *Bref Laudatif de
Leon XIII* (12 Aout 1878), which reads: Vous êtes attachés avec une dili-
gence nouvelle à étudier les Livres sacres des Chinois et les ouvrages des
sages antiques. Vous en avez extrait les Vestiges très clairs des dogmes et
des traditions de notre sainte religion, lesquels vestiges prouvent qu'elle a
été depuis longtemps annoncée dans ces régions et que, par son antiquité,
elle précède de beaucoup les écrits des sages dont les Chinois tirent la
règle et l'enselgnement de leur religion. (Bernard-Maître, op. cit., p. 152)

12. de Prémare, op. cit., p. 22. Voici quel sera le plan de cet ouvrage.—
I. J'expliquerai d'abord différents points dont la connaissance est necessaire
pout l'intelligence du livre.—I. Je parlerai de Dieu en tant que UN et
Trine.—III. Je traiterai (la question) de l'état de Nature integre et
innocente.—IV. Puis de l'état de Nature corrompus, et séparement, de la
rebellion des Anges et de la chute d'Adam.—V. De l'état de Nature réparée
par Jesus-Christ. Ce point, Dieu aidant, sera traité assez longuement tant
à cause de l'importance du sujet que de l'abondance de la matière.

13. Ibid., pp. 8f. Le fin ultérieure et derniere à laquelle je consacre
cette Notice (sa Grammaire), c'est de faire en sorte, si je puis, que toute
la terre sache que la Religion chrétienne est aussi ancienne que le monde,
et que le Dieu-homme a été très certainement connu de celui ou de ceux
qui ont inventé les hieroglyphes de Chine et composé les Kings.

14. Ibid., p. 55.

15. Ibid. Je dois avertir encore une fois les lecteurs que je ne pretends
point que Tien ou Chang-ty soit le "vrai Dieu" que, nous Chrétiens, nous
adorons. C'est pourquoi je traduirai toujours la lettres Tien par le mot
"Ciel" et les caracteres Chang-ty par le "Supreme-Seigneur." Quant à ce
que les Chinois entendent par Tien et Chang-ty, je le laisse au jugement
des savants et surtout à celui de la S. Congregation de la Propagande (of
the Vatican), et même, quant a mon jugement privé, si j'ose en forumuler
un sur cette matière, j'y renoncerai sans retard et sincerement, de qu'il me
consterna qu'il est même un peu désagréable a la sainte Église, hors de
laquelle il n'y a point de salut.

16. Ibid., p. 392. *"ces traditions confuses furent, dans des temps posterieurs, mises par écrit, et amalgamées tant bien que mal, mais offrant encore des souvenirs reconnaissables."*

17. Ibid., p. 152. *"un visage d'homme, un corps de Serpent."*

18. Ibid., p. 204.

19. Ibid., p. 205.

20. *Chuang Tzu.* Cf. ibid., p. 226. Un homme vil meurt pour amasser du bien. Les philosophes meurent pout acqueirir de la renommée. Le nobles meurent pour conserver leur demeure. Le Saint meurt pout sauver l'Univers.

21. Ibid., pp. 247ff.

22. Ibid., pp. 259ff.

23. *Chuang Tzu.* Cf. ibid., p. 330. L'agneau aimela societé, mais il fuit la foule seditieuse. Quand on s'empare de lui, il ne pousse aucun bêlement; quand on le tue, il ne crie point; durant sa vie, il ne manque a aucun devoirl; par sa mort, il remplit toute justice.

24. Ibid., pp. 338ff.

25. Ibid., pp. 401–402. "Apres avoir constate l'identité des Chinois (Sères) et des Syriens, il s'agit de savoir comment ces peuples de l'extrême Orient se sont eux-mêmes appeles Tsin. Ils auraient pris ce nom des Pheniciens ou des Triens, dont le nom en hebreu est Tsyrim, de Tsir, Tyr leur Capital. Les Chinois n'ayant pas de 'r,' its en ont fait Tsin. En identificant les Tsin, ou Chinois, ou Sères de l'Orient avec les Tsir ou Syriens de l'Occident, il ne faudrait pas en conclure que la conlnie chinoise est partie de la Syrie. Il faut dire plutot que ces deux peuples, partis de l'Asie contrale, se sont separés pour aller l'un en Orient et l'autre en Occident." Ibid., pp. 402ff. (Tr.: After having established the identity of the Chinese (Seres) and the Syrians, it is a matter of knowing how these peoples in the Far East were themselves called Tsin. They could have taken this name from the Phoenicians or the Trians, whose name in Hebrew is Tsyrian, from Tsir, Tyr, which was their capital. Chinese have no sound 'r' and their name became 'Tsin.' In identifying the Tsin or the Chinese or the Seres of the Orient with the Tsir or the Syrians of the Occident, it would not be necessary to conclude that the Chinese colony was a part of Syria. Rather, one would say that these two peoples belonging to central Asia separated, one heading towards the Orient and the other towards the Occident.)

26. Ibid. *"identité des 10 premières génération chinoises avec les 10 génération bibliques d'avant le Déluge."*

27. Adam (Homme et Terre Rouge ou Orangée) = Hoang (Terre Rouge ou Orangée), Ty (le Seigneur ou Patriarche). Eve (ou la Vie) = Louy (celle qui entrainte les autres dans son propre mal), Tsou (la grande Aïeule).

28. For a balanced criticism to the Prémarian approach offered by a contemporary Jesuit Antoine Gaubil, see Brucker, "Le B. Antoine Gaubil. Correspondance scientifique d'un missionaire français à Pékin," *Revue du Monde Catholique*, 1884, cf. Bernard-Maître, op. cit., pp. 166f.

29. de Prémare, op. cit., p. 55. *"ne l'a jamais accusé de s'être trompé, ni d'avoir mal compris les anciens livres; au contraire, tous lui ont décerné les plus grands éloges."*

30. Bernard-Maître, op. cit., pp. 135f.

31. Ibid., p. 143.

32. Cf. chapt. 5.

33. Cf. chapt. 8; Bernard-Maître, op. cit., p. 107.

34. Pascal, *Pensées*, petite édition de M. Bunschvig, p. 569. Lequel est le plus croyable des deux, Moïse ou la Chine? Il n'est pas question de voir cela en gros. Je vous dis de quoi aveugler et de quoi éclairer. Par ce mot seul, je ruine tous vos raisonnements. "Mais la Chine obscureit, dites-vous," et je reponds: "La Chine obscureit, mais il y a clarté a trouver; cherchez-la." Il faud donc voir cela en détail, il faut mettre papiers sur table. . . . Différence d'un livre recu d'un peuple, ou qui forme un peuple. Cf. Bernard-Maître, op. cit., p. 138.

35. Leibniz, "Novissima Sinica" (1698–1699), quoted in Bernard-Maître, op. cit., p. 139. Je redoute que bientŏt, sous les rapports, nous ne soyons inferieurs aux Chinois; il sera presque nécessaire de recevoir des missionnaire de chez eux pour en apprendre l'usage et la pratique de la theologie naturelle, de même que nous leur envoyons des missionnaires pour leur enseigner la theologie révélée.

36. Alfred W. Wasson, *Church Growth in Korea*, New York, 1934, pp. 18–21.

37. J. S. Gale, "A History of the Korean People," a series of articles on *The Korea Mission Field*, March 1916–October 1926. [Similar stories are found in Richard Rutt, *James Gale and His History of the Korean People*, (Seoul: Royal Asiatic Society, 1972)—Ed.]

38. Cf. chapts. 4 and 5.

39. Chu Tzu, *Commentary on the Chung-yung*.

40. Cheng I-ch'üan, *T'ai-chi T'u-shuo*. See also Chu Tzu *Wen-chi*, vol. 46 and Chu Tzu *Hsing-li chüan-shu*, vol. 49.

41. Chu Tzu, *Yü-lui*, vol. 1.

42. Cf. Bernard-Maître, op. cit., p. 107.

43. Chou Yü-t'ung, *Chu Hsi*, 2nd ed., 1933, Shanghai, pp. 38–43.

44. Cf. chapt. 7.

45. Cf. Bernard-Maître, "Loexégèses Leibnizienne du systeme philosophique de Tschou-hi," op. cit., Locon VIII, pp. 153ff.

46. Quoted in Bernard-Maître, ibid., pp.160f. Les Chinois appellent la Li (par excellence) l'Être, la Substance, l'Entité. Cette Substance, selon eux, est infinis, éternelle, incrée, incorruptible, sans principe et sans fin. Elle n'est pas seulement le "principe physique" du Ciel, de la terre et des autres choses corporelles; mais encore "le principe moral" des vertus, des habitudes et des autres choses spirituelles. Elle est invisible, elle est parfaite dans sons être au souverain degré; elle est même toute sorte de perfections. Ils l'appellent aussi "l'unité sommaire" ou supreme, parce que comme dans les nombres l'unité en est le principie et qu'elle n'en a point, aussi dans les substances, dans les essences de l'univers, il y en a une qui est souvrainement une, oui "n'est point capable de division" quant à son entité et qui est le principe de toutes les essences qui sont et qui peuvent être dans le monde ... La Li est le "grand Vide" ou Espace, la capacité immense, parce que dans cette Essence universelle toutes les essences particulières sont renfermées. Mais ils l'appellent aussi la "souveraine plénitude" parce qu'elle remplit tout et ne laisse rien de vacant. Elle est étendue au dedan et au dehors de l'univers ... C'est ainsi que nous expliquons l'immensité de Dieu, il est partout et tout est dans lui. Ils appellent la Li "la Nature" des choses, je crois que c'est comme nous disons que Dieu est la "Natura naturante."

47. The Hŏnjong Anti-Christian document prepared by the Royal Scholar Cho Inyong in October, the 5th year of Hŏnjong by the order of the Queen Regent.

48. Cf. chapt. 11.

49. *"Ta-ya,"* in *Shih-ching* (Book of Odes)

50. *Yŏrha ilgi.* Cf. chapt. 3.

51. *Ch'ŏnhakko kŭp Ch'ŏnmunhak Mundap*, English translation by Gale, "A Korean View of Christianity by An Chungbok (1712–1791)," *Korea Magazine*, I, 1917, pp. 262–268. "The foreign missionary claims to worship *T'ien* or God and, in that respect, we are at one, but we do it in a right and proper way, while his is a wicked and deceitful way, and I oppose it. For the Western missionary to call his teaching 'the Religion of God' is most foolish, not to say blasphemous. They think that, if they claim for their teaching the name of the Supreme Ruler of the Universe, no one will dare to oppose them on account of that all-prevailing name. It is like using the name of the Emperor in order to accomplish one's private ends,

a very clever trick, indeed! The Sages of China were very high and very great, and yet they never pretend to equal God Himself. How foolish are these foreign missionaries to speak of their Founder in such extravagant and unreasonable terms!"

52. Cf. chapt. 3.

Chapter Nine

1. Cf. chapts. 1, 2, 3, and 4.

2. Cf. chapt. 4.

3. According to *Samguk sagi* (History of the Three Kingdoms), Buddhism was introduced into the Kingdom of Koguryŏ in 372 C.E.; into the Kingdom of Paekche in 384 C.E.; and into the Kingdom of Silla in 528 C.E.

4. Cf. chapt. 3.

5. Cf. chapts. 7 and 10.

6. Cf. chapt. 11.

7. Cf. Son Chint'ae, *Chosŏn Minjok Munhwa ŭi Yŏngu*, Seoul, 1948, pp. 172f.

8. Cf. chapt. 7.

9. Cf. chapts. 10 and 11.

10. *Samguk sagi*, vol. 4, the paragraph on the 15th year of the era of King Pŏphŭng.

11. *Samguk yusa*, vol. 3, Paragraphs on Hwangnyong-sa Nine-Story Stupa.

12. Cf. Ko Yusŏp, *Hanguk T'ap'a ŭi Yŏngu*, Seoul, 2nd ed. 1954, pp. 9f.

13. *Samguk yusa*, vol. 3, Paragraphs on Hwangnyong-sa Nine-Story Stupa.

14. *Nihon shoki*.

15. Imanishi doubts the authenticity of the will. He places the date of this "false" document half a century later than the date adopted in *Koryŏ sa*. Cf. Imanishi Ryu, "Korai Taiso Gunyo Jitsu-cho ni tsuite," *Toyo Gakuho*, vol. 8, and his posthumous publication *Korai-shi Kenkyu*. But his assumptions were proved to be erroneous by recent scholarship. Cf. Yi Pyŏngdo, *Kuksa Taegwan*, Seoul, 1952, pp. 155f.

16. *Koryŏ sa*, Sega II, Yonsei University Press, vol. I, p. 55.

17. Sŏng Hyŏn, *Yongje Ch'onghwa*.

18. *Koryŏ sa*, Biographies VI, on Ch'oe Sŭngno.

19. Cf. chapt. 3.

20. Cf. chapts. 3 and 7.

21. *Royal History of the Yi dynasty*, Chŏngjong vol. In the 2nd year of Chŏngjong, quoted in Yi Sangbaek, *Hanguk Munhwasa Yŏngu Nongo*, Seoul, 1956, p. 77f.

22. *Royal History of the Yi dynasty*, T'aejong vol. In the 8th year of T'aejong.

23. Ibid.

24. T'aejong vol. 16. In the 8th year of T'aejong.

25. T'aejong vol. 15, Kyeyu Paragraph.

26. Cf. Nohomiya Keiji, "Korai no Hatsikuankai ni Tsuite," *Chosen Gakuho*, no. 9, 1956, pp. 235–250.

27. *Koryŏ sa*, Sega II.

28. Mishina Akihite, "Yong-dong Kami Sho-ko," *Chosen Gakuho*, no. 10, 1956, p. 169; Ninomiya Keiji, "Korai-cho no Jogen Nendokai ni Tsuite," *Chosen Gakuho*, no. 12, 1958, pp. 111–122.

29. Cf. chapt. 6.

30. Cf. chapt. 11.

31. Cf. ibid.

32. Compare the Catholic translation of Lord of Heaven *T'ien-chu* with this Buddhist *T'ien-chu*.

33. Cf. chapt. 11.

34. Cf. chapt. 6.

35. Cf. chapt. 11.

36. Cf. Karl Ludwig Reichelt, *Truth and Tradition in Chinese Buddhism*, English translation, Shanghai, 1927, pp. 44f and passim.

37. Yasukazu Suematsu, "Inscriptions on the Back of Mirŭk Buddha and the Amida Buddha in the Kam San Temple 719 C.E. and 720 C.E.," Appendix 2, pp. 450ff.

38. *Samguk yusa,* vol. 2, the Era of King Hyoso, Paragraph on Chukchirang.

39. *Samguk sagi,* vol. 50, Biographies X.

40. *Taisho Taizokyo,* vol. 15, *Zoku Koshoten,* 24, *Shyaku Zizo Biography.*

41. Cf. *Samguk yusa,* vol. 5, Sinju 6, Milbon ch'oesa.

42. Ibid.

43. *Taisho Taizokyo,* vol. 50, *Kaito Koshoten,* 1, *Shaku Hoku.*

44. Cf. chapt. 11.

45. Cf. C. H. Hamilton, *Buddhism: A Religion of Infinite Compassion,* New York, 1952, pp. 133–135; Takakusu Junjiro, *Azia Minzoku no Chusin Shiso* (The Central Thought of Asian Peoples), Tokyo, 1942, p. 133. [The author has some reason to believe that K'uei-chi, the famous Fa-hsiang master of the T'ang dynasty in China, was a Korean monk, just like his rival Wŏnch'ŭk was. –Ed.]

46. Cf. *Samguk yusa,* vol. 4, *Wŏnhyo Pulbae* and passim; *Kosŏnsa T'anghwat'odap pi;* and *Sung Kao-sheng chuan,* vol. 4.

47. *Samguk yusa,* vol. 5, *Kamt'ong* 7.

48. See some examples. Kyugi: *Amit'a-kyŏng ŭigi* in one volume, *Pulsŏl Amit'a-kyŏng t'ongch'an so,* in three volumes. Wŏnhyo: *Muryansu-kyŏng chongyo* in two volumes, *Pulsŏl Amit'a-kyŏng so* in one volume, and *Yusim allakto* in one volume. Kyŏnghŭng: *Muryangsu-kyŏng yŏnŭisŏlmun ch'an* in three volumes.

49. Cf. Rudolf Otto, *India's Religion of Grace and Christianity Compared and Contrasted,* English tr., New York, 1930, pp. 19f.

50. K. L. Reichelt, op. cit., p. 133.

51. *Transactions, the Korea Branch of the Royal Asiatic Society,* vol. V, part 1, Seoul, 1914, pp. 1–39.

52. Ibid., p. 30.

53. See ibid., p. 2.

54. Ibid., pp. 14, 15, 26f, and passim.

55. Cf. Andrea Eckardt, *A History of Korean Art,* English ed., London & Leipzig, 1929, p. 471; Sekino Tadasi, *Chosen no Kenchiku to Geijutsu* (Architecture and Fine Arts in Korea), Tokyo, 1942, pp. 82f.

56. Gordon, op. cit., p. 19. To prove her point she wrote a book, *Temples of the Orient and Their Message,* London.

57. Eckardt, op. cit., pp. 2, 4, 7, and 27ff.

58. Ibid., p. 28.

59. Ibid.

60. Ibid., p. 32.

61. Ibid.

62. Reichelt, op. cit., p. 132.

63. Ibid., p. 30. "Here it is asserted that the spiritual life which, just at that time, had developed in Turkestan and the north-western part India came to have a stimulating effect on the West as well as on the East. In other words, we stand here before one of the main sources of the spiritual life of the West as well as of the East. On the possibility of Western influences in the formative period of Mahayana, Professor K. B. Westman points out that such a possibility cannot be denied, since in Hanishka's kingdom (i.e., Punjab and Afghanistan) at that time Hellenistic and Persian civilization was not unknown. The religious art, there introduced into Mahayana, was essentially Hellenistic (Gandhara art). There may have been other influences as well from the Hellenistic mystical religions of the Near East. Such a hypothesis might explain the similarity in many of the customs and paraphernalia of worship between Mahayana and Greek and Roman Catholicism, since it is well known that the ancient church borrowed many of these things form these Hellenistic religions. That the Indian Bhakti movement, which advocates an inward consecration to the deity, through prayer and meditation, has also been operative in connection with the later development of Mahayana on Indian ground, is now generally acknowledged, and that China, through its many pilgrims who went to India, took its share from this rich spring, is also certain."

64. Takakusu Junjiro, *Azia Minzoku no Chusin Shiso*, op. cit., pp. 10f.

65. Cf. chapts. 5 and 8.

66. Pak Chiwŏn, *Yŏrha ilgi*; cf. chapt. 5.

Chapter Ten

1. Johannes Bettray, *Die Akkommodationsmethode des P. Matteo Ricci, S.J. in China*, Rome, 1955, p. 267. Ricci hätte mehr hinweisen Können auf die möglichen historischen Zusammenhänge [des Taoismus] mit dem Christentum und hätte daraus ohne Zweifel Argumente geformt für den Übertritt zum Christentum. So aber sieht er im Taoismus praktisch nur Negatives und lehnt das System ebenso wie den Buddhismus ab.

2. Cf. chapt. 7.

3. Bernard-Maître, *Sagesse Chinoise et Philosophie Chrétienne*, op. cit., p. 143. Et comme par la crainte et le respect qu'ils ont pour lui [*T'ien*], ils n'osent pas l'appeler directement par son propre nom, ils ont coutume de l'invoquer sous le nom ciel suprême, de ciel bienfaisant, de ciel universel.

4. In Korean Buddhism, Confucius is worshipped as Yŏdong Posal.

5. Cf. chapt. 7.

6. Bernard-Maître, op. cit., p. 42.

7. Ibid., p. 43. On a pu comparer sans trop d'exagération l'enseignnement de Mei-ti [Mo-ti] a celui de Jesus-Christ: tous deux reclament en effet de l'homme, l'amour de Dieu et celui du prochain, mais chez Mei-ti c'est l'amour du prochain et prime. Il est certain que sa doctrine, fondée qu'elle est sur le theme général du traditionalisme du théisme des lettres, ne laisse pas de se zapprocher curieusement du théisme et du spiritualisme occidentaeux.

8. Ibid., pp. 44–45. Pourtant son systeme philosophique était, fondamentalement, le dévelopement logique de celui de Confucius, auquel il tient de très près, malgré le divergences. La principale différence vient de ce que Mei-ti ne cherche pas seulement a justifier sa theorie par l'autorite des anciens sages, mais par le raisonnement et la dialectique. Les vieilles conceptions des Scribes et des Devins sur le Saint, l'Homme supérieur et leur vertu que Confucius avait conservées, pieusement, sont abandonnees completement par Mei-ti; il n'emprunte à celui-ci que ce qui'il à créé d'original, cette notion d'altruisme ou de Jenn et il la développe, il la pousée à l'extrême en un amour universel. Chez Mei-ti, l'Amour ne s'étend plus aux hommes en quelque sort par rang et par classe, se dégradant à mesure qu'on s'éloigne du centre, c'est-a-dire de soi et de sa famille; dans l'Amour universel, tous, proches et distants, sont également confondus, et seul l'amour qui ne fait pas de distinction sauvera le monde. Ce principe doit être applique jusqu'au sacrifice de soi-même.

9. Yale University Library has a substantial collection of these materials in its rare book room.

10. Ko Hung, *Pao-p'o-tzu*, vol. 3.

11. Cf. Henri Doré, *Researches into Chinese Superstitions*, vols. I–X, translated by M. Kennelly and, later, by D. J. Finn, Shanghai, 1914–1933. Though voluminous, Doré's collection is merely a fraction of the extant letter charms in China. Doré's are mainly from the South to the Yang-tzu River. Cf. Kubo Noritada, "Dokyo to Nihon Minkan Shinko," *Minzokugaku Kenkyu*, vol. 18, no. 3, September 1947, p. 37.

12. Ko Hung, op. cit., vol. 4, Chin-tan-p'ien.

13. J. J. M. de Groot, *Universismus*, Berlin, 1918, passim.

14. Cf. Kubo, op. cit., p. 37.

15. *Ts'eng-wen-cheng-kung Chia-shu*, II, dated on June 19, Tao-kwang 25th year, as quoted in Kubo, ibid.

16. *Samguk sagi*, vol. 21, the 7th and 8th years of the era of King Yŏngnyu of Koguryŏ.

17. *Samguk yusa*, vol. 3, Report on King Pojang.

18. *T'ang-shu*, Tung-i-ch'uan, Kaoli paragraph.

19. *Chiu-t'ang-shu*, Kaoli-ch'uan.

20. Cf. Andrea Eckardt, op. cit., pp. 122–136; *Chosen Ko-fun Heki-kwa Shi-fu* (Mural Paintings in Old Tombs of Koguryŏ Period), published by the Korean Royal Household Museum, Seoul, 1916; SekinoTadashi, *Chosen no Kenchiku to Geijutsu*, op. cit., pp. 119–157. Yi Pyŏngdo, "A Study on the Mural Paintings of Ancient Tomb at Kangsŏ, especially on the Wall Paintings of the Taemyo," *Tongbang Hakchi* (Journal of Far Eastern Studies), vol. I, March 1954, pp. 371–423.

21. Cf. Sekino, *Shina Ega-shi*, Appendix, p. 238.

22. Yi Pyŏngdo, ibid., p. 125.

23. Eckardt, op. cit., p. 128. "Buddhist influence might be inferred from the lotus-flowers which occur in the Sam-Sil-Ch'ong or 'Tomb of the Three Chambers,' but it should be remembered that in pre- and extra-Buddhist art the lotus-flower has always been a favorite motive in sculpture, painting, and handicrafts . . . The shape of the flower too is unusual and is not met with in later Korean art."

24. Cf. de Groot, *Universalismus*, op. cit., pp. 367f.; *Lu-shih-ch'un-ch'iu, Yu-shih-lan; Shi-chi, T'ien-kuan-shu; Huai-nan-tzu, T'ien-wen-hsun,* etc.

25. The plant has more fancy names in Taoist scriptures. They are: "Divine Mushroom," "Plant for Immortality," "Plant for Longevity." According to Ko Hung, there are several species in the medicine for the immortals. They are gold, silver, cinnabar, and many kinds of mushrooms. The plant the angel is picking must be one of those mushrooms. Cf. Yi Pyŏngdo, op. cit., pp. 137f.

26. *Samguk sagi, Paekche pongi.*

27. Cf. chapt. 9.

28. There may have been two Hwangnyong-sa Temples, though the historical accounts are often confused. One was with the character Hwang meaning "yellow," while the other with a character Hwang meaning "emperor." Both characters are identical in pronunciation.

29. Cf. Mishina Akihite, "Yon-dong Kami Sho-ko," *Chosen Gakuho*, no. 10, 1956, p. 169.

30. *Samguk sagi*, vol. 2, Ki-i. Manp'a sikchŏ.

31. Cf. chapt. 9.

32. *Koryŏ sa*, Sega II.

33. The text has no date.

34. Cf. Reichelt, op. cit., pp. 130.

35. Cf. chapt. 7.

36. *Samguk sagi*, *Somun chŏn*; *Samguk yusa*, Pojang pongno passages.

37. *Samguk yusa*, vol. 4, *Silla pongi* 4.

38. *P'ungnyu* or "*P'ung-ryu*" is a transliteration of *puru* or *pŏl* ("nation"), an old Korean vocabulary. Therefore, the *P'ungnyudo*, here, must be interpreted as the "national faith or religion." And we believe that *Hwarangdo* was the name given to the religious body of this "national faith" or "*P'ungnyu*."

39. Ko Hung, *Shen-hsien-chuan*, Paragraph on P'eng-tsu.

40. Wŏnhyo, *Mirŭk Sangsaeng Chongyo*, *Taisho*, vol. 38.

41. *Samguk yusa*, vol. 3, Mirŭk Sŏnhwa Paragraph.

42. *Samguk yusa*, vol. 2, Chukchirang in the era of King Hyoso.

43. Cf. chapt. 11.

44. Cf. chapt. 7.

Chapter Eleven

1. Iryŏn's *Samguk yusa* was written in circa 1270 C.E. and edited and published by his disciple Mugŭk sometime after his death. The commentaries inserted in the text may have come from Mugŭk, instead of the author himself.

2. Translated by Kim Chewŏn from the *Samguk yusa* edited by Ch'oe Namsŏn. Quoted from Kim Chewŏn, "Han Dynasty Mythology and the Korean Legend of Tangun," *Archieves of the Chinese Art and Society of America*, III, 1948–1949, pp. 43–48.

3. Cf. M. Garnet, *Chinese Civilization*, New York, 1930, p. 207; Kim Chewŏn, op. cit., footnote 8.

4. Cf. chapt. 7.

5. In Eastern books, commentaries are inserted in the text but kept usually in brackets or similar devices to make it clear that the added words are not found in the original texts. Iryŏn's comments follow this tradition. As is suggested in our footnote 1 above, the real commentator may have been Mugŭk.

6. The Buddhist critics on Riccian Catholicism in China indicated that Ricci's *T'ien-chu* was no other than this Buddhist *T'ien-chu*. Cf. chapts. 5, 7, and 9.

7. See below.

8. The Korean favorite name for the mountains *"paek"* or *"park"* may have some religious significance. Cf. Ch'oe Namsŏn, *Asi Chosŏn*, Seoul, 1926. But his approximation of *"park"* or "luminousness" to the notion of Sun-worship is an exaggeration and a mistake. For good paraphrases from Ch'oe's book in French translation, see You, Eul-Sou, *Le Confucianisme en Corée*, Paris, 1939, pp. 3–12.

9. Buddhist *Chesŏk*, or *Ti-shi* in Chinese pronunciation, was retransferred to Taoist *Shang-ti* here.

10. The extant text *Yongnak, 15th year, Kyŏngju Chogak* is unfortunately a very poor imprint, full of mistakes.

11. *Chŏntan* tree is repeatedly referred to in the Buddhist scriptures *Fo-hua-ching* (*Saddharmapundarika Sutra*). The Buddhist concordance *Chih-chü-i-t'u-chi* lists the text concerning *chŏntan*.

12. Kwŏn Kŭn, *Ŭngjesi*. These poems were composed by Kwŏn Kŭn in response to the poems of the Emperor Hwang Wu-ti of Ming, China, at the request of the emperor, on the occasion of Kwŏn's visit to the court as an ambassador of Korea in 1397 C.E. The grandson's commentary was published in 1461.

13. The 1442 version mentions "the *Old Record*" of Tangun. But the Yi Sŭnghyu's 1287 version definitely gives the title of the record as *Tangun pongi*.

14. *Samguk yusa*, vol. I, North *Puyŏ* passage.

15. Cf. Chŏng Inbo, *Chosŏn sa Yŏngu*, Seoul, 1946, pp. 35f.

16. Cf. chapt. 9.

17. *Samguk sagi*, vol. 17, Tongch'ŏn-wang paragraph.

18. Of course, this Korean *hsien* is not identical with the Taoist *hsien*. We know this because Silla's Ch'oe Ch'iwŏn sufficiently testifies that the national religion or the religion of *P'ungnyu* "adopted" the teachings and practices of Buddhism and Confucianism as well as those of Taoism to enrich itself. See chapt. 10. It is true that the Korean *hsien* took a Chinese

costume, but Ch'oe Ch'iwŏn tries to explain that the *hsien* story goes beyond the introduction of Taoism into the society.

19. Yi Pyŏngdo, "Asadal and Chosŏn," *Universitas Seoulensis Collectio Theseon*, vol. 2, 1956, Seoul, pp. 2f.

20. Imanishi Ryu, *Chosen Koshi no Kenkyu*, Tokyo, 1934, pp. 1–130, et al.

21. Cf. Sin Ch'aeho, "Chosŏn Yŏksa sang Ilch'ŏnnyŏn rae Cheil Taesagŏn," in Yi Sŏngŭn, *Hwarangdo Yŏngu*, Seoul, 1949, pp. 207–232.

22. An Chŏngbok, *Tongsa kangmok*.

23. Cf. Chŏng Inbo, op. cit., vol. 2, pp. 281–285, 292, 293–298.

24. *Kŏm* is the Korean pronunciation of this character. The original meaning of this character is economical. The Chinese pronunciation is *Chien.*

25. *Chul* in *kŏm-chul* is an entirely Korean vocabulary, and therefore, found in Korean dictionaries only. It is composed of *Chu* and the Korean phonetic symbol for the "l" sound so as to produce the sound effect of *chul.*

26. In view of the linguistic affiliation, the Korean *Ul-kŏm* or *Ung-kŏm* may have some relationship to the Ural-Altaic 'Ulgan' or 'Ulgen.' Cf. Mircea Eliade, *Traité d'Histoire des Religions*, Paris, 1949, pp. 65ff. The "k" of *kŏm* or *kam* is not aspirated in Korean, and therefore, it is virtually the same as "g" in '-gan' or '-gen.'

27. Yi Pyŏngdo, *Kuksa Taegwan*, 6th edition, Seoul, 1952, p. 451.

28. Cf. chapt. 10.

29. Yi, op. cit.

30. A. Irving Hallowell, *Bear Ceremonials in the Northern Hemisphere*, Philadelphia, 1926.

31. Cf. J. Batchelor, "On the Ainu Term Kamui," *Transactions, Asiatic Society*, Japan, no. 16, pp. 17–32. See also Hallowell, op. cit., p. 49.

32. Cf. Heinrich Koppermann, "Die Verwantschaft des Indogermanischen mit dem Koreanischen und der Ainusprache," *Anthropos*, vol. XXIII, Wien, 1928; *Die Eurasische Sprachfamilie, Indogermanische Koreanish und Verwandtes,* Heidelberg, 1933. Koppermann tries to establish a linguistic relationship between the Korean language and the Indogerman family on the basis of the Korean "Zahlwörten und grammatischen Affixen."

33. Cf. Mircea Eliade, *Le Chamanisme et Les Techniques Archaïques de L'Extase*, Paris, 1951, p. 18 and 32; Wilhelm Schmidt, *Der Ursprung der Gottesidee*, Freiburg, 1949, pp. 245–248 and 687–688.

34. *Samguk yusa*, vol. 1, North *Puyŏ* passage.

35. Ibid., Koguryŏ chapter.

36. *Han-yüan-suo* in *Hou-han-shu; Chin-shu Ssu-i-ch'uan; T'ung-tien Pien-fang-men*.

37. Cf. Yi Pyŏngdo, op. cit., p. 32.

38. Ibid., et passim.

39. Tangun worshipped the Heaven on behalf of the nation. The stone altar on the Manisan in Kanghwa Island is still believed to be the altar of Tangun.

40. Cf. *Wei-chih*, Han-ch'uan Mahan paragraphs.

41. See below.

42. Cf. *Wei-chih, Hui-ch'uan*.

43. Cf. *Wei-chih, Sanhan-ch'uan*.

44. These documents, collected by Ma Tuan-lin (1245–1325 c.e.) in his *Wen-hsien-t'ung-k'ao*, were translated into French. Cf. *Ma-tuan-lin, Ethnographie des Peuples Étrangèrs à la Chine; Ouvrage composé au XIIIe Siecle de Notre Ére*, tr. pour la premiére fois du Chinois avec un Commentaire Perpetual par le Marquis d'Hervery de Saint-Denys, Genéve, 1876–82, vol. I, Orientaux.

45. Cf. W. Schmidt, *Der Ursprung des Gottesidee*, op. cit., especially III, pp. 331–498; bk. IV, pp. 70–75, 274, 444–454; VII, pp. 609–701; IX, pp. 3–794; X, pp. 1–758; XI, pp. 1–712. See English translation: *The Origin and Growth of Religion: Facts and Theories*, tr. by H. J. Rose, New York, 1972. -Ed.

46. Mircea Eliade, *Traité d'Histoire des Religions*, Paris, 1949, pp. 46–66. Tr. from *Patterns in Comparative Religion*, tr. by Rosemary Sheed, New York, 1958, pp. 59–61. -Ed.

47. Thomas Ohm, "Die Himmelsverehrung der Koreaner," *Anthropos*, XXXV–XXXVI, 1940–1941, pp. 830–840.

48. Ibid., p. 830. Der Glaube an den Himmel (*Hananim, Hanalnim* oder *Hanŭnim*) (der Wortgebrauch ist nach Gegenden verschieden) ist in Korea nach wie vor allgemein. Wohl gibt es bereits junge Leute genug, die nicht mehr an ihn glauben oder sogar ihre Witze über ihn machen. Aber im allgemeinen sind die Koreaner noch von seinem Dasein überzeugt. Es ist ihnen etwas Selbstverständliches.

49. Andreas Eckhardt, "Die Familie in Korea," *Internationale Woche für Religions-Ethnologie* 5, Tagung 1929, Paris, 1931, p. 181.

50. Thomas Ohm, op. cit., pp. 831f. Alle Koreaner sehen in *Hanŭnim* das höchste Wesen. Fragt man sie aber näher nach der Wesenheit und den Eigenschaften dieses Wesens, so erlebt man Enttäuschungen. Nebelhaft nur und verschwommen sind die Vorstellungen von ihm. Es fehlt dem Begriff vom "Himmel" Bestimmtheit und Anschaulichkeit, eine Tatsache, die wohl damit zusammenhängt, dass die Koreaner *Hanŭnim* wenig verehren und sich infolgedessen kaum theoretisch mit ihm beschäftigen. Ausserdem spüren die Koreaner kein Bedürfnis, sich alles und jedes recht klar und verständlich zu machen.

Die Leute wissen nicht einmal zu sagen, ob *Hanŭnim* persönlich oder unpersonlich, geistig oder materiell ist *bzw.* ob man unter *Hanŭnim* den Himmel im geistigen oder physischen Sinn zu verstehen hat. Man hört hier gegensätzliche Auffassungen.

Nach Andreas Eckhardt versteht der Koreaner unter *Hanŭnim* eine Art "Himmelskraft, Weltseele, Naturgeist." Johannes Kim meinte ähnlich, die alten Koreaner hätten den Himmel einfach als Geist verehrt. Erst später sei Gott aus ihm geworden.

Ein anderer Koreaner erklärte mir aber—es war am 16. 9. 1936 in Hamheung—dass die Leute unter *Hanŭnim* unbedingt einen persönlichen Gott verstünden. Mit *Hanŭnim* sei nicht der blaue Himmel gemeint, sondern der Schöpfer (*tjo-multju*). Hulbert deutet die Auffassungen der Koreaner ähnlich. Er meint sogar, die Koreaner seien, soweit ihre *Hanŭnim*-Verehrung in Betracht komme, strikte Monotheisten. Die Attribute, die man *Hanŭnim* beilege, stimmten mit jenen Jahwes überein. Einige von den mehr unwissenden Koreanern leugneten zwar, dass *Hanŭnim* unfassbar sei, wobei sie zur Bekräftigung ihrer Ansicht auf den sichtbaren Himmel verwiesen, schrieben dem *Hanŭnim* dann aber doch wieder väterliche Sorge für die Menschen und vergeltende Macht gegenüber dem Bösen bei. Cf. H. B. Hulbert, *The Passing of Korea*, op. cit., p. 405.

51. Ohm, op. cit., pp. 832–833. Aus dem Gesagten dürfte hervorgehen, dass wir durch direkte Befragung der Koreaner über das Wesen *Hanŭnims* nicht zum Ziele kommen. Aber vielleicht erreichen wir mehr, wenn wir die Tätigkeit *Hanŭnims* betrachten. Die Koreaner schreiben dem Himmel die Weltregierung zu. *Hanŭnim* ist der Herr des Himmels und der Beherrscher des Universums. Er wisse alles. Sprüche wie: "Der hohe Himmel hört (weiss), was auf Erden ist," sind allen geläufig.

Von *Hanŭnim* kommt alles Gute und nichts Böses. Grosses Unglück und bitter Leid wird auf seine Gnade oder seinen Willen zurückgeführt.

Ferner glauben die Koreaner, dass *Hanŭnim* das Gute belohnt und das Böse bestraft. Wie mir Lehrer Kim in Tokwon erzählte, sagt man noch jetzt zu bösen Leuten: "*Hanuri mu-sop-tji ani-nia!*" (Ist der Himmel nicht zu fürchten?) Wenn einer schuldlos ist, erklärt er: "*Hanuri kubo posinta*" (Der Himmel schaut herab").

52. Ibid., p. 833. Über das Verhältnis *Hanŭnim's* zu den Naturgeistern darf man wohl bei aller sonstigen Zurückhaltung folgendes sagen: Ein

Naturgeist im Sinne der anderen vielen Naturgeister, die in Korea verehrt werden, ist *Hanŭnim* nicht. Das beweisen die Aussagen über ihn und die ihm zugeschriebenen Eigenschaften und Tätigkeiten. *Hanŭnim* steht auf einer ganz anderen Ebene als die Naturgeister.

53. Cf. Eliade, op. cit., p. 53.

54. Ohm, op. cit., p. 835.

55. Hulbert, op. cit., p. 404.

56. Eliade says: "Shamanism is a complex religious phenomenon whose morphological and historical study has scarcely been begun." V. Ferm, ed., *Forgotten Religions*, New York, 1950, p. 300. But he himself has contributed greatly to the cause.

57. Mircea Eliade, *Shamanism: Archaic Techniques of Ecstasy*, tr. by Willard R. Trask, Princeton, 1972, pp. 8–12.

58. C. A. Clark, *Religions of Old Korea*, op. cit., p. 173.

59. Eliade, op. cit., p. 18. M. A. Czaplicka, *Aboriginal Siberia: A Study in Social Anthropology*, Oxford, 1914, p. 198.

60. Eliade, op. cit., p. 32; Czaplicka, op. cit., p. 198.

61. Cf. Akiba Takashi and Akamatsu Joji, *Chosen Bujoku no Kenkyu*, Tokyo, vol. 2, p. 123.

62. L. O. Hartman, *Popular Aspects of Oriental Religions*, New York, 1917, p. 20, and 33–44.

63. Cf. chapter 8.

64. Ohm, op. cit., pp. 834–835: "Sehr bezeichnend für das Berhältnis der Koreaner zum Himmel ist das Erlebnis eines Dieners der Mission in Wonsan.
Gelegentlich einer Reise traf dieser Diener in einem Wirtshaus einen Bonzen, der bei dem Ausbruch eines Gewitters eigrig den Rosenkranz zu beten begann und dabei die Worte murmelte: "Namu Amida Pul" ("Ich setze mein Vertrauen auf Amida Buddha!"). Als aber einmal der Blitz in der Nähe einschlug, fiel er ganz aus seiner buddhistischen Rolle und rief voll Angst aus; *Hanŭnim toadjusio* ("Himmel hilf").
In dem Augenblick höchster Not bleibt also doch Gott allein übrig. Man flüchtet zu ihm, als ob man zur Erkenntnis käme, dass all anderen Geister und Götter, auf die man sonst verträut, Schwachheit und Tauschung seien. *Hanŭnim* ist die letzte Zuflucht. Er überragt schliesslich doch alle anderen Götter und Geister."

65. Ibid., p. 834. In grosser Not gehen die Koreaner wohl ganz still in die einsamen Berge, wo sie dann tief gebeugt beten: *Hanŭnim kubo-bososo* ("Himmel, neige dich zu mir herab") oder "Schau unser Elend an" und zugleich ein "vollkomenes Opfer" darbringen.

Wenn einer überfallen wird, ruft er: "*Hanŭnim*, lass mich leben." Wenn einer in Lebensgefahr ist, so ruft er: *Hanŭnim*, rette mich. Bei grossem Hunger betet man wohl: *Hanŭnim*, gib mir zu essen, wobei man sich die Hände reibt. Abgeklagte pflegen zur Beteuerung ihrer Unschuld zu sagen: "Der Himmel weiss, dass ich das nicht getan habe. . . .

66. Ibid., p. 834.

67. Cf. chapter 5.

68. Ohm, op. cit., p. 831. "Also *Hanŭnim* ist *coeli dominus*, die wörtliche Übersetzung des chinesichen Tchontju [T'ien-chu]."

69. Cf. L. G. Paik, op. cit., pp. 241f. [At present, while Catholics in Korea use the term "Hanŭnim," most Protestants prefer the term "Hananim," claiming that "Hananim" means not only the "Lord of Heaven" but also "the one and only Lord."—Ed.]

Bibliography

The following list contains the titles of those books and papers that have been cited in the preceding pages. [The more recent references related to the present subject are added at the end of the list under the subtitle of "Further References."—Ed.]

In Western Languages

Aimé-Martin, M. L. de (ed.). *Lettres Édifiantes et Curieuses.* 4 vols. Paris, 1838–1843.

Asvaghosha. *Discourse on the Awakening of Faith in the Mahayana,* tr. by D. T. Suzuki. Chicago, 1900.

Batchelor, J. "On the Ainu Term Kamui." *Transactions, Asiatic Society, Japan,* No. 16, pp. 17–32.

Berdyaev, Nicholas. *The Meaning of History.* English tr., New York, 1936.

Bernard-Maître, Henri. *Sagesse Chinoise et Philosophie Chrétienne.* Paris, 1935.

Bettray, Johannes. *Die Akkommodationsmethode des P. Matteo Ricci S.J. in China.* Rome, 1955.

Beyerhaus, Peter. *Die Selbständigkeit der Jungen Kirchen als Missionarisches Problem.* Barmen, 1956.

Boullaye, H. Pinard de la. *L'Étude Comparée des Religions.* Tome II, 2ᵉ ed. Paris, 1925.

Broadman, E. P. *Christian Influence upon the Ideology of the T'aiping Rebellion 1851–1864.* Madison, Wis., 1952.

Brou, P. "Les Jésuites Sinologues de Pékin et leur Éditeurs de Paris," *Revue l'Histoire des Missions.* Tome II. Paris, 1934.

Buhlmann, Walbert. *Die Christliche Terminologie als Missionmethodologisches Problem.* Schöneck-Bechenrid (Switzerland), 1950.

Cassirer, Ernst. *Language and Myth.* English tr., New York, 1946.

Chang, Carsun. *The Development of Neo-Confucian Thought.* New York, 1958.

Chavannes, E. *Mission Archaeologique dans la Chine Septentrionale.* Paris, 1909.

Clark, *The Korean Church and the Nevius Methods.* New York, 1930.

———. C. A. *Religions of Old Korea.* New York, 1932.

Courant, Maurice. *Bibliographie Coréene, Tableau Litteraire de la Corée, Contenant la nomenclature des Ouvarage publies dans ce pays jusqu'en 1890.* Paris, 1894.

Cronin, Vincent. *Wise Man from the West.* London, 1955.

Czaplicka, M. A. *Aboriginal Siberia: A Study in Social Anthropology.* Oxford, 1914.

Dallet, Charles. *Histoire de l'église de Corée, Précédée d'une Introduction sur l'Histoire, les Institutions, la Langue, le Moeurs et Coutumes Coréennes,* 2 vols., Paris, 1874.

Devred, *The Catholic Church in Corea.* English Version. Hong Kong, 1924.

Doré, Henri. *Researches into Chinese Superstitions,* vols. I–X, tr. by M. Kennelly and later on by D. J. Finn. Shanghai, 1914–1933.

Dudon, Paul. *Saint Ignace de Loyola.* Paris, 1934.

Eckhardt, Andrea. *A History of Korean Art.* English ed., London and Leipzig, 1929.

D'Elia, Pasqualé M. (ed.). *Fonti Ricciane: Documenti originali concernenti Matteo Ricci e la Storia delle prime reazioni tra l'Europe e la Cina (1579–1615).* 3 vols. Rome, 1942–49.

Eliade, Mircea. "Le Problème de Chamanisme," *Revue de l'Histoire des Religions.* t. CXXXI, 1946, pp. 5–42.

———. *Traité D'Histoire des Religions.* Paris, 1949. (English tr. Rosemary Sheed. *Patterns in Comparative Religion.* New York, 1958.)

———. "Shamanism," *Forgotten Religions.* Ed. by Vergilius Ferm. New York, 1950, pp. 297–308.

———. *Le Chamanisme et Les Techniques Archaïques de L'Extase.* Paris, 1951. (English tr. Willard R. Trask. *Shamanism: Archaic Techniques of Ecstasy.* Princeton, N.J., 1972.)

Gale, J. S. *Korea in Transition*. New York, 1909.

———. "A History of the Korean People." *The Korea Mission Field Magazine*, March 1916–1926, intermittently.

Gordon, Mrs. E. A. "Some Recent Discoveries in Korean Temples and Their Relationships to Early Eastern Christianity." *Transactions of the Korea Branch of the Royal Asiatic Society*, Vol. V, Part I. Seoul, 1914.

Gouvea, Alexandre de. *Extractum Epistolae Excellentissimi Admodumque Reverendi Episcope Pekinensis Ad Illustrissimum Episcopum caradrensem (dated 1797)*, No date of publication.

Graf, Olaf. "Ein Abriss der Religionsgeschichte Koreas." *Christus und Die Religionen Der Erde, Handbuch der Religionsgeschichte*, ed. by Franz König, 3 vols. Wien, 1951, pp. 375–391.

Grajdanzev, Andrew J. *Modern Korea*. New York, 1944.

Griffis, William Elliot. *Corea, the Hermit Nation*, 7th ed., New York, 1904.

Groot, J. J. M. de. *Universismus: Die Grundlage der Religion und Ethik des Staatwesens und der Wissenschaften Chinas*. Berlin, 1918.

Gustafson, J. M. *Community and Time* (Doctoral Dissertation Submitted to Yale University). New Haven, Conn., 1955.

Gützlaff, C. F. A. *Journal of Three Voyages along the Coast of China in 1831, 1832, with Notices of Siam, Corea and the Loo-Choo Islands*. London, 1834.

Hallowell, A. I. *Bear Ceremonialism in the Northern Hemisphere*. Philadelphia, 1926.

Hamel, Hendrik. *An Account of the Shipwreck of a Dutch Vessel on the Coast of the Isle of Quelpart (in 1652), together with the Description of the Kingdom of Corea*, English tr., Republication by the Korea Branch of the Royal Asiatic Society, Transactions, Vol. IX, Seoul, 1918.

Harnack, Adolf. *The Mission and Expansion of Christianity in the First Three Centuries*. English tr. by James Moffat. New York, 1908.

Hartenstein, Karl. *Die Mission als Theologisches Problem*. Berlin, 1933.

Hartman, L. O. *Popular Aspects of Oriental Religions*. New York, 1917.

Hentze, Carl. *Altchinesische Bronzen und Kultdarstellungen*. Antwerp, 1947.

———. *Die Sakralbronzen und ihre Bedeutung in den fruhchinesischen Kulturen*. Antwerp, 1947.

Hogbin, H. I. *Experiments in Civilization: The Effects of European Culture on the Native Community of the Solomon Islands*. London, 1933.

Hu, Shih. *The Chinese Renaissance.* Chicago, 1934.

Hulbert, H. B. *The Passing of Korea.* New York, 1906.

Huonder, Anton. *Der Chinesische Ritenstreit.* Aachen, 1921.

———. *Der heilige Ignatius von Loyola und der Missionsberuf der Gesellschaft Jesu.* Aachen, 1922.

Jones, G. H. "The Spirit Worship of the Koreans." *Transactions of Korea Branch of the Royal Asiatic Society,* Vol. II, Part II. Seoul, 1901.

Kim, Chewŏn: "Han Dynasty Mythology and the Korean Legend of Tangun." *Archives of the Chinese Art Society of America,* III, 1949–49.

Kortholt, Ch. *Leibnitti epistolae ad Diversos.* II. Leipzig, 1734.

Kraemer, Hendrick. *The Christian Message in a Non-Christian World.* New York, 1946.

———. *Religion and Christian Faith.* Philadelphia, 1956.

Latourette, K. S. *A History of Christian Missions in China.* New York, 1929.

———. *The Chinese: Their History and Culture.* New York, 3rd revised ed., 1947.

———. *A History of the Expansion of Christianity.* 7 vols., New York, 1937–45.

Launay, Adrien. *Martyrs Français et Coréens 1838–1846, Beatifiés en 1925.* Paris, 1925.

Ma, Tuan-Lin (1245–1325). *Ethnographie des Peuples Étrangères à la Chine, Ouvrage Compose au XIIIe Siecle de Notre Ère,* by Marquis d'Hervey de Saint-Denys. Vol. I., Orientaux. Genève, 1876–82.

McCune, G. M. *Korea Today.* Boston, 1950.

McLeod, John. *Voyage of His Majesty's Ship Alceste to China, Corea and the Island of Lew Chew: with an Account of Her Shipwreck,* 3rd ed. London, 1820.

Merkel, Franz Rudolf. *G. W. von Leibniz und die China-Mission.* Leipsig, 1920.

Moffat, James. "Syncretism." Hasting's *Encyclopedia of Religion and Ethics.*

Nida, Eugene A. *God's Word in Man's Language.* New York, 1952.

Niebuhr, H. Richard. *The Social Sources of Denominationalism.* New York, 1929.

Ohm, Thomas. "Die Himmelsverehrung der Koreaner." *Anthropos*, XXXV–XXXVI, 1940–41, pp. 830–40.

Osgood, Cornelius. *The Koreans and Their Culture*. New York, 1951.

Otto, Rudolf. *India's Religion of Grace and Christianity*. English tr. New York, 1930.

Paik, L. G. *The History of Protestant Missions in Korea 1832–1910*. Pyeng Yang [Pʻŏngyang] (Korea), 1929.

Pascal, B. *Pensées*. (Petite édition de M. Brunschvig).

Pope, Liston. *Millhands and Preachers*. New Haven, 1942.

Prémare, Josephe-Henri (ou Marie). *Vestiges des Principaux Dogmes Chrétiens Tirés des Anciens Livres Chinois*. Tr. by A. Bonnetty and Paul Perny. Paris, 1878.

Radin, Paul. *Primitive Religion: Its Nature and Origin*. New York, 1937.

Reichelt, K. L. *Truth and Tradition in Chinese Buddhism: A Study of Chinese Mahayana Buddhism*. Tr. from Norwegian. Shanghai, 1927.

Reischauer, A. K. *Studies in Japanese Buddhism*. New York, 1917.

Rhodes, Harry A. (ed.). *History of the Korea Mission: Presbyterian Church U.S.A. 1884–1934*. Seoul, 1934.

Saussaye, Chantepie de la. *Lehrbuch der Religionsgeschichte*. Vol. I. Tübingen, 1925.

Schaarb, Julins Jakob. *Geschichte und Begriff, eine Kritische Studie zur Geschichtemethodologie von E. Troeltsch und Max Weber*. 1945.

Schmidlin, Josef. *Katholische Missionsgeschichte*. Steyr, 1925.

Schmidt, Wilhelm. *Der Ursprung der Gottesidee*. Münster-Freiburg, 1949.

———. *Handbuch der Vergleichenden Religionsgeschichte*. Münster, 1930.

Schurhammer, Georg. *Das kirchliche Sprachproblem in der Japanischen Jesuitmission des 16 u. 17 Jahrhunderts*. Tokyo, 1928.

Sohm, Rudolf. *Kirchengeschichte im Grundriss*. 2 Aufl., 1888.

Soltau, T. Stanley. *Korea, The Hermit Nation and Its Response to Christianity*. New York, 1932.

Speer, R. E. *Report of a Visit to Korea*. New York, 1897.

Suzuki, D. T. *Outlines of Mahayana Buddhism*. Chicago, 1908.

Thauren, Johannes. *Die Akkommodation in Katholischen Heidenapostolat*. Münster, 1927.

Toynbee, A. J. *A Study of History*. Vols. I–X. London, 1933–1952.

Troeltsch, Ernst. *Die Absolutheit des Christentums und Die Religionsgeschichte*. Tübingen, 1929.

Tschackert, Paul. "Syncretism." *New Schaff-Herzog Encyclopedia of Religious Knowledge*.

Underwood, H. G. *The Call of Korea*. New York, 1908.

——. *The Religions of Eastern Asia*. New York, 1910.

Underwood, Mrs. L. H. *Fifteen Years among the Top-Knots*. New York, 1904.

Vicaire-Général de Soissons (ed.). *Choix des Lettres Édifiantes*. 3 Vols. Paris, 1808.

Wasson, Alfred W. *Church Growth in Korea*. New York, 1934.

Youn, Eul Sou. *Le Confucianisme en Corée*. Paris, 1939.

In East Asian Languages

I. Literature to 1882 C.E.

   (I)   Korean

      1) Historical Records, Annals, Historical Geographies:

         Ch'oe Hwan (ed.). *Kyŏngguk taejŏn* (Great Collection of National Code).

         Chŏngjong sillok (The Royal History of the Yi Dynasty During the Reign of King Chŏngjong).

         Hŏnjong kihae ch'oksa yunŭm (Government Anti-Heresy Declaration.)

         Hyojong sillok.

         Hyŏnjong sillok.

         Injong sillok.

         Iryŏn. *Samguk yusa* (Memorabilia of the Three Kingdoms).

         Kim Chongsŏ and Chŏng Inji. *Koryŏ sa* (History of the Koryu Dynasty).

         Kim Pusik. *Samguk sagi* (The History of the Three Kingdoms).

         Kukcho pogam (The Handbook of the Royal Court of the Yi Dynasty).

Sŏ Kŏjŏng. *Tongsa kangmok* (Analytical History of Korea).

Sunjo sillok.

T'aejong sillok.

Tongguk yŏji sŭngnam (Korean Gazetteer).

Yun Hoe, Sin Saek, and Maeng Sasŏng. *P'aldo chiriji* (Geography of the Eight Provinces in Korea).

2) General Sources:

An Chŏngbok. *Ch'ŏnhakko kŭp Ch'ŏnhak mundap* (A Study on Catholicism and Questions and Answers on Catholicism).

Chŏng Ch'o, et al. *Nongsa chiksŏl* (Lectures on Agriculture).

Chŏng Tojŏn. *Chosŏn kyŏngguk chŏn* (Administrative Codes of Chosŏn).

———. *Pulssi chappyŏn* (Discourses on Buddha).

———. *Sambong chip* (Complete Works of Sambong).

Chŏng Yakchong. *Chugyo yoji* (Introduction to Catholic Doctrines).

Hong Yangho. *Igye chip* (Writings of Igye).

Hwang Sayŏng. *Hwang Sayŏng paeksŏ* (Hwang Sayŏng Silk Letter).

Kakhun. *Haedong kosŭng chŏn*, Taisho. Vol. 50, no. 2065.

Kim Sunŭi, et al. *Kogŭm ŭibang yuch'wi* (Medical Prescriptions Ancient and Modern).

Kwŏn Nam. *Kwon Kŭn Ŭngjesi chu* (Commentaries on Kwon Kŭn's Response Poems).

Kyŏnghŭng. *Muryangsu kyŏng sŏlmun ch'an.*

Kyugi (K'uei-chi). *Amit'a kyŏng ŭigi.*

———. *Pulsŏl Amit'a kyŏng t'ongch'an so.*

Pak Chehyŏng. *Kŭnse chosŏn ch'onggam* (Historical Survey on the Recent Development of Political Affairs in Korea).

Pak Chiwŏn. *Yŏrha ilgi* (Journal of the Travel to Je-ho).

Sŏ Kŏjŏng, et al. *Tong munsŏn* (Korean Literary Works).

Tosŏn. *Tosŏn Ŭlyong kyong.*

Wŏnhyo. *Mirŭk sangsaeng chongyo.*

——. *Muryangsu kyŏng chongyo.*

——. *Pulsŏl Amit'a kyŏng so.*

——. *Yusim allakto.*

Yi Ik. *Sŏngho sasŏl* (Fragmentary Comments of Sŏngho).

Yi Kyugyŏng. *Oju yŏnmun* (Essays on the Five Continents).

Yi Sugwang. *Chibong yuse* (Analytical Discourses on Various Subjects by Chibong).

Yi Sŭnghyu. *Chewang ungi* (Rhymed Record of Emperors and Kings).

(II) Chinese

   1) Historical Records:

   Chin-shu.

   Chiu T'ang-shu.

   Fan Yeh, at al. *Hou Han-shu.*

   Ma Tuan-lin. *Wen-hsien T'ung-kao.*

   Lu-shih Ch'un-ch'iu.

   Ssu-ma Ch'ien. *Shih-chi.*

   T'ung-tien.

   Tzu-ch'ih T'ung-chien.

   Wei-chih.

   Wu-shu.

   2) General Sources:

   Asvaghosha. *Ta-sheng ch'i-hsin lun.*

   Ch'eng I-ch'uan. *T'ai-chi T'u-shuo Chieh.*

   Chi-ch'ü-i-t'u-ching.

   Chou-li.

   Chu Hsi. *Hsing-li ch'üan-shu.*

   ——. *Wen-chi.*

   ——. *Yü-lui.*

   ——. *Chung-yung chu-chieh.*

Fa-hua-ching (Saddharma-pundarika-sutra).

Han-yü. *Chi-shang-chun-fu-jen-wen.*

Hua-hu-ching.

Huai-nan-tzu.

Hui Chiao. *Kao-seng-chuan.*

I-ching.

Ko Hung. *Pao-p'o-tzu.*

———. *Shen-hsien-chuan.*

Kuang-hung-ming-chi.

Kung-ko-che.

Leng-yen-ching Chu-chieh.

Mou-tzu. Li-huo-lun.

Pan-jo-po-lo-mi-to (Prajnaparamita).

San-pao-chi.

Shan-hai-ching.

Shih-ching.

Sung Kao-seng-chuan.

T'ai-p'ing-ching.

T'ai-shang-kan-ying-p'ien.

Tao Hsüan. *Hsü kao-seng chuan. Taisho* 50, no. 2060.

T'ao Hung-ching. *Ti-wang-nien-p'u; Chen-ling-wei-yeh-t'u.*

Ts'eng-kuo-fan. *Ts'eng*-wen-cheng-kung Chia-shu.

3) Literature Related to the Jesuit Mission in China

Didacus de Pantoja. *Ch'i-ko Ch'üan-shu* (Seven Mortifications).

Feng Pao-pao. *Ou-lo-pa Kuo-yü-ti-t'u* (European Map).

Feng Ping-cheng. *Sheng-shih-ch'u-jao.*

Matteo Ricci. *Chiao-yu-lun* (The Treatise on Friendship).

———. *Chi-jen shih-pien* (Ten Discourses of a Stranger).

———. *Erh-shih-wu-chang-chü* (The Twenty-five Chapters).

———. *K'un-yü-wan-kuo-ch'üan-t'u* (World Maps).

———. *Shan-hai-yü-ti-t'u* (World Map).

———. *Shu-li-ching-yün* (Textbook on Mathematics).

———. *Ssu-shih-erh-chang-chü* (The Forty-two Chapters).

———. *T'ien-chu-shih-i* (True Record of the Lord of Heaven).

———. *T'ien-wen-shu* (On Astronomy).

——— and Hsu-kuang-chi. *Chi-ho-wen-pen* (Introduction to Euclid Geometry).

Ruggieri. *T'ien-chu shih-lu* (True Record of the Lord of Heaven).

von Bell, Johannes Adam Schall. *Cheng-chieh-t'u chi Ch'i-cheng-li Pi-li* (Manual of Calendar Making).

———. *Chu-chih-ch'un-cheng* (General Survey of Scientific Knowledge of the West).

———. *Shih-hsien-li* (Calendar).

(III) Japanese

Hirata Atzutane. *Hon-kyo kai-hen.*

———. *Ko-shi sei-bun* (Complete Works of Hirata Atzutane).

Nihon shoki.

II. Literature since 1882

Abe Yoshio. "Hayashi Razan no Jukyo to Chosen" (Hayashi Razan's Confucianism and Korea). *Chosen Gakuho* 10, 1956: 1–45.

Akiba Takashi and Akamatsu Joji. *Chosen Buzoku no Kenkyu* (Studies on Shamanism in Korea). 2 vols., Tokyo, 1938.

Ch'oe Namsŏn. *Assi Chosŏn* (Ancient Korea). Seoul, 1926.

———. *Paektusan Ch'amgwangi* (Journey to Mount Paektu). Seoul, 1926.

———. *Chosŏn Yŏksa* (History of Korea). Seoul, 1931.

Chŏng Inbo. *Chosŏn sa Yŏngu* (Study of Korean History). 2 vols., Seoul, 1946.

———. *Tamwŏn kukhak sango* (Tamwŏn's Manuscripts in Korean Studies). Seoul, 1955.

Chou Yü-t'ung. *Chu Hsi.* Shanghai, 1934.

Hiaku Nanun (Paek Namun). *Chosen Shakai Keizai-shi* (Social Economic History of Korea). Vol. 1, Tokyo, 1933.

Hwang, Peter. *Cheng-chiao-feng-pao.* Shanghai, 1904.

Hyŏn Sangyun. *Chosŏn yuhak sa* (History of Korean Confucianism). Seoul, 1947.

Imanishi Ryu. *Chosen Koshi no Kenkyu* (Study of Ancient History of Korea). Tokyo, 1934.

———. "Korai Taiso Gunyo Jitsu-cho ni tsukite," (On the Ten Important Precepts of the T'aejo of the Koryŏ Dynasty). *Toyo Gakuho,* vol. 8.

Kim Wŏnyong. *Hanguk Kohwalja Kaeyo* (On the Movable Type Printing of Old Korea). Seoul, 1955. (with English resume)

Ko Yusŏp. *Hanguk T'ap'a ŭi Yongu* (Studies on the Korean Stone Pagodas), 2nd ed. Seoul, 1954.

Kubo Noritada. "Dokyo to Nihon Minkan Shinko" (Taoism and Popular Belief of Japanese People). *Minzokugaku Kenkyu* 18, no. 3, 1947.

Lo Erh-kang. *T'ai-p'ing-t'ien-kuo Shih-hua* (Pictorial History of the T'ai-p'ing Rebellion). Nanking, 1956.

———. *T'ai-p'ing-t'ien-kuo Shih-liao K'ao-shih-chi* (Sourcebook on the History of the T'ai-p'ing Rebellion). Peking, 1956.

Mishina Akihite. "Yemaek Shoko" (A Study on Yemaek People). *Chosen Gakuho* 2, 1951: 121–154.

———. "Yondong Kami Shoko" (A Study on the Yondong God). *Chosen Gakuho* 10, 1956: 163–177.

Muraoka Noritsugu. *Shinto-shi* (History of Shintoism). Tokyo, 1956.

Nakayoshi Isao. "Shiragi Kanzan-ji Sekizo Miroku, Amita-zo ni Tsuite" (On the Stone Statues of Mirŭk and Amita Buddhas of Silla Kamsan Temple). *Chosen Gakuho* 9, 1956: 275–288.

Ninomiya Keiji. "Korai no Hatsikuankai ni Tsuite" (On the P'alkwanhoe of the Koryŏ Dynasty). *Chosen Gakuho* 9, 1956: 235–251.

———. "Korai-chio no Jogen Nendokai ni Tsuite"(On the Sang-won Yŏndŭnghoe of the Koryu Dynasty). *Chosen Gakuho* 12, 1958: 111–122.

Sekino Tadasi. *Chosen no Kenchiku to Geijutsu* (Architecture and Fine Arts in Korea). Tokyo, 1942.

Sin Ch'aeho. "Chosŏn Yŏksa sang Ilch'ŏn-nyŏn nae Cheil Taesagŏn" (The Largest Disaster in a Thousand Years of Korean History). In Yi Sŏngun, *Hwarangdo Yŏngu* (Studies on *Hwarangdo*). Seoul, 1949, pp. 207–232.

Son Chint'ae. *Chosŏn Minjok Munhwa ŭi Yŏngu* (Studies on the Culture of Korean People). Seoul, 1948.

———. *Kuksa Kaeyo* (Outline of Korean History). 7th ed. Seoul, 1955.

Suematsu Yasukazu. *Shiragi-shi no Sho-mondai* (Problems of the Silla History). Tokyo, 1954 (English resume).

Takakusu Junjiro. *Azia Minzoku no Chusin Shiso* (The Central Thought of Asian Peoples). Tokyo, 1941.

Tanaka Hitenaka (tr.). "Chosen ni okeru kiristo-kyo Ten-rai Hogoku-sho" (Report on the Evangelism of Christianity in Korea). *Chosen Gakuho* 10, 1956: 189–238.

T'ang Yung-t'ung. *Han Wei Liang-chin Nan-pei Ch'ao Fo-chiao Shih* (History of Buddhism of the Han-wei, Liang-chin, North and South Dynasties). Vol. 1, 2nd ed. Peking, 1955.

Tokiwa Daijo. *Shina ni okeru Bukkyo to Jukyo, Dokyo* (Buddhism, Confucianism and Taoism in China). Tokyo, 1930.

Yamaguchi Masayuki. "Yakuchu Ou Shiei Hakusho" (Translation and Notes on Hwang Sayŏng's Silk Letter). *Chosen Gakuho* 2, 1951: 121–154.

Yi Nŭnghwa. *Chosŏn Kidokkyo kŭp Oegyo sa* (History of Christian Churches in Korea and Diplomacy). Seoul, 1922.

Yi Pyŏngdo. *Kuksa Taegwan* (An Outline of Korean History). 6th ed. Seoul, 1952.

———. "Kang-sŏ Kobun Pyŏkhwa ŭi Yŏngu" (A Study on the Mural Paintings of Ancient Tomb at Kangsŏ). *Tongbang Hakchi* 1, 1954: 119–157.

———. "Asadal kwa Chosŏn." *Universitas Seoulensis Collectio Theseon*, Vol. 2, 1956, Seoul, 1–8.

Yi Sangbaek. *Hanguk Munhwasa Yŏngu Nongo* (Studies on Cultural History of Korea). Seoul, 1948.

Yi Sŏngun. *Hwarangdo Yŏngu* (Studies on *Hwarangdo*). Seoul, 1949.

Further References

Baker, Donald. "A Confucian Confronts Catholicism: Truth Collides with Morality in Eighteenth Century Korea." *Korean Studies Forum* 6, 1979–80.

———. "Morality and Metaphysics in Korean Neo-Confucianism." *Journal of Korean Thought* 1, 1996.

Best, Jonathan W. "Tales of Three Paekche Monks Who Traveled Afar in Search of the Law." *Harvard Journal of Asiatic Studies* 51, no. 1, 1991.

Buswell, Robert E., Jr. *The Korean Approach to Zen: The Collected Works of Chinul.* Honolulu: University of Hawaii Press, 1983.

————. *The Formation of Ch'an Ideology in China and Korea: The Vajrasamadhi-Sutra—A Buddhist Apocryphon.* Princeton, N.J.: Princeton University Press, 1989.

Chan, Wing-tsit, trans. *Reflections on Things at Hand: The Neo-Confucian Anthology Compiled by Chu His and Lü Tsu-ch'ien.* New York: Columbia University Press, 1967.

Chosŏn wangjo sillok. 48 vols. Seoul: Kuksa P'yŏnch'an Wiwŏnhoe, 1960.

Chung, Chai-sik. "The Rise of Neo-Confucian Orthodoxy and the Problems of Conformism in Yi Korea." *Korean Social Science Journal* 12, 1985.

Clark, Donald N. *Christianity in Modern Korea.* Lanham, Md. and London: University Press of America, 1986.

de Bary, William Theodore, et al. *Sources of Chinese Traditon.* New York: Columbia University Press, 1960.

————, and JaHyun Kim Haboush, eds. *The Rise of Neo-Confucianism in Korea.* New York: Columbia University Press, 1985.

Grayson, James H. *Early Buddhism and Christianity in Korea: A Study in the Implantation of Religion.* Leiden: E. J. Brill, 1985.

————. *Korea: A Religious History.* Oxford: Larendon, 1989.

Haboush, JaHyun Kim. *A Heritage of Kings: One Man's Monarchy in the Confucian World.* New York: Columbia University Press, 1988.

Han, U-gŭn. *The History of Korea.* Honolulu: University of Hawaii Press, 1970.

Han, Ugŭn, and Songmu Yi. *Saryorobon Hanguk Munhwasa* (History of Korean Culture through the Historical Sources). 4 vols., Seoul: Ilchisa, 1985.

Hangukhak Taebaekwa Sajŏn. 3 vols. Seoul: Ŭryumunhwasa, 1972.

Hunt, Everett N., Jr. *Protestant Pioneers in Korea.* Maryknoll, N.Y.: Orbis, 1980.

Kalton, Michael. "An Introduction to Silhak." *Korean Journal* 15, no. 5, 1975.

Kang, Wi Jo. *Ilbon T'ongch'i-ha Hanguk-ŭi Chonggyo-wa Chŏngch'i* (Korean Religions and Politics under the Rule of Japan). Seoul: Taehan Kidokkyo Sŏhoe, 1977.

Keel, Hee Sung. *Chinul: The Founder of the Korean Sŏn Tradition.* Berkeley, Calif.: Institute of Buddhist Studies, 1984.

Kendall, Laurel, and Griffin Dix. *Religion and Ritual in Korean Society.* Berkeley: University of California, Center for Korean Studies, 1987.

Kim, Kyung Jae. *Christianity and the Encounter of Asian Religions: Method of Correlation, Fusion of Horizon, and Paradigm Shifts in the Korean Grafting Process.* Netherlands: Uitgerverij Boekencentrum, 1994.

Kister, Daniel A. *Korean Shamanist Ritual: Symbols and Dramas of Transformation.* Budapest: Académiai Kiadó, 1997.

Kŭm, Changt'ae. "Chosŏn Hugi Yuhak Sŏhak kanŭi Kyorinonjaeng kwa Sasangjŏk Sŏnggyŏk" (Confucian-Catholic Doctrinal Debates in Later Chosŏn Period and their Intellectual Characteristics). *Kyohoesa Yongu* 2, 1979.

Ledyard, Gari. *The Dutch Come to Korea.* Seoul: Royal Asiatic Society, Korea Branch, 1971.

Lee, Ki-baek. *A New History of Korea.* Translated by Edward W. Wagner with Edward J. Shultz. Cambridge, Mass.: Harvard University Press, 1984.

Lee, Peter H., et al. *Sourcebook of Korean Civilization.* 2 vols. New York: Columbia University Press, 1993 and 1996.

Min, Kyŏngbae. *Hanguk Kidokkyohoe-sa* (A History of the Korean Church). Seoul: Yonsei University Press, 1972.

Moffett, Samuel H. *The Christians of Korea.* New York: Friendship Press, 1962.

Oh, Kang-nam. "Sagehood and Metanoia: Confucian-Christian Encounter in Korea." *The Journal of American Academy of Religion,* vol. LXI, no. 2, 1993: 303–320.

Rogers, Michael C. "*P'yŏnnyŏn T'ongnok*: The Foundation Legend of the Koryŏ State." *Journal of Korean Studies* 4, 1982–83.

Yi, T'aejin. "The Socio-Economic Background of Neo-Confucianism in Korea of the 15th and 16th Centuries." *Seoul Journal of Korean Studies* 2, 1980.

Yu, Tongsik. *Hanguk Mugyo ŭi Yŏksa wa Kujo* (The History and Structure of Korean Shamanism). Seoul: Yonsei University Press, 1986.

Yun, Sasoon. *Critical Issues in Neo-Confucian Thought: The Philosophy of Yi T'oegye*. Translated by Michael Kalton. Seoul: Korea University Press, 1990.

Walker, Hugh. "The Weight of Tradition: Preliminary Observations on Korea's Intellectual Response." *Korea's Response to the West*. Kalamazoo, Mich.: Korea Research Publications, Inc., 1971.

Weems, Benjamin B. *Reform, Rebellion and the Heavenly Way*. Tuscon: University of Arizona, 1964.

Glossary

An Chŏngbok　安鼎福
Amenominakanushi　天御中
Amit'a kyŏng ŭigi　阿彌陀經義記
An-shih-kao　安世高

Chajang　慈藏
Chaui　慈懿
Ch'ang-i　昌意
Chang Tsai　張載
Chang Yŏngsil　蔣英實
Ch'angnyong　蒼龍
chen-ju　眞如
Chen-ling-wei-heh-t'u　眞靈位業圖
Chen-chiao-feng-pao　正敎奉褒
Cheng-chieh-t'u　政界圖
Cheng I-ch'uan　程伊川
Cheng-meng　正蒙
Cheng Hsüan　鄭玄
Cheng Ming-tao　程明道
Chesŏk　帝釋
Chewang ungi　帝王韻記
ch'i　氣
Chi-hsiang-chün-fu-jen-wen　祭湘君夫人文
chi-jen　畸人
chien　儉

Chi-jen shih-pien 畸人十篇
Ch'i-ko ch'i-shu 七克七書
chia-lan 伽藍
chiang-chün 將軍
chiang-chung 降衷
Chiao-yu-lun 交友論
chüeh 覺
chieh 劫
chih-ts'ao 芝草
chih-jen 至人
chin-tan 金丹
Ching 經
Chinja 眞慈
Chinji 眞智
ch'ilsŏnggak 七星閣
Ch'iung-sang 窮桑
Cho Kwangjo 趙光祖
Cho Nungbong 趙凌奉
Cho Taesŏn 趙泰選
Cho Yundae 趙允大
Ch'oe Ch'anghyŏn 崔昌賢
Ch'oe Ch'iwŏn 崔致遠
Ch'oe Hang 崔恒
Ch'oe Nanhŏn 崔蘭軒
Ch'oe Yun 崔潤
chŏn-tan 栴檀
Ch'ŏndogyo 天道敎
Ch'ŏnju 天主
Chŏng Ch'o 鄭招
Chŏng Inji 鄭麟趾
Chŏng Mongju 鄭夢周
Chŏng Tojŏn 鄭道傳
Chŏng Tuwŏn 鄭斗源

Chǒng Yakchong　丁若鐘
Chǒngja　貞慈
Chǒngjong　正宗
Ch'ǒnnyong　天靈
ch'ǒnsin　天神
Chosǒn　朝鮮
Chosǒn kyǒngguk chǒn　朝鮮經國典
Chou Tun-i　周敦頤
Chou Wen-mo　周文謨
Chu Hsi　朱熹
Chu-chih ch'ün-cheng　主制群徵
Chu-tzu chia-li　朱子家禮
chu-tsun　主尊
Chuang-tzu　莊子
Chugyo yoji　主教要旨
Chujak　朱雀
Chukchirang　竹旨郎
Chumong　朱蒙
chün　君
ch'ün-chen　群眞
Ch'ung-hsü-ssu　崇虛寺
Chungjong　中宗
Chung-yung　中庸

Erh-shih-wu chang-chu　二十五章句

Fa-hua-ching　法華經
Fa-pen-nei-ch'uan　法本內傳
fen-shen　分身
feng-shui　風水
Fu-hsi　伏羲
fu-jen　夫人

Habaek   河伯
Han Yü   韓愈
Hanŭl   하늘
hanŭnim   하느님
Haeburu   解夫婁
Haemosu   解慕漱
Hirata Atzutane   平田篤胤
hoguk pulgyo   護國佛敎
Hŏnjong   憲宗
Hŏnjong Kihae Ch'ŏksa Yunum   憲宗己亥斥　邪綸音
Hong Kyŏngnae   洪景來
Hong Yangho   洪良浩
Hon-kyo kai-hen   本敎外篇
hsi-ho   義和
hsi   犧
hsiang   祥
hsien   仙
Hsien sa   仙史
hsien-rang   仙郎
hsien-che   賢者
hsin-jen   信人
hsing   性
Hsüan-hsiao   玄囂
Hsüan-tsang   玄奘
Hsü-kuang-chi Chi-ho yüan-pen   徐光啓　幾　何原本
Hua-hu-ching   化胡經
hua-hsien   化仙
Huang-ti   黃帝
Hui-chiao   慧皎
Hui Shih-chi   惠士奇
hwalinwŏn   活人院
Hwang Sayŏng   黃嗣永
Hwanghae   黃海

Hwangnyong-sa　皇龍寺
Hwanin　桓因
Hwanung　桓雄
Hwarang　花郎
Hwarangdo　花郎道
Hyojong　孝宗
Hyŏnjong　顯宗
hyŏnmu　玄武
hyungsŏ　凶書

i　義
I-ching　易經
I-hsing　一行
Ibullan　伊弗蘭
Igye chip　耳溪集
In nae ch'ŏn　人乃天
Injong　仁宗
Iryŏn　一然
Izanagi　伊邪那歧
Izanami　伊邪那美

jen-ai-ch'ing-ching　仁愛清淨
jiriki　自力
Ju-te-ya　如德亞

Kaema　蓋馬
Kaesomun　蓋蘇文
Kai-huang　開皇
kam　坎
Kamimimushibi　神皇産靈
kamsil　坎室
kamt'o　坎土
kamyŏ　堪與
Kando　間島

K'ang-hsi　　康熙

K'ang-seng-hui　　康僧會

Kang Wansuk　　姜完淑

Kaoli ch'uan　　高麗傳

kidowŏn　　祈禱院

Kim Cho　　金銚

Kim Chongjik　　金宗直

Kim Chongsŏ　　金宗瑞

Kim Ch'unch'u　　金春秋

Kim Pŏmu　　金範佑

Kim Sunui　　金循義

Kim Taegŏn　　金大建

Kim Tam　　金淡

Kim Yŏsam　　金汝三

Kim Yuji　　金有智

Kim Yusin　　金庾信

Ko Hung　　葛洪

Kogŭm ŭibang yuch'wi　　古今醫方類聚

Kojong　　高宗

Koguryŏ　　高句麗

Koryŏ sa　　高麗史

Koullun　　昆崙

Ku T'ing-lin　　顧亭林

Ku-kung-yen　　賈公彦

Kukcho Pogam　　國朝寶鑑

Kungye　　弓裔

kunja (chün-tzu)　　君子

Kung-kua-ko　　功過格

Kuang-hung-ming-chi　　廣弘明集

Kŭnch'ogo　　近肖古

Kun-yu Wan-kuo ch'uan-t'u　　坤輿萬國全圖

Kung-kung　　共工

K'ung-Meng-Cheng-Chu　　孔孟程朱

P'aldo chiriji 八道地理誌

pŏmjong 梵鐘

Pongi 本紀

Pao-p'o-tzu 抱朴子

Pŏphŭng 法興

park 밝

Pu-chou 不周

pu-mieh 不滅

Puyŏ 扶餘

Pul 佛

Pulsŏl Amit'a kyŏng so 佛說阿彌陀經疏

Pulsŏl Amit'a kyŏng t'ongch'an so 佛說阿 彌陀經 通贊疏

p'ungnyu 風流

P'ungnyudo 風流道

Pyŏn Ch'omun 卞招文

P'yŏngan 平安

P'yŏngyang 平壤

Samguk sagi 三國史記

Samguk yusa 三國遺事

Samsin 三神

samun nanjok 斯文亂賊

San-pao-chi 三寶記

San-wei 三危

Sang-li-pei-yao 喪禮備要

Sansindang 山神堂

Sejong 世宗

shan 善

Shan-hai-ching 山海經

shan-jen 善人

Shan-lung 善龍

Shan-tao 善導

Shang-ch'ing 上清

Shang-shu 尙書

Shang-ti 上帝

Shao-hao 少昊

Shen-hsien Fang-shu 神仙方術

shen-jen 神人

Shen-nung 神農

shen-tsun 仙尊

Shen-t'ien sheng-shu 神天聖書

sheng 聖

Shi-hsien-li 時憲曆

Shi-pen 世本

Shi-tzu 尸子

shih-che 使者

Shih-ching 詩經

Shu 書

Shu-ching 書經

Shu-li ching-yün 數理精蘊

Silla 新羅

Sillok 實錄

Sin 神

Sin Ch'aeho 申采浩

Sin Saek 申穡

Sin Sukchu 申叔舟

sinmungo 申聞鼓

sipchangsaengdo 十長生圖

Sŏ Kŏjŏng 徐居正

Sŏ Kyŏngdŏk 徐敬德

Sŏ Sangyun 徐相崙

sodo 蘇塗

Sohyŏn 昭顯

soin (hsiao-jen) 小人

Sŏin 西人

Sŏkch'ong 釋聰

Sŏkkuram   石窟庵
Sŏllang   仙郎
Somun   蘇文
Sŏndŏk   善德
Sŏninwanggŏm   仙人王儉
Sŏng Sammun   成三問
Sŏnghwangdang   城隍堂
Sŏngho sasŏl   星湖僿說
Sŏnggyungwan   成均館
Sŏnjong   善宗
sonnyŏ   孫女
Sŏnsa   仙史
ssu-shen-t'u   四神圖
sui-yüan   隨緣
Sundo   順道
Sunjo   純祖

Ta-hsien   大仙
Ta-ming-lu   大明律
Ta-t'ung-li   大統曆
T'aejong   太宗
taemyo   大墓
Taewŏngun   大院君
T'ai-chi   太極
T'ai-ch'in   太秦
T'ai-ch'ing   太清
T'ai-hao   太昊
t'ai-ho   太和
T'ai-p'ing-ching   太平經
T'ai-p'ing t'ien-kuo   太平天國
T'ai-shang   太上
T'ai-shang kan-ying-p'ien   太上感應篇
Tai-sheng-pen   戴聖本

Tai-te-pen 戴德本

Takamimusubi 高皇産靈

T'an-k'o-chia-lo 曇柯迦羅

T'akna 託羅

T'ang-shu 唐書

Tanggol 黨骨/丹骨/堂骨

Tanguk 丹國

Tangun 檀君/壇君

Tangungi 檀君記

Tangun pongi 檀君本紀

Tanung 檀雄

Tao 道

T'ao Hung-ching 陶弘景

Tao-chia 道家

Tao-chiao 道敎

Tao-cho 導綽

Tao-hsien-lun 道賢論

Tao-jen 道人

Tao-li-t'ien 忉利天

tariki 他力

Ti-wang-nien-p'u 帝王年譜

ti-yü 地獄

t'ien 天

T'ien-chu 天主

T'ien-chu shih-i 天主實義

T'ien-chün 天君

T'icn-ti 天帝

t'ien-t'ang 天堂

t'ien-wang 天王

Tong munsŏn 東文選

Tongdo sŏngnip ki 東都成立記

Tongguk t'onggam 東國通鑑

Tongguk yŏji sŭngnam 東國輿地勝覽

Tonghak   東學
Tongbang kogi   東方古記
Tosŏn   道先
Tosŏn ŭlyong kyŏng   道先乙用經
Tou-ssu   陡斯 (Deus)
Ts'eng Kuo-fan   曾國藩
Tu-jen-shang-pin-miao-ching   度人上品妙經
T'ung-kou   通溝
T'ung-shu   通書
tzu-jan   自然
Tzu-ji-t'ung-chien   資治通鑑
Tzu-min   慈愍

ung   熊, 雄
ungnyŏ   熊女
Ungyu   鷹遊

Wanggŏm   王儉
Wanggŏn   王建
Wang Yang-ming   王陽明
Wei-chih   魏志
Wei Chih-nan   維柢難
Wŏnhyo   元曉
Wŏnsullang   元述郎
wu   無
wu-chi   無極
Wu-li-i   五禮儀
wu-wei   無爲
Wu-yüeh   吳越

Yaksa yŏrae   藥師如來
yang   羊
yangban   兩班

Yemaek　濊貊

Yen Jo-chu　閻若璩

Yen-k'ang　延康

Yesong　禮訟

Yi Chungbae　李中培

Yi Hwang (T'oegye)　李滉（退溪）

Yi I (Yulgok)　李珥（栗谷）

Yi Ik　李瀷

Yi Kyugyŏng　李圭景

Yi Mansu　李晚秀

Yi Pangwŏn　李芳遠

Yi Sŭnghun　李承薰

Yi Sunji　李純之

Yi Sunsin　李舜臣

Yi Wan　李浣

Yin-hsi　尹喜

Yo-lung-ko　躍龍閣

Yŏjok　女狄

yŏn　燃

Yŏndŭnghoe　燃燈會

yong　龍

yŏng　靈

Yonghwasamhoe　龍華三會

Yŏngyang　嬰陽

Yŏngnyu　榮留

Yŏnggo　迎鼓

Yŏrha ilgi　熱河日記

Yü-hsien-lun　喩賢論

Yü-huang　玉皇

Yü-nü　玉女

Yü-ching　玉京

Yü-ch'ing　玉清

Yüan-shih-t'ien-tsun　元始天尊

Yuhwa   柳花

Yusim allakto   遊心安樂道

Yun Chich'ung   尹持忠

Yun Hoe   尹淮

Yun Saung   尹士雄

Index

253

Sŏ Kyŏngdŏk, 25
"Some Recent Discoveries in
Korean Temples and Their
Relationships to Early Eastern
Christianity" (Gordon), 138–
139
Somun, 150
Sŏndŏk, Queen, 129–131, 137
Songdo, 133
Sŏngmyŏng, King, 131–132
Sŏng Sammun, 25
Song Si-yul, 116
Sŏninwanggŏm (Kim Pusik), 162
Sŏnjong, 136–137, 152
Sŏnjong, King, 161
Sŏnsa, 150, 161–162
Sorae, seed-bed of Protestant
Christianity, 14
Sŏ Sangyun, 13–14
Sparrowhawk, 36–38
Suares, Joseph, 34
Sun Ch'o, 98
Sundo (Buddhist missionary), 127
Sung dynasty (China), 67, 99
Surangama Sutra, 158
syncretism: defined, 83–90; in
China, 100–101

T'aebek, Mount, 156
T'aejo, King, 132, 135, 149
T'aejong, King, 24, 133–134
Taewŏngun, Regent, 4
Ta-hsien, 97
T'ai-ping Rebellion, 101
Takakusu, 140
T'ang dynasty (China), 139
tangol, 155–156, 168
Tangun, 162–163, 165; Chewang
ungi, 159–160; foundation
myth, 93; linguistic analysis of
term, 155–156, 166–167;
Samguk yusa, 156–159

Tangungi, 160
Tangun pongi, 159, 160–161
Tangun Wanggŏm. See Tangun
T'ang-shu, 147
T'ang-shu Kaoli ch'uan, 147
Tanung, 159
Taoism, 91–92; animism, 95; and
Buddhism, 96, 97–98; and
Confucianism, 62–63; ethics,
143–145; Ricci opposes, 61–64,
141; symbolism, 147–148; the-
ism, 141–143
Ta-shih-chih, 137
temper, 44
theistic influence, 108
Thomas, Robert Jermain, 46, 47
Thomas, St., 139
T'ien-chu shih-i (Ricci), 35, 61–
63, 65, 67, 70
T'ien-chu shih-lu (Ruggieri), 60, 65
tolerance, 85–87
Tongbang kogi, 160–161, 162
Tongguk t'onggam, 25
Tongguk yŏji sŭngnam, 25
Tonghak revolt, 92, 93, 153
Tong munsŏn, 25
Tongnae Port, 42
Tongsa kangmok (An Chŏngbok),
162–163
Tosŏn, 149
Tosŏn ŭlyong kyŏng, 149–150
totemic behavior, 165–166
Toynbee, A. J., 85–86
transmigration, 87
treaties, 48
trinity: in Buddhism, 128; Chris-
tian, 111–112; Tangun, 163–
164; Taoism, 164
Troeltsch, E., 86
Ts'eng Kuo-fan, 146
Tschackert, Paul, 83
Tsiou, Jacques. See Chou Wen-mo